THE FIFTEEN WEEKS

THE
FIFTEEN
WEEKS

(February 21 - June 5, 1947)

Joseph M. Jones

New York

THE VIKING PRESS

1955

For

Clergue and Clarissa

COPYRIGHT © 1955 BY JOSEPH M. JONES
FIRST PUBLISHED BY THE VIKING PRESS IN SEPTEMBER 1955
PUBLISHED ON THE SAME DAY IN THE DOMINION OF CANADA
BY THE MACMILLAN COMPANY OF CANADA LIMITED

Library of Congress catalog card number: 55-8923

PRINTED IN U.S.A. BY THE VAIL-BALLOU PRESS, INC.

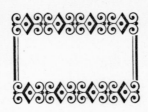

CONTENTS

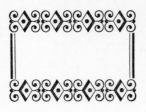

FOREWORD

S INCE the early days of the Fifteen Weeks I have known that I should write this book, that some day I would write it. All who participated in the extraordinary developments of that period were aware that a major turning in American history was taking place. The convergence of massive historical trends upon that moment was so real as to be almost tangible, and it was plain that in that *carrefour* of time all those trends were being to some degree deflected. How much of what was sensed and felt at that moment would find its way into histories written years later wholly from dusty records? How much of the atmosphere and drama would be recaptured? Indeed, so few were the records, so unlikely the source of many of them, and so unorthodox were many of the procedures, how would historians ever be able to find out what really happened? These questions occurred to me at the time and led me to prepare myself for writing this book.

Equally compelling was the spectacle of the government of the United States operating at its very finest, efficiently and effectively, and of the American people responding to leadership in a manner equally splendid. To observe this closely was to be filled with deep pride and thanksgiving. It seemed important to describe that spectacle in detail as a pattern and as an inspiration for the future.

I am proud to say that this book was written at Yale University during my residence as a Fellow in the Department of Political Science. I am deeply grateful to those who made possible the grant which was made to me, and to the faculty and staff of the Department of Political Science for their unfailing courtesy and helpfulness.

J. M. J.

May 30, 1955

PROLOGUE

IN WASHINGTON

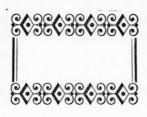

IN WASHINGTON

THE comfortable, dowdy old structure at Seventeenth Street and Pennsylvania Avenue, known as State, War, and Navy, was soon to lose her distinction as hostess to the Secretary of State and as center of the relations of the United States with the world. War and Navy had abandoned her long ago. Now, in early 1947, the State Department too was leaving her for new quarters, gaudier, more commodious, even air-conditioned, in a questionable part of town. After years of stubborn rearguard resistance to White House encroachments on space, the move was decided—one of George Catlett Marshall's first acts as Secretary of State. Even now files were being packed in Old State and room assignments were being made in New State at Twenty-first Street and Virginia Avenue. But on the gray Friday afternoon of February 21, 1947, Old State, unlike most of her tenants to whom the prospective parting brought anguish and a sense of personal loss, wore her regrets with silence and dignity. There was nothing that afternoon in the cables, or in circulating memoranda, or even in anybody's mind to suggest that the most revolutionary advance in United States foreign policy since 1823 would occur within the next fifteen weeks, and that the last days of State Department tenancy at Seventeenth and Pennsylvania would be a period of intense activity leading to great historical accomplishment.

Mr. Marshall had left his office earlier than usual that afternoon to go to Princeton, New Jersey, where he would the next day attend a celebration of Princeton's Bicentennial, receive a degree of Doctor of Laws, and make his first public address as Secretary of State. He had been gone only a short while when the private secretary to Lord Inverchapel, British Ambassador in Washington, telephoned to request an immediate appointment. As the matter appeared urgent and Secretary Marshall was not expected to return to his office until Monday morning, Dean Acheson, Undersecretary of State, was consulted on what to do.

Acheson was reluctant to ask the Secretary to return to his office late Saturday unless it was necessary. Only a month earlier General Marshall had returned from his long and grueling mission to China, to assume immediately the burdens of his new office. In less than two weeks he was to leave for a Conference of Foreign Ministers in Moscow, which would last no one knew how many weeks or months. He deserved, Acheson thought, at least part of a weekend off if it could be managed. Inquiry at the Embassy disclosed that the Ambassador wanted to deliver to the Secretary two notes concerning a decision of the British government to end aid to Greece and Turkey. Acheson therefore arranged that H. M. Sichel, First Secretary of the British Embassy, should at once bring over copies of the notes and discuss them with Loy Henderson, Director of the Office of Near Eastern and African Affairs, and John D. Hickerson, Deputy Director of the Office of European Affairs. Whatever staff work might be required could be started over the weekend, and the Ambassador could call on Secretary Marshall Monday morning, deliver the notes formally, and discuss the problem. Meanwhile the Secretary and the President would be informed.

As Jack Hickerson had another appointment he could not break on short notice, Loy Henderson alone received Mr. Sichel forty-five minutes later. Henderson and Sichel had known each other casually for some time. This day they greeted each other cordially, but there was no preliminary badinage. Sichel drew from his dispatch case copies of two notes and handed them to Henderson, who began to read the note on Greece.

The British government recalled that previous exchanges of views had resulted in the mutual understanding that for military and strategic reasons Greece and Turkey should not be allowed to fall under Soviet control, and mentioned the informal agreement reached between Secretary of State Byrnes and Foreign Minister Bevin in Paris the previous summer that Great Britain would extend chiefly military aid and the United States chiefly economic aid, though the possibility of United States military aid to Greece had not been excluded. Greece was now in most urgent need, and the British government thought it should be decided how much economic aid the United States intended to give and what form it should take.

The Greek economic situation, the note continued, was on the point of collapse. Unless help from the outside was forthcoming there was certain to be widespread starvation and consequent political disturbances.

Experts appointed by the United Nations, the British government pointed out, had estimated the relief needs of Greece for 1947 at £21 million, but this figure would be wholly inadequate for the political objective of maintaining internal stability. A more adequate figure would be £40 million. In addition, the Greek armed forces were in serious need of re-equipment and reorganization to permit assault on the rebels in the spring. Reorganization, re-equipment, and six months' military operations would require £20 million in foreign exchange in addition to the £2 million of equipment the British government planned to give Greece. The British government felt that the military problem should be urgently considered by the Combined Chiefs of Staff. The restoration of public confidence in Greece was essential to recovery, and confidence depended upon the ability of the Greek government to assert its authority effectively over the rebel bands.

In Total, Greece needed in 1947 between £60 million and £70 million ($240 to $280 million) in foreign exchange, and for several years thereafter would require substantial outside aid. But Great Britain would be unable to offer further financial assistance after March 31. The British government hoped the United States would be able to provide enough aid to enable Greece to meet its minimum needs, civilian and military, assuming as of April 1 the burden theretofore borne chiefly by Great Britain.

The note concerning Turkey was even briefer. The British government recalled that Secretary of State Byrnes had told the British Minister of Defense on October 15, 1946, that the United States would do everything possible to aid Turkey economically and hoped the United Kingdom would furnish military aid. The British government had subsequently studied the Turkish military situation, and the United States and British Embassies in Ankara had studied the economic problems. The British government was of the opinion that it was of the utmost importance for Turkey to maintain its independence, but that in their present state the armed forces could not resist effectively aggression by a first-class power. The Turkish government needed advice on the organization and equipment of the army and aid in procuring the modern weapons decided upon. Great Britain would be unable to provide much equipment for the army; it could help with the navy and air force if financial arrangements could be made.

Turkey needed to carry on a program of economic development, which would improve the military situation, and needed at the same time to re-equip its army. Turkey could do one or the other with its own resources, but not both. Great Britain was unable to offer further financial assistance. The obligation therefore devolved upon the United States or the International Bank. The British government suggested that joint studies be undertaken of measures necessary to bring Turkey to a reasonable state of preparedness, and solicited the views of the United States on how the program of Turkish reorganization could be financed. If it should be agreed, the British government would be prepared to send a military, naval, and air mission, as had been requested by the Turkish government.

Sichel had handed over his messages without portentousness or expectation. Henderson wondered, as with mounting excitement he read the two notes, whether Sichel fully appreciated the seriousness and significance of the information he was conveying. Sichel knew very well; his blandness of manner came from his training in the

British Diplomatic Service. Moreover he was merely reporting another of the many British withdrawals that were then taking place around the world under the scourge of necessity—India, Burma, Egypt, Palestine—withdrawals that opened vast breaches in the system of political, diplomatic, and military defense by which Britain had for so long maintained a measure of stability in the world. Greece and Turkey were of great importance, but so were the others. He was merely reporting *another* breach. He therefore had no precedent, no reason for supposing that he might be transmitting a spark that would ignite a historical situation and propel the United States promptly into that breach.

The facts were clear, and there was very little discussion. Shortly Sichel took his leave, and Henderson, ascertaining by telephone that Hickerson was free, hurried down the hall to see him.

Reading the messages, Hickerson realized at once, as had Henderson, that Great Britain had within the hour handed the job of world leadership, with all its burdens and all its glory, to the United States. To most people in the United States, Greece and Turkey were only remote places on a map with incidental historical, touristic, or cultural associations, but not to Henderson and Hickerson. They lived daily, hourly—had so lived for several years—with the problems arising out of the crumbling of British power from the Eastern Mediterranean to the South China Sea and the relentless probing and pressing of the Soviet Union into situations of weakness everywhere in Europe and Asia. They were acutely aware of the strategic importance of Greece and Turkey to the security of three continents. The British had borne the chief responsibility for strengthening and sustaining Greece and Turkey and the countries of the Middle East generally. The United States had helped too, had in fact authorized $451 million in aid to Greece alone since the war, but this was nearly used up, and the operations of the United Nations Relief and Rehabilitation Administration in Greece were due to end within a few weeks. At a time when Greece was on the point of collapse the government in Washington had no funds and no authority to help that country meet its budget needs, or re-equip its army, or undertake the reconstruction of its war-shattered industry, agriculture, and public works. The Greek government had only $14 million of free foreign exchange in its Treasury.

The situation in Turkey was not immediately dangerous, but it would become so if Greece fell, and in any case it was clear that Turkey was headed for grave financial troubles if it built up its defenses and modernized its economy simultaneously. The United States government had no funds and no authority to help Turkey.

Now British aid to Greece was to cease within six weeks, and Britain could not be expected to help Turkey carry its increasing burdens. These were the only new facts added to the situation as a consequence of Sichel's call, but they were devastating facts. They meant that the struggle in Greece against Communist domination would be hopeless, and that Turkey's position as a friend of the West, resistant to Soviet pressure, would become untenable.

Loy Henderson and Jack Hickerson did not discuss this situation on the afternoon of February 21. Each knew it by heart, and each knew the other knew it. (Before going home late that evening Henderson and his staff prepared a memorandum containing most of the facts.) Whisking up copies of the *aides-mémoires* left by Sichel, they walked rapidly downstairs to lay the new facts before Dean Acheson.

This sudden spark set off a dazzling process which within fifteen weeks laid the basis for a complete conversion of American foreign policy and of the attitudes of the American people toward the world. It was clear to many at the time that an enduring national conversion to the role of world leadership was taking place. It is even clearer now. This is the story of what happened during those fifteen remarkable weeks, told by one who was close enough to the situation to know how and why policy was made without sharing responsibility for its determination. It is a story of American democracy working at its finest, with the executive branch of the government operating far beyond the normal boundaries of timidity and politics, the Congress beyond usual partisanship, and the American people as a whole beyond selfishness and complacency. All three faced the facts of international life fearlessly and without sentimentality, made identifiable contributions to the development of a new American foreign policy, and worked together to accomplish a national acceptance of world responsibility.

This transformation was not something that was simply willed and accomplished, but a sudden response to the most compelling world situation ever to confront the nation in time of peace. For decades massive historical caravans had been observed moving slowly toward predictable destinations: Great Britain toward loss of Empire and inability to maintain the balance of power in Europe and order in Asia; Western continental Europe toward instability and weakness; the United States toward economic and military pre-eminence in political isolation; and the Soviet Union toward a fundamental challenge of Western civilization. Suddenly during the Fifteen Weeks of 1947 it was discovered that all four caravans were on the point of arrival. According to a logical projection of historical trends, these destinations would shortly be reached and the world stage set for an inevitable war between two titans, the Soviet Union, astride Europe and Asia, and America standing alone.

The conversion of United States foreign policy was long overdue. The United States had emerged from World War I as a great world power, yet had refused to help maintain world order through collective security or otherwise; as a great industrial power and the world's greatest creditor nation, yet had continued economic policies appropriate to an isolated, debtor nation. These policies and attitudes had yielded during World War II to full political involvement in world affairs as a member of a powerful team, to the wise generosity of Lend-Lease, and after the war to membership in the United Nations and enormous appropriations for relief and rehabilitation abroad. But there had been no genuine national conversion to the attitudes and policies and specific requirements— political, military, or economic—of world leadership, no confirmed acceptance of its continuing responsibilities on a scale commensurate with the need.

Popular American support of the United Nations during its first two years of existence was sentimental and unrealistic, an escape from the responsibilities of our unique power. It was grounded in the feeling that the splendid machinery of the United Nations, generously stoked with funds, would automatically assure world peace and economic and social well-being without any drastic change in United States economic policies and without bold, sacrificial, risk-taking actions by the United States alone on the world stage. In the years that have since passed much has been learned about the great strength of the United Nations, but also about its limitations in dealing with many of the modern forms of aggression: infiltration, subversion, economic pressures, wars of nerves, aid to rebel groups, tactics that can often be dealt with effectively only by prompt single-power intervention to supply economic, political, and military support. We have also learned the limitations of the United Nations as a channel for large-scale United States aid abroad. And we have also found that, as in the case of Korea, United Nations action requires vigorous and determined leadership. But in 1946 this perspective had yet to be gained.

Other American attitudes lagged far behind reality in 1946 and early 1947, weighing down policy decision and action. The war was over, victory had been won, a long period of peace lay ahead. Public sentiment during the war had been aroused in favor of our Russian allies, whose victories we had for years celebrated and whose setbacks we had mourned as our own. We were reluctant to believe that Soviet behavior at postwar conferences, the clamping down of Soviet control in Central Europe and the Balkans, Communist infiltration in Western Europe, and Soviet pressures in the Middle East formed a pattern of aggressive expansion dangerous to our own security. To believe this was to give up thoughts and plans for normal living, to face up to new tensions and sacrifices, to accept in the atomic age that had opened the possibility of a new and more horrendous war.

Wartime cordiality waned in 1946, and voices were raised to warn against the new danger; but others urged patience and tolerance, and most Americans, perplexed and edging slowly toward fear, withheld judgment. Crises arose—over Poland, over Trieste, over Tripolitania, over Iran, Turkey, and China, over the shooting down of American planes—but each was dealt with singly by the

USSR

government and largely forgotten by the public. Official policy toward the Russians stiffened markedly in early 1946 on specific issues, but neither President Truman nor Secretary of States Byrnes nor other government leaders who saw the pattern of inexorable Soviet pressure described it whole to the American people, explained what it meant to their security, or outlined a policy for dealing with it. To have done so would have made the Russians even more intractable, and we had not wholly despaired of their willingness to call a halt to expansion short of acquiring the keys to world domination.

But during this time Soviet leaders, reviving the aims and methods of the czars and operating in league with Communist agents and supporters abroad, had deployed their diplomacy, propaganda, military pressures, and economic weapons in persistent efforts to break through the Iran-Turkey-Greece barrier to the south and establish Soviet power in the eastern Mediterranean, the Middle East, and the Indian Ocean. In 1946 they had been at least temporarily frustrated in Iran; they had been resisted by the Turks, who had more determination than effective military or economic strength; but Greece, according to unanimous reports streaming into the State Department, was in February 1947 within weeks of an economic, moral, and military collapse that would leave power to the local armed Communist bands, which, supported by Greece's Communist neighbors to the north, were already successfully defying the authority of the government in large parts of the country. If Greece fell to Communist control and Soviet domination, Turkey, three-quarters encircled, would also fall in time, as would Iran. The whole of the Middle East, South Asia, and North Africa would be laid open to Soviet adventuring. Western Europe, already on the brink of political and economic disaster, could hardly hope to survive the material and psychological shock of a Soviet breakthrough into the Mediterranean and the Indian Ocean.

Rapidly, in an orderly manner, and with virtually no dissent, the executive branch of the government decided to act. Having paved the way through consultations with congressional leaders, President Truman, before a joint session of Congress on March 12, announced in a sweeping declaration that it would henceforth be the policy of the United States "to support free peoples who are resisting attempted subjugation by armed minorities or by outside pressures." President Monroe, a hundred and twenty-four years earlier, had committed the United States to protection of the American Hemisphere against foreign encroachment. President Truman committed the United States to support all free peoples and announced that our support would primarily be in the form of economic and financial aid essential to economic stability and orderly political processes. Journalists, noting that the commitment compared in its boldness and sweeping implications with the Monroe Doctrine, promptly labeled it the Truman Doctrine. In the ensuing weeks aid to Greece and Turkey was voted in Congress by large bipartisan majorities. But, more important, the Doctrine set off in the United States a process of official policy development and an intense and mature public debate on the nation's role in the world. This led us very shortly to assume heavy responsibilities for financing European recovery and subsequently to world-wide programs to help build up the economic, social, political, and military strength of free nations.

President Truman could have decided to ask Congress for a modest appropriation for economic aid to Greece, transferred to Greece obsolete American military equipment out of existing stocks, ignored the problem of Turkey, which was not immediately pressing —in short, he could have tried to muddle through with stopgap measures. That he did not try to do so, that he recognized that a full turn in history was necessary and called the turn, that he chose the occasion of Greece to accept in the name of the United States the world-wide responsibilities of great power, that he attracted broad public support and accomplished conversion of American foreign policy and attitudes, the pages that follow should show.

By 1955 the shadow of war had by no means disappeared from the earth, but such strength had been built in Europe and the Middle East, as a consequence of United States leadership, aid, and commitment of power, as to discourage localized aggression, make Communist subversion and infiltration far more difficult, and improve the chances of winning a major war to the point where the launching of such a war by Soviet leaders had become considerably less likely. The Soviet-Communist challenge to Western civilization continued, but the terms and prospects had altered. The premium on peaceful competition had been increased. The doors had been held open to peaceful change, and thus to hope.

In this book an effort is made to set forth in detail the situation that gave rise to the developments of the Fifteen Weeks, and to tell the intimate story of what happened in Washington during those weeks, and why. But first let us glance at the highlights of that extraordinary period: three occasions and three speeches.

PART I

THREE OCCASIONS AND THREE SPEECHES

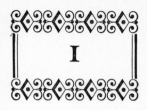

I

THE CAPITOL, WASHINGTON, D.C., MARCH 12, 1947

THE Speaker of the House, Joseph Martin, at 12:16 p.m. on March 12, 1947, declared the House in recess subject to the call of the Chair. The House and Senate were shortly to meet in joint session to hear a Special Message to be delivered in person by the President of the United States, Harry S. Truman.

The confusion in the House Chamber was greater than usual. The representatives occupying the front ranks on the House floor were in process of evacuating them to accommodate the expected guests, members of the Senate, and the President's Cabinet. Dozens of ex-congressmen, exercising their prerogatives on this special occasion, loitered in conversation with old friends on the periphery of the Chamber. Every clerk, secretary, or functionary on Capitol Hill whose familiar face would get him past a guard at a door was on the floor. One Democratic representative had planted himself, with his small daughter on his lap, in a seat on the center aisle.

The gallery seats, except those few kept free by vigilant door-keepers, had long since been taken, and distinguished visitors were now being packed in on the steps. The warm and sparkling day had brought out in their spring finery all the wives of high official-dom who could wangle a ticket from their husbands. The diplomatic gallery was jammed. At the west end of the Chamber the central gallery reserved for the White House was overflowing with Cabinet wives, White House staff, and guests. Mrs. Truman, arriving in the company of a friend five minutes before one o'clock, was trying rather unsuccessfully to pick her way unrecognized down the packed steps to her seat in the front row when a White House aide, belatedly recognizing her and appreciating the indignity of the situation, with authority and a firm voice cleared a path for the wife of the President.

Meanwhile, at 12:45 p.m., the Speaker had called the House to order, and although very little order resulted the doorkeeper announced the President *pro tempore* of the Senate and members of the United States Senate. Senator Arthur Vandenberg, flanked by the Secretary of the Senate and the Sergeant at Arms, walked down the center aisle and mounted the Speaker's rostrum; some fifty senators straggled behind him and took the good seats courteously yielded to them by their colleagues in the House. The Speaker of the House and the President *pro tempore* of the Senate each appointed three members to a committee of six to conduct the President of the United States into the Chamber.[1] At 12:57 the doorkeeper announced the Cabinet of the President of the United States. Two by two they entered—headed by Dean Acheson, Acting Secretary of State (General Marshall was in Moscow), and John Snyder, Secretary of the Treasury, followed by James Forrestal, Secretary of the Navy, and Robert Patterson, Secretary of War, and the others—and progressed rather stiffly to the seats left for them in the front row.

At 1 p.m. the doorkeeper announced the President of the United States, and, as all in the Chamber rose and applauded, President Truman, escorted by the committee of senators and representatives and carrying a black folder under his arm, strode briskly down the aisle. Leaving his escort in the House well, he mounted to the Clerk's desk below the Speaker's rostrum and acknowledged with a broad smile the continuing ovation. As the applause died away he opened his black folder and, after turning for a moment to address the Chair behind him, began to read. His voice was flat and not impressive, but this day he spoke with a newly acquired forcefulness,

---

[1] Senators Connally, Taft, and White; Representatives Halleck, Eaton, and Rayburn.

tripping only occasionally. And what he had to say was impressive indeed.

"Mr. President, Mr. Speaker, Members of the Congress of the United States, the gravity of the situation which confronts the world today necessitates my appearance before a joint session of the Congress. The foreign policy and the national security of this country are involved."

It had been just nineteen days earlier that the first in the chain of events leading to this appearance of the President before Congress had occurred, the official news that the British government could no longer aid in sustaining and strengthening Greece and Turkey. On the fourth day after Sichel's call (the four days covered a weekend) the State Department had ready a documented statement of position approved by Secretary Marshall. On the fifth day this position had been endorsed by the Secretary of War and the Secretary of the Navy and approved by the President. On the sixth day it had been laid by the President before congressional leaders of both parties, none opposing. On the seventh day a working party in the State Department had been appointed to draw up a detailed program of aid, draft a message to Congress for the President, and work up a program of public information. In the twelve following days all this had been done, the proposed program had been approved by the Cabinet and discussed again with congressional leaders, and the message had been polished and approved in the White House for final delivery. It had all gone like clockwork. No one in the government had opposed. No one had dragged his feet. Veterans in government service had never seen anything like the unanimity of view, and this on a matter recognized as a major turning point in American history. Nor had they ever before witnessed such efficiency in the government as that with which the job was done.

Now the President was displaying the end product to Congress, to the American people, to the world.

"One aspect of the present situation . . . concerns Greece and Turkey . . ."

President Truman described the tragic physical, financial, and

economic condition of war-wrecked Greece, the threat to the very
existence of the Greek state posed by the activities of the Communist-led terrorists in the north, the inadequacies of the Greek
army, the urgent appeal of the Greek government to the United
States. The British government, he said, could give no further
financial or economic help after March 31. The question had been
considered as to how the United Nations might assist in this crisis,
but the situation was an urgent one requiring immediate action,
and the United Nations and its related organizations were not in a
position to extend help of the kind required.

"Greece must have assistance if it is to become a self-respecting
democracy.

"The United States must supply this assistance.

"There is no other country to which democratic Greece can turn.

"No other nation is willing and able to provide necessary support for a democratic Greek government."

Mr. Truman emphasized that the Greek government had asked
for our assistance in utilizing effectively the financial and other aid
we might give to Greece and in improving its public administration.
"It is of the utmost importance that we supervise the use of any
funds made available to Greece," he said—and here he was interrupted by the first applause—"in such a manner that each dollar
spent will count toward making Greece self-supporting, and will
help to build an economy in which a healthy democracy can
flourish."

The future of Turkey as an independent and economically sound
state, the President continued, was clearly no less important to
the freedom-loving peoples of the world than the future of Greece.
Turkey, having been spared the disasters of war, was in much
better condition than Greece, but nevertheless needed our support
"in order to effect that modernization necessary for the maintenance
of its national integrity. That integrity is essential to the preservation
of order in the Middle East." If Turkey was to have the help it
needed, the President concluded, the United States would have to
supply it, for we were the only country able to do so. This was

brief treatment indeed, but it is all the message contained about Turkey.

Up to this point President Truman had said things that had been more or less expected as a consequence of news leaks, discussions with congressmen over the previous two weeks, and background information officially given to the press. It was unique in our history that a President should ask Congress for an appropriation in time of peace to help foreign countries maintain their "integrity and independence"—financial aid to accomplish frankly political purposes—but it was a not illogical extension of Lend-Lease. But all the President had said thus far was but prologue. Now came the main drama.

"I am fully aware of the broad implications involved if the United States extends assistance to Greece and Turkey. . . .

"One of the primary objectives of the foreign policy of the United States is the creation of conditions in which we and other nations will be able to work out a way of life free from coercion. . . . To insure the peaceful development of nations, free from coercion, the United States has taken a leading part in establishing the United Nations. The United Nations is designed to make possible lasting freedom and independence for all its members. We shall not realize our objectives, however, unless we are willing to help free peoples to maintain their free institutions and their national integrity against aggressive movements that seek to impose upon them totalitarian regimes. This is no more than a frank recognition that totalitarian regimes imposed on free peoples, by direct or indirect aggression, undermine the foundations of international peace and hence the security of the United States. . . .

"At the present moment in world history nearly every nation must choose between alternative ways of life. The choice is too often not a free one. One way of life is based upon the will of the majority, and is distinguished by free institutions, representative government, free elections, guaranties of individual liberty, freedom of speech and religion, and freedom from political oppression. The second way of life is based upon the will of a minority forcibly imposed upon the majority. It relies upon terror and oppression, a controlled press and radio, fixed elections, and suppression of personal freedoms.

"I believe that it must be the policy of the United States to support free peoples who are resisting attempted subjugation by armed minorities or by outside pressures.

"I believe that we must assist free peoples to work out their destiny in their own way.

"I believe that our help should be primarily through economic and financial aid, which is essential to economic stability and orderly political processes."

Here, in its essense, was the Truman Doctrine. There was at this point no applause. It was as though the President's listeners were stunned, some perhaps dismayed, by the sweep, the boldness, of the President's utterance. The President went on.

"It is necessary only to glance at a map to realize that the survival and integrity of the Greek nation are of grave importance in a much wider situation. If Greece should fall under the control of an armed minority, the effect upon its neighbor, Turkey, would be immediate and serious. Confusion and disorder might well spread throughout the entire Middle East. Moreover, the disappearance of Greece as an independent state would have a profound effect upon those countries in Europe whose peoples are struggling against great difficulties to maintain their freedoms and their independence while they repair the damages of war. Collapse of free institutions and loss of independence would be disastrous not only for them but for the world. Discouragement and possibly failure would quickly be the lot of neighboring peoples striving to maintain their independence. Should we fail to aid Greece and Turkey in this fateful hour, the effect will be far reaching to the West as well as to the East. We must take immediate and resolute action."

President Truman asked Congress to appropriate $400 million for aid to Greece and Turkey and to authorize the detail of American civilian and military personnel to Greece and Turkey, at the request of those countries, to assist in the tasks of reconstruction and to supervise the use of United States aid. He also asked authorization to train selected Greek and Turkish personnel in the United States.

"This is a serious course upon which we embark. I would not recommend it except that the alternative is much more serious. . . . The seeds of totalitarian regimes are nurtured by misery and want. They spread and grow in the soil of poverty and strife. They reach their full growth when the hope of a people for a better life has died. We must keep that hope alive. The free peoples of the world look to us for support in maintaining their freedoms. If we falter in our leadership, we may endanger the peace of the world —and we shall surely endanger the welfare of our own nation. Great responsibilities have been placed upon us by the swift course of events. I am confident that the Congress will face these responsibilities squarely."

It is customary, when the President has finished delivering a message to Congress, for those present to rise, applaud, and remain standing while the President and his Cabinet take their leave from the Chamber. There was no exception on this occasion, but the applause had a bewildered quality about it. There was no vocal acclaim, no rebel yells. The President was solemn as he acknowledged the applause, except that a fleeting smile accompanied a special look and bow toward Mrs. Truman in the west gallery. He shook hands with Senator Vandenberg and Speaker Martin and descended from the rostrum, briefly clasped a few outstretched hands as he made his way to the door, and hesitated long enough to shake the hand of the little girl who had twisted on her father's lap throughout the speech and was now carried in his arms.

The President retired from the House Chamber at 1:21 p.m., followed by his Cabinet, and Speaker Martin declared the joint session dissolved. Mr. Truman motored directly to the Washington airport and boarded the *Sacred Cow* for a flight to Key West, where he would vacation for a few days and await the reaction to his message.

The reaction was not slow in coming. It was tremendous, somewhat confused, and on the whole favorable. But that is a matter to be considered in a later chapter.

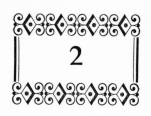

THE DELTA COUNCIL, CLEVELAND, MISSISSIPPI, MAY 8, 1947

THE Greece-Turkey aid bill was well along toward final passage in Congress and missions were being assembled for Athens and Ankara when on May 7, 1947, Dean Acheson, accompanied by Francis Russell, chief of the Department's Office of Public Affairs, boarded a DC-3, assigned by the Air Force to the Secretary of State, to fly to Cleveland, Mississippi, where, the following day, he was to deliver a major address on foreign policy before the Delta Council. The moving stream of human woe and government trouble the world over had swelled steadily during the previous eight weeks and was now swirling ahead in full flood, sweeping away comfortable premises and inundating preconceptions of the postwar world. The President's Doctrine of March 12 had been broad enough *in conception* to contain the floodwaters, but the specific project of aid to Greece and Turkey had sandbagged only a tributary to the main stream, which was now out of banks.

The most acute and dangerous situations were developing throughout Europe, especially in France, Italy, and Britain. Economic reconstruction was grinding toward a halt, and, with inflation mounting, the stream of farm products to the cities and raw materials to industries was drying up. Governments were spending precious and limited reserves of gold, dollars, and other foreign exchange at an

24

alarming rate, to pay not for reconstruction materials but for food and fuel. Strikes and social disorders abounded. Communism's rapid advance had been stunningly checked in most continental European countries by the psychological barriers thrown up by President Truman on March 12, which had a powerful influence upon the government change in France on May 4 and in Italy on May 13, when the Communists were eliminated from the government coalitions and their ministers disappeared from the Cabinets. But Communist voting strength, organization, and plans to take over remained intact. And as the Moscow Conference progressed (March 10–April 24), it became clear that Soviet policy was set against the economic recovery of Europe—for reasons that were obvious. The worsening situation in Western Europe cast a lengthening shadow over the deliberations of late February on aid to Greece and Turkey and contributed to the breadth of the President's policy statement of March 12, but recognition within the government of the specific character and proportions of the crisis confronting Western Europe did not crystallize until later in March. Just how that came about, and why, will be considered later.

There are some who contend that the highest officers of the government should restrict their speech-making to times when they have something to say; that official speeches at the top level should be more consciously used as a vehicle to project or foreshadow desired policy development and to enlist public discussion as a helpful partner in its realization; and that if a top official has something important to say it doesn't matter very much whether it is pitched to the immediate listening audience gathered together for an "occasion," for his real audience is the nation and the world, and those physically present who may not appreciate the importance of what he says will be satisfied to hear a distinguished man utter solemn phrases. Many would have considered Cleveland, Mississippi, to be one of the least promising places in the country from which to call the attention of the American people to their responsibilities for European reconstruction. Acheson did not. He was committed to speak before the Delta Council, he had something to say, and with the authority of the President he flew down to say it.

The Delta Council is a remarkable organization of farmers and small businessmen who live in the Mississippi Valley between Vicksburg and New Orleans. Most of them have a world outlook and a modern attitude toward agriculture. Cotton remains the main crop, and cotton requires world markets, hence the traditional internationalism of the delta. But the Delta Council has been an important factor in introducing dairy herds, beef cattle, new crops, and in developing improved plant and animal strains, with the result that a purely cotton economy has been transformed, and the delta is one of the most progressive and prosperous regions in the South. Once a year from seven to ten thousand citizens of the delta—members of the Council accompanied by their wives, sisters, cousins, grandparents, and babes in arms—congregate for a day of speeches, spreads, and visiting.

Arriving in Greenville, Mississippi, in the late afternoon of May 7, Acheson and Russell were met at the airport by their hosts, Mr. and Mrs. William T. Wynne, taken to their hotel for a wash-up, and then to the Wynnes' home for a julep party and reception, followed by dinner with a large company. Among the guests were Mr. and Mrs. Hodding Carter, Jr. Carter, courageous and able editor of the *Delta Democratic Times,* had been awarded the Pulitzer Prize for the best editorial of 1945. The next morning Mr. and Mrs. Wynne drove their guests through the delta country to see the cattle feeding knee-deep in new grasses and clovers developed for that area, then proceeded to Cleveland, where, on the grounds of the Teachers College, the Delta Council was meeting. A great number of tables had been set up under the trees, and the large gathering of people ate lunch in the shade. Afterward all who could be accommodated crowded into the nearby gymnasium. There, in the early afternoon on May 8, in a little college in a little farming town in southern Mississippi, Dean Acheson talked about the grim facts of international life and the requirements of international reconstruction. His words were heard only by those in the gymnasium, by the overflow crowd who listened to the loudspeaker installed outside, and by those few in the delta who, on this hot and humid afternoon, may have had their radios tuned to the local broadcast.

But Acheson was speaking to a much wider audience: to the staff of the Department of State, to the Cabinet and the whole government hierarchy, to the Congress, to the American people. And he was also assuring the governments and peoples of Europe that the government of the United States recognized their problem and its own responsibility in true perspective. Acheson had told the President, "I am going to throw up a ball and it's going to have to come down somewhere."

Acheson gave every appearance of enjoying himself thoroughly. Conforming to the weather and the informal attire of his audience, he removed his coat. He did not read the text he had brought with him, but managed to deliver it almost verbatim from brief notes he had made on the plane the day before on the backs of the pages opposite. He contrived, nevertheless, to put it over in a way that held the unwavering attention of every man, woman, and child on the crowded basketball floor. These were farming people, most of whom had never given a thought to international finance, and yet they were spellbound by his analysis of an intricate world economic problem.

"You who live and work in this rich agricultural region," he began, "must derive a certain satisfaction from the fact that the greatest affairs of state never get very far from the soil. When Secretary of State Marshall returned from the recent meeting of the Council of Foreign Ministers in Moscow he did not talk to us about ideologies and armies. He talked about food and fuel and their relation to industrial production, and the relation of industrial production to the organization of Europe, and the relation of the organization of Europe to the peace of the world. The devastation of war has brought us back to elementals, to the point where we see clearly how short is the distance from food and fuel either to peace or to anarchy."

He then proceeded to describe "some of the basic facts of international life with which we are primarily concerned today in the conduct of foreign relations." The first, he said, was that most of the countries of Europe and Asia were in a state of physical destruction or economic dislocation, or both. The second was that two of the greatest workshops of Europe and Asia—Germany and Japan—had barely been able even to begin the process of reconstruction because of the lack of a peace settlement. The third was that unforeseen disasters—what the lawyers call "acts of God"—had occurred to the crops of Europe—droughts, storms, floods, and excessive cold—slowing down the pace of reconstruction, impeding recovery of export trade, and necessitating the expenditure of reserves of gold and foreign exchange for food and fuel.

The accumulation of these grim developments, Acheson continued, had produced a disparity between production in the United States and production in the rest of the world that was staggering in its proportions. During 1947 the United States, responding to the world's need, would export goods and services totaling $16 billion—this figure representing one month's work for each man and woman in the United States and one month's output from every farm, factory, and mine. In return the world would be able to supply us with goods and services of only half that amount, totaling $8 billion, leaving a deficit of $8 billion.

"How are foreigners going to get the U.S. dollars necessary to cover a likely difference of nearly the same amount next year? These are some of the most important questions of international relations today."

In 1947 Acheson went on to explain, more than $5 billion of the difference would be covered by loans and grants-in-aid already authorized by Congress, and the remainder by private investments, remittances of American citizens abroad, and by foreign countries drawing down their extremely limited reserves of gold and foreign exchange. "But what of next year, and the year after that? Continued political instability and 'acts of God' are retarding recovery to a greater degree than had been anticipated. The extreme need of foreign countries for American products is likely, therefore, to continue undiminished in 1948, while the capacity of foreign countries to pay in commodities will be only slightly increased. Under existing authorizations, considerable sums will be available to offset next year's deficit. But these funds will taper off rapidly during the latter part of 1948. The need, however, will decline very little, if at all."

Acheson put the question, "What do these facts of international life mean for the United States and for United States foreign policy?" They meant first, he said, that the United States was going to have to take as large a volume of imports as possible from abroad in order to narrow the financial gap between what the world needed and what it could pay for. They meant, second, that "the United States is going to have to undertake further emergency financing of foreign purchases if foreign countries are to continue to buy in 1948 and 1949 the commodities which they need to sustain life and at the same time rebuild their economies. Requests for further United States aid may reach us through the International Bank, or through the Export-Import Bank, or they may be of a type which existing national and international institutions are not equipped to handle and therefore may be made directly through diplomatic channels. But we know now that further financing, beyond existing authorizations, is going to be needed. No other country is able to bridge the gap in commodities or dollars."

Acheson had three more points to make. One was that since world demand exceeded supply we were going to have to concentrate our emergency assistance in areas where it would be most effective in building world political and economic stability, in promoting human freedom and democratic institutions, in fostering liberal trading policies, and in strengthening the authority of the United Nations. Free peoples seeking to preserve their independence and democratic institutions and human freedoms against totalitarian pressures would therefore receive top priority. Another thing we would have to do, he said, would be to push ahead with the reconstruction of Germany and Japan. Finally, in order to carry out an effective policy of relief and reconstruction, the government would need the extension by Congress of certain executive powers, due to expire on June 30, over the domestic sale, transportation, and exportation of a limited list of commodities.

In concluding, Acheson recalled a story that had been going the rounds about a man who, after listening to an extended lecture on the grave financial and economic difficulties of Western Europe and Great Britain, remarked, "And, just think, all the trouble was caused by a blizzard." Said Acheson, "I think we will all agree that something more than a blizzard has caused Europe's current difficulties. But last winter's blizzard did show up the extremely narrow margins of human and national subsistance which prevail in the world today, margins so narrow that a blizzard can threaten populations with starvation and nations with bankruptcy and loss of independence. Not only do human beings and nations exist in narrow economic margins, but also human dignity, human freedom, and democratic institutions. It is one of the principal aims of our foreign policy today to use our economic and financial resources to widen these margins. It is necessary if we are to preserve our own freedoms and our own democratic institutions. It is necessary for our national security. And it is our duty and our privilege as human beings."

It is doubtful that many of the people gathered there knew they had heard a history-making speech calculated to speed up and alter the direction of major policy development in Washington and Europe. There is nothing unusual in this. Official speeches are legion, and in terms of policy development they may mean much or they may mean little. The public seldom knows how closely, if at all, the shining wheel on public display is geared into intentions, prior agreement and approval, staff work, and actual plans. The importance of any speech depends, in fact, upon the official action that precedes and follows. What this was, in the case of the Acheson speech, will become clear in the body of this book.

Acheson was not interrupted once during his speech. The applause when he finished was standing, generous, and polite. After a round of hand-shaking, he and Francis Russell descended from the improvised stage, were driven in a station wagon to a nearby airport, and took off for Washington.

3

HARVARD UNIVERSITY,
CAMBRIDGE, MASSACHUSETTS, JUNE 5, 1947

ROBERT FISKE BRADFORD, Governor of Massachusetts, dressed in a cutaway and top hat and escorted by a company of lancers, whose mounts, the Governor complained, had to be hired for the occasion, arrived by limousine at the Harvard Yard at 8:45 a.m. on June 5, 1947, and the 296th Harvard Commencement officially began. The Yard was already filling up with candidates and professors in academic gowns and alumni in their best clothes. The weather could not have been more perfect.

At 9:30 the Yard bell began to toll, and candidates for degrees, in caps and gowns, assembled under their respective marshals. Shortly afterward, with the Harvard band leading the way, they marched in procession and lined up on both sides of the walk around the Yard and the pathway leading from the Yard to Widener Library.

The official party that left Widener for procession to the Yard and thence back to the Tercentenary Theatre was led by the University Marshal, Dr. Reginald Fitz, and the Special Sheriff of Middlesex County, Loring R. Kent, whose presence symbolized, as it had since 1642, the ties between Harvard and the county. Following, in order, were President Conant, members of the Board of Overseers, Governor Bradford and his military staff, the deans of several departments, the thirteen honored guests, professors, and local dignitaries. The guests who were to receive honorary degrees included Secretary of State George C. Marshall, General Omar N. Bradley, J. Robert Oppenheimer, T. S. Eliot, Hodding Carter, Jr. (whom we have already met at the Delta Council), and William F. Gibbs, the naval architect. Amid the colorful gowns and hoods of scholars, the splendid uniforms and decorations of military officers, and the cutaways and top hats of dignitaries, the gray sack suit, white shirt, and blue necktie of George C. Marshall stood out in dramatic contrast. He wore no hat, no ribbon or button of his many military honors. He had chosen to appear simply as the Secretary of State; but his white-haired, soldierly figure commanded attention. Deeply tanned, his face lined and stern, he nodded tightly right and left as he passed the ranks of the graduating class, as though reviewing troops. As he came into view in the Tercentenary Theatre, the outdoor auditorium in the adjoining quadrangle, the eight thousand people assembled there under the elms broke into loud applause. Officials and distinguished guests took their places on the huge platform constructed on the steps of Memorial Church, with a large red shield inscribed VERITAS centered above the Ionic columns behind them; and the candidates for degrees filed into the seats reserved for them in the front ranks below.

The Sheriff of Middlesex County called the assembly to order by striking the stage three times with his scabbard, and there followed the usual Commencement proceedings—the benediction, the welcome by the President, three brief speeches by members of the graduating class, a rendition by the University choir, all leading up to the presentation of the candidates by the deans to the President for degrees. The honorary degrees came last. When his name was called, George C. Marshall rose and faced President Conant for his citation:

"An American to whom freedom owes an enduring debt of gratitude, a soldier and statesman whose ability and character brook only one comparison in the history of this nation."

As President Conant completed this eloquently brief comparison with George Washington, the audience rose in a great ovation. Mr. Marshall bowed, accepted his degree from the University Marshal, and sat down. The speech that launched the Marshall Plan was to be given, along with many others, that afternoon.

The short speech which Secretary Marshall carried in his pocket had not been entirely satisfactory to him when he left Washington the afternoon before with Mrs. Marshall and General and Mrs. Bradley to fly to Boston to spend the night with President Conant in Cambridge. He had agreed eight days earlier with his staff that a speech of this general nature should be made on an early occasion, and a day or two later had decided to take advantage of his presence at the Harvard Commencement exercises to give it there. But he had not liked the pitch of the last part—the vital part—of his draft speech, and had already rewritten it once. Going up on the plane he revised it again, and liked it better. Late that afternoon Undersecretary Acheson's office in Washington, reaching by telephone the Secretary's Executive Assistant in Cambridge, appealed to him to extract the final version from the Secretary and authority to release it. This was done. The State Department was thus able to issue a text to the press on the evening of June 4, but with no release time specified, as it was not known whether the Secretary would speak during the morning, afternoon, or evening.

It is a Harvard custom for the alumni to hold an annual spread in the Yard following the morning's exercises, while the President, Overseers, honored guests, and others are entertained at the Chief Marshal's spread in the Fogg Museum. Afterward the alumni have a review and procession, by classes, followed by the annual meeting and the day's speech-making under the gavel of the president of the Alumni Association. On this 1947 occasion Laird Bell of Chicago presided, President Conant and Governor Bradford made brief addresses, and then came the turn of a number of the honored guests. Thus was Secretary Marshall introduced to the Harvard Alumni and given a chance to make a few remarks.

The Secretary launched into his prepared statement with intense earnestness: "I need not tell you gentlemen that the world situation is serious. That must be apparent to all intelligent people. I think one difficulty is that the problem is one of such enormous complexity that the very mass of facts presented to the public by the press and radio make it exceedingly difficult for the man in the street to reach a clear appraisment of the situation."

With broad and vivid brush strokes he proceeded to paint the picture of Europe, physically wrecked and with the entire fabric of its economy dislocated. The breakdown of the business structure of Europe during the war was complete, he declared, and the system of division of labor between farms and cities, the basis of modern civilization, was in danger of collapse. The town and city industries were not producing enough goods to exchange with the food-producing farmer. The farmer, unable to find the goods for sale which he desired to purchase, was producing less and less for sale. Instead he was withdrawing fields from cultivation, feeding more grain to his stock, and consuming more of his food himself. Meanwhile people in the cities were short of food and fuel, and governments were being forced to use their foreign money and credits to procure these necessities abroad, exhausting reserve funds urgently needed for reconstruction.

"The truth of the matter is that Europe's requirements for the next three or four years of foreign food and other essential products —principally from America—are so much greater than her present ability to pay that she must have substantial additional help or face economic, social, and political deterioration of a very grave character. The remedy lies in breaking the vicious circle and restoring the confidence of the European people in the economic future of their own countries and of Europe as a whole. The manufacturer and the farmer throughout wide areas must be able and willing to exchange their products for currencies the continuing value of which is not open to question. . . .

"It is logical that the United States should do whatever it is able to assist in the return of normal economic health in the world, without which there can be no political stability or assured peace. Our policy is directed not against any country or doctrine but against hunger, poverty, desperation, and chaos. Its purpose should be the revival of a working economy in the world so as to permit the emergence of political and social conditions in which free institutions can exist. Such assistance, I am convinced, must not be on a piece-meal basis as various crises develop. Any assistance that this government may render should provide a cure rather than a palliative. Any government that is willing to assist in the task of recovery will find full cooperation, I am sure, on the part of the United States government. Any government which maneuvers to block recovery of other countries cannot expect help from us. Furthermore, governments, political parties, or groups which seek to perpetuate human misery in order to profit therefrom politically will encounter the opposition of the United States."

Now came the explicit pitch to Europe. "It is already evident that, before the United States government can proceed much further in its efforts to alleviate the situation and help start the European world on its way to recovery, there must be some agreement among the countries of Europe as to the requirements of the situation and the part those countries themselves will take in order to give proper effect to whatever action might be undertaken by this government. It would be neither fitting nor efficacious for this government to undertake to draw up unilaterally a program designed to place Europe on its feet economically. This is the business of Europeans. The initiative, I think, must come from Europe. The role of this country should consist of friendly aid in the drafting of a European program and of later support of such a program so far as it may be practical for us to do so. The program should be a joint one, agreed to by a number, if not all, European nations."

The Secretary then reverted to his opening theme. "An essential part of any successful action on the part of the United States is an understanding of the character of the problem and the remedies to be applied. Political passion and prejudice should have no part. With foresight, and a willingness on the part of our people to face up to the vast responsibility which history has clearly placed upon our country, the difficulties I have outlined can and will be overcome."

This was the end of the Secretary's prepared speech, but at this point he paused, removed his eyeglasses, looked out over the hushed assembly, and with great intensity emphasized his last point with remarks that do not appear in any official version.

"But to my mind it is of vast importance to our people to reach some general understanding rather than to react to the passions and prejudices of the moment. We are too remote from all these countries to grasp at all the real significance of the situation. It is virtually impossible, merely by reading or looking at photographs, to grasp the real significance, and yet the whole world's future hangs on a proper judgment, hangs on a realization by the American people of what can best be done, of what must be done."

It was around 9 p.m. in London when Secretary Marshall finished speaking. Before going to sleep that night, Ernest Bevin, Great Britain's Minister for Foreign Affairs, read and reread and studied with mounting excitement the full text of the speech, which, unknown to Marshall, had by prearrangement been rushed to him through unofficial channels with a specific suggestion as to its powerful intent. It was Bevin who, in his own words, "seized the offer with both hands" and took the initiative in organizing Europe's response. Out of offer and response grew the mammoth four-year Marshall Plan for European Recovery.

Although these three occasions and three speeches were the highlights of the Fifteen Weeks, policy development during the period was a continuous fabric made in courageous response to a rapidly evolving pattern of external events, each advance stimulated and made possible by the action preceding. It is the purpose of the body of this book to describe as faithfully as possible this continuous process during the Fifteen Weeks and to interpret the significance of the whole and of its parts. But first it is necessary to examine the "wider situation" out of which the developments of the Fifteen Weeks had grown.

PART II

"A MUCH WIDER SITUATION"

"It is necessary only to glance at a map to realize that the survival and integrity of the Greek nation are of grave importance in a much wider situation. If Greece should fall under the control of an armed minority, the effect upon its neighbor, Turkey, would be immediate and serious. Confusion and disorder might well spread throughout the Middle East.

"Moreover, the disappearance of Greece as an independent state would have a profound effect upon those countries in Europe, whose peoples are struggling against great odds to maintain their freedoms while they repair the damages of war."

—President Truman
in his Message to Congress, March 12, 1947.

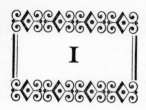

I

BALANCE OF POWER AND IMPERIAL SYSTEM

PRESIDENT TRUMAN told his Cabinet on March 7 that he was faced with a decision more serious than had ever confronted any President. The British notes concerning Greece and Turkey brought home dramatically and with compulsion the awful truth that many of the most familiar and important furnishings of the world in which the American Republic had grown to maturity had vanished. It was indeed a much wider situation than Greece and Turkey that confronted the United States. It was the widest situation we had ever been obliged to deal with as a nation.

Throughout our history power in the world had been divided among a number of countries, and in that dispersal of power had lain a measure of our security. But the balance of power—the dominant, controlling power in Europe, in Asia, in Africa, in the islands and on the seas—had remained continuously in the hands of Great Britain and her European allies, whose heritage and basic beliefs we shared. After 1823 Great Britain had found it to her interest to leave the Western Hemisphere to its own free and independent development, to respect our Monroe Doctrine, and to help enforce respect by others. Thus, isolated from the main currents of world politics, we had been left free to grow in security, and free, also, to cultivate the illusion that our happy state was the special gift of geography and Providence and that order in the world was a natural condition.

39

Then, within the space of twenty-five years, 1914–1939, had come two German challenges to the benevolent power system by which we had lived but which we did not understand. In both cases we became involved in European war only when it was evident that Great Britain and her allies could not without our aid prevent the domination of Europe by a country possessing an authoritarian political system and a detestable ideology hostile to human freedom and the independence of nations. But neither during nor after World War I or World War II did we understand the structure and meaning of the aging and weakened power system that had brought us security, that had supported in the world such concepts as human freedom, national independence, freedom of the seas, liberal trading practices, and that we had intervened to protect. During that time we did not build the foundations of a stable new order based upon a balance of power. After the first war we withdrew into isolation, leaving the British-dominated world power system little changed in appearance but in fact fatally weakened and without the buttress of our political, economic, and military strength. In the late 1930s three totalitarian powers, all with a profound contempt for human freedom—Germany, Japan, and the Soviet Union—had virtually all the military force in existence. Thus there was a second challenge, more hideous, more powerful, and again we became a defender of the free world system, of which we were inescapably a part. And though victory over the enemy was won in 1945, the bases, the essential conditions of a free and stable world order, had disappeared so completely that the United Nations organization we helped to bring into being was denied a solid foundation. The policy of unconditional surrender had brought about the destruction of the power of Germany and Japan, automatically increasing the power of the USSR in Europe and Asia.

There remained in the whole world but two great powers in the prewar sense of the term—the United States and the Soviet Union —in fact, super-powers, which were separated by an unbridgeable ideological chasm: the one the champion, the other the denier and sworn destroyer, of the values, institutions, and methods of Western civilization. And at this point the United States had largely demobilized its armed forces.

There existed not even a semblance of a balance of power in Europe. Great Britain was exhausted and impoverished, permanently weakened. Germany did not exist; France was barely alive; defeated Italy did not count; and the smaller countries were not important. It was clear that never again could the British marshal enough power in Europe to restore balance and maintain it. Outside power—that of the United States—was required. For hundreds of years British diplomacy had been backed up by a world-wide imperial system, unchallenged naval supremacy, manufacturing superiority, and a vast control over the world's finances, raw materials, and markets. Now her empire was in liquidation; naval supremacy had passed to the United States and was in any case largely superseded by air power; manufacturing superiority had disappeared; Britain had become a heavy debtor nation and the pound sterling inconvertible; and the United States was the giant of the economic and financial world.

The Soviet Union, unique in its power position in two continents, had demonstrated beyond any doubt that it was aggressive and expanding, and that its immediate design for dominion included as much of Europe and Asia and North Africa as it could get away with short of war with its Western allies. As the Russians had rolled the Germans back westward from Stalingrad, they had consistently subordinated military objectives to long-range political goals, whereas the United States and Great Britain had usually done the opposite. The consequence was that the Red armies had "liberated" or occupied all of Central Europe westward to the Elbe and all of the Balkans except Greece. In violation of agreements with their allies, Soviet leaders had then set in motion in the countries under their physical control that horrendous process of installing local Communist puppet dictatorships in which human beings lose their dignity and nations their capacity for independence. In a dreary and almost continuous round of postwar conferences among heads of states and foreign ministers, the United States and Great Britain had wrestled for the souls of the captive countries of Central Europe and the Balkans and had tried to reach agreement upon peace settlements for Germany and Austria, without success. Wherever Soviet control had been extended, it stayed and reinforced itself.

The wartime alliance was clearly dead, and remained only to be officially buried. The bad public manners of the Russians toward their allies at the San Francisco Conference progressed in succeeding months to vituperation, slander, and thence to full-scale, official propaganda warfare against the West. Stalin himself, in a public speech on February 9, 1946, formally launched the cold war on capitalist countries.

In France and Italy, Moscow-directed Communist parties, profiting from growing social unrest due to hunger, cold, inadequate housing, and bad working conditions, gained strong voting support and were aggressively extending the tentacles of their organization and control in industry, the armed forces, the government. In both countries the Communist party was a member of the government coalition and Communist ministers were in the cabinet, directing the activities of a number of government departments. The head of the Italian Communist party, Palmiro Togliatti, and the head of the French Communist party, Maurice Thorez, conferred openly with Molotov at the Paris Peace Conference in the summer of 1946. In other countries of Western Europe the Communist menace, while less acute, was rising. The Red Army, aided by a fifth column, could have taken the continent of Europe in two weeks.

The immediate prospect in South Asia and Africa was a degree less dangerous; the longer-range outlook was more so. For a century and a half British power and diplomacy had dominated, held together, and protected South Asia and Africa. Now British power was no longer equal to the task. Half the world was breaking down into defenseless, nationalistic fragments, and these were in danger of being picked up one by one by Soviet Russia.

The foundation of Britain's nineteenth-century imperial system was control of India and her organization and use of the resources and manpower of that vast subcontinent. Immediately clustered about the British-Indian sun were Ceylon, Burma, and Malaya, under British rule. In the countries on the perimeter—Iraq, Persia, Afghanistan, Tibet, and Siam—British diplomacy worked overtime and usually with success to prevent a serious challenge to vital British interests. To the southeast were the satellite empires of France and the Netherlands, Western democracies that no longer challenged Britain in Europe or abroad. Beyond these were still more British possessions—Australia, New Zealand, and a galaxy of smaller islands and bases. To the northeast was China, where British concessions dominated the principal ports, British gunboats the rivers, and British merchants and shipping the foreign trade. To the west was the continent of Africa, where the pattern was one of direct colonial rule by Great Britain and kindred Western European powers that had made peace with her. Ringing the African continent were British and allied bases, which imposed order and protected the trade routes from the east to Britain and Western Europe.

Last but by no means of least importance in this scheme of things was the protected "life-line" through the Red Sea, the Suez Canal, the Mediterranean, and the Strait of Gibraltar. The control or friendly neutrality of the Middle East was essential. The Ottoman Empire, menaced by Russia, awed and pressured by British naval supremacy, economic power, and diplomacy, maintained friendly relations with Britain and offered no lasting or important challenge to British security and British aims. Egypt was British-occupied. When the Ottoman Empire was broken up after World War I, British-French dominance in the Middle East was assured by a complex system of colonies, protectorates, mandates, and alliances, maintained by diplomatic skill and economic and political support. Russia was kept out of the Mediterranean as it had been out of the Indian Ocean. And Greece, occupying a crucial position in the Mediterranean between Europe and the Middle East, was aided, supported, and maintained in friendly independence.

This imposing imperial system was not based upon power alone. The spread of British influence and control was accompanied by protection of human rights, freedom under law, institutions designed to grow toward freedom, and liberal trading practices. Her policies were considered moral and enlightened by the progressive leaders of

the age. Half the world was held together and protected and removed from the white heat of great power rivalry by a force that
was both skillful and benign. Two great continents were kept open
to trade and settlement, open to development, open to the growth
of religion, open to the growth of the ideas and institutions and
trade with the West.

After the devastation of World War II in Europe and Asia the
power that had supported the imperial system was broken and the
morality and the fact of rule by one people over another was everywhere challenged. Each day's cables, each day's newspapers and
broadcasts, brought the story: From the Mediterranean eastward to
the Sea of Japan nationalism was successfully asserting itself. In the
very heart of the British Empire six independent states were emerg-
ing: India, Pakistan, Burma, Ceylon, Nepal, and Afghanistan.
Revolutionary movements were challenging French and Dutch control in Indochina and Indonesia, with good prospects of success.
The Philippines had achieved independence; Thailand had thrown
off British influence. Victorious China had freed herself of Western
controls. In the Middle East, colonies were moving toward self-
government, mandated countries toward independence, all toward
nationalistic self-assertion that weakened alliances. The Union Jack
had been hauled down with great ceremony from the Cairo citadel,
the green and white flag of Farouk I hoisted, and British troops
concentrated at Suez, their future status under negotiation. Syria,
Lebanon, Iraq, Jordan, Saudi Arabia, and Yemen had achieved
(or were soon to achieve) full independence. Palestine, then ravaged
by violence, was soon to make way for the new state of Israel. What
was clearly happening was the sudden disappearance of the imperial
system and the rise of independent, weak, nationalist states. This
had happened in Europe hundreds of years earlier—and had led to
centuries of bloody, nationalistic strife.

Moreover, in 1947, the prospects for strength and stability within
each nationalistic unit were bleak. Effective self-government requires
experience, discipline, and at least fair economic conditions. Democratic self-government requires in addition a high degree of literacy,
a reasonable standard of living, and a substantial middle-class—

assets that are in short supply throughout Asia. Only Japan possesses all these assets; several nations have none. Underlying these deficiencies, and the political instability they cause, are poverty, ignorance, undernourishment, and disease. Improvement in these conditions depends upon the efficient use and development of resources, including human resources. This requires outside capital and technical assistance, but capital will not invest where there is not political stability. There is thus a vicious circle in Asia, with political instability causing poor economic conditions and poor economic conditions causing political instability, which frightens away investment that might improve economic conditions.

Pressing down into this weakness, into this riot of nationalist disunity and self-assertion, was the expanding power of the Soviet Union. Ever since a Russian czar had married the daughter of the last Byzantine emperor four centuries earlier, the Russians had felt a sense of mission in Asia, as a result of which Imperial Russian control was extended from European Russia throughout north and central Asia. This expansionist urge, far from being reversed by the Bolshevik revolution, was merely reinforced by it. The chief practical difference was that the tactics of infiltration and propaganda were added to the standard forms of nineteenth-century expansionism. Monolithic in power and ideology, with a fanatical historical sense of mission, the USSR hung over fragmentized Asia in 1947, as it does today, like a dark and heavy sky over a patchwork countryside. In Manchuria, North China, and North Korea, Communist rain was coming down in sheets. Over the rest of China great spattering drops were falling. In northern Indochina a Communist-led nationalist revolution was raging. Communist agents trained in Moscow were busily organizing trouble throughout Southeast Asia. Each month brought new portents of the approaching storm.

To the restless continent of Africa the advancing storm was still distant thunder. The Russians had failed in postwar efforts to get control of the former Italian colonies of Libya and Eritrea. But the dependent peoples of Africa sensed that European rule was no longer backed, as it had been in the past, by military power for coercion and protection, by capital for development, or by an un-challenged political system, and they were accordingly pressing hard for greater control over their affairs; the colonial powers, for their part, were trying, in haste and with limited resources, to pro-mote development and to build local strength. Should the Com-munists take over government in the homeland of a single colonial power—in France or Britain or Belgium, in Portugal or Spain—its possessions in Africa would become beachheads in a poorly de-fended continent and the whole structure would be in danger.

Such was the wider situation in early 1947. Partly articulated and partly sensed from a knowledge of history and an evaluation of the stream of current information, it exercised an all-pervasive, con-trolling influence upon the decisions underlying the Truman Doctrine and determined the breadth of the President's expression of policy. An era, a power system, that had lasted hundreds of years, that had not been perfect but had brought a degree of balanced order out of chaos, had ended. A new era was beginning, and if there was to be any check upon the expansion of the Soviet Russian empire, the United States would have to throw its great weight into the balance.

The barrier to the direct and immediate extension of Soviet power and influence into the Mediterranean, North Africa, and South Asia, was the land mass extending from the borders of Afghanistan westward to the Adriatic, comprising Iran, Turkey, and Greece. It was accordingly against these three countries that, beginning in 1945 and extending through 1948, the Soviet Union persistently deployed the powerful pressures of its diplomacy, its propaganda, and its apparatus for subversion; these were rein-forced in Iran by direct armed intervention and in Greece by armed intervention of an indirect variety.

If the Soviet Union could gain control of Iran, not only would it command the oil riches of the Persian Gulf, but, more important, through that country—which has been described as the "Suez Canal of revolution"—it would be able to play a direct, open, and powerful role in the political evolution of the weak, newly independent coun-tries of the Middle East and South and Southeast Asia.

Centrally located Turkey, anchored in Europe but extending far into Asia, astride the Dardanelles and commanding the Black Sea and the eastern Mediterranean—this was the real prize. For hundreds of years every holder of power in Europe had recognized the Turkish Straits as the key to still more power in Europe and Asia and had tried to secure control of it, meaning control of Turkey on both sides of the Straits. Catherine the Great had been obsessed by it, Napoleon had called it the key to world rule. Kaiser Wilhelm, Hitler, and Stalin had lusted after it. And needless to add, for a century and a half Great Britain and France had been keenly aware of it and were determined that it should not fall into hostile hands. In 1945, with British power crumbling and French power nonexistent, the Russians took a leaf from the history of the czars and began a drive to secure control of the Turkish Straits, which, if successful, would give them control of the eastern Mediterranean, dominion over the trade routes from Europe to the East, and the possibilities of infinite mischief in North Africa and the Middle East. The oil reserves of the Middle East and the uranium mines of Africa would be within grasp. And Soviet control of Greece would be a steppingstone to this end.

The backwash of these developments on Western Europe would be devastating—psychologically, politically, economically, and militarily. The entire continent of Europe would be fatally weakened in the face of an even more powerful Communist drive.

The danger of these Soviet moves was not generally realized by the American people, and in the weeks following March 12, 1947, it was a familiar complaint that the bold proposal to aid Greece and Turkey had been launched abruptly on an unsuspecting public without the danger and provocation being proportional. But Soviet actions in and intentions toward Iran, Turkey, and Greece had been a matter of serious official concern for more than a year and a half, and in 1946 there had been two major crises involving decisions to resist Soviet expansion. In order to understand the Fifteen Weeks, we must consider in more detail the 1946 crises over Iran and Turkey and the troubles of Greece.

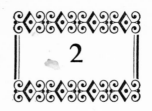

NEAR BREAKTHROUGH IN IRAN

IN EARLY March of 1946 Averell Harriman, having resigned as Ambassador to the Soviet Union, returned from Moscow and called on President Truman at the White House. The President was extremely worried over the possibilities of war with the Soviet Union and asked Harriman to go as Ambassador to London, where his wide experience would be helpful in maintaining a united front with the British. Harriman had been out of the country almost continuously since early 1941 and was reluctant to accept another foreign assignment, but under the circumstances he could not refuse.

The immediate danger point was Iran, though it was only one part in the ominous pattern of Soviet expansionist pressure extending from Teheran to Trieste, and the ruthless communization of the Balkans and Central Europe already under Red Army control.

Russian and British troops had simultaneously invaded Iran in August 1941 in order to put the country out of reach of mounting Nazi influence and to secure the fullest use of Iranian communications and transport from the Persian Gulf to Russia's back door. The Russians occupied the northern provinces, the British the central and southern portions of the country, Teheran and Meshed being left in a small neutral zone. The pro-German Reza Shah Pahlevi abdicated, and his son was accepted as his successor. A Tripartite Treaty of Alliance between Iran, the Soviet Union, and Great Britain was signed on January 29, 1942, one provision of which was that "the forces of the Allied Powers shall be withdrawn from Iranian territory not later than six months after all hostilities between the Allied Powers and Germany and her associates have been suspended by the conclusion of an armistice or armistices." The Allies also pledged themselves to "respect the territorial integrity, sovereignty, and political independence of Iran." About a year after the signing of this treaty, 30,000 U.S. noncombatant troops of the Persian Gulf Command moved into Iran under the auspices of the British treaty arrangement to speed up the transmission of supplies to the Soviet Union.

The signing of the armistice with Japan on September 2, 1945, fixed the final date for evacuation of all foreign troops from Iran at March 2, 1946. That date had passed when the President spoke to Harriman. British and American troops had been withdrawn; the Soviet troops were still there. Moreover the Moscow radio had announced on March 1 that the military evacuation of certain parts of Iran would begin on the following day but that in other parts troops would remain "until the situation was clarified." Iran had formally protested to the Soviet Union on March 3, Great Britain on March 4, and the United States on March 6. The Iranian Prime Minister, Qavam-es-Saltaneh, who was negotiating in Moscow, protested again to Molotov and Stalin personally and left for Teheran. Meanwhile verified reports had been received in Washington that, instead of withdrawing, additional Soviet troops with large numbers of tanks and other heavy combat equipment were pouring southward from the Soviet border to Tabriz and thence moving westward toward the Turkish and Iraqi borders and southeastward toward Teheran. The U.S. air attaché in Iran observed Russian Sherman tanks only twenty-five miles from Teheran. The State Department immediately asked the Soviet government whether these reports were true and published its communication on March 12. The *New York Times* of the following day carried a banner headline reading: "Heavy Russian Columns Move West in Iran; Turkey or Iraq May Be Goal; U.S. Sends Note." The situation was extremely dangerous.

This was, of course, an old story to the Iranians. For more than two hundred years Iran had been squeezed between rival Russian and British imperialisms, subjected by both to continual intervention, amputation, division into formal or *de facto* spheres of influence, and after 1860 to economic exploitation. The British had been interested primarily in preventing Russian (and later, German) influence from reaching the Persian Gulf and India, and secondarily, though importantly, in oil. The Russians had persistently sought to extend their influence and control to the Persian Gulf and the Indian Ocean; and in the 1944 they also became interested in oil. The difference between the two imperialisms, and it was an enormous difference, was that the British had learned that their interests were best served, as Sir Eyre Crowe had pointed out in a famous memorandum to the Cabinet in 1907, by identifying themselves with "the primary interests of the majority of other nations," these primary interests being, first, independence, and, second, trade. Britain must protect the open door, Sir Eyre wrote, and at the same time display "a direct and positive interest in the independence of small nations," recognizing herself as "the natural enemy of any nation which threatened the independence of smaller countries." Harold Nicolson, in his classic book *Diplomacy*, pointed out in 1939 that this principle coupled with a democratic system at home had tended during the previous hundred years to render British policy, and therefore British diplomacy, more "liberal" than those of certain other powers. The Russians were one of these "certain other powers." Under the czars they had extended and protected their interests in Asia through annexation or thinly disguised puppet governments; the Communists merely added to czarist policies and methods greater boldness, crudity, and new techniques.

When the Iranian crisis occurred in 1946 the Iranians had already been subjected for a year and a half to the most flagrant Soviet pressure and intervention designed to insure continuing Russian control when and if Red troops should be withdrawn. In September 1944, when the end of lengthy negotiations between the Iranian government and British and American oil companies in regard to oil concessions in southeast Iran was in sight, a Soviet Vice-Commissar for Foreign Affairs accompanied by a large staff arrived in Teheran and demanded exclusive mineral and oil rights in all the northern provinces. He also offered to supply experts in all branches to assist in administering the government of Iran. Thoroughly alarmed, the Iranian government terminated all oil negotiations, and later the Iranian parliament (Majlis) passed a law prohibiting any government official from negotiating oil concessions with any foreign government. The British and American negotiators accepted the situation and left the country. The enraged Soviet Vice-Commissar stayed long enough to organize mass demonstrations by the Communist-controlled Tudeh party and violent press campaigns against the Iranian government both in Iran and the Soviet Union. When he left he warned publicly that Iran would someday repent its refusal to negotiate.

His threat was not an idle one, for there shortly began a campaign, directed by Soviet agents, aided by the Tudeh party, and protected by the Red Army in northern Iran, to bring the central government in Teheran to heel. Their objective was to establish, under the duress of military occupation, local Communists in complete political control in an autonomous (not independent) Azerbaijan, secure its recognition by Teheran, bring about the "election" of a large bloc of Communist deputies to the Majlis, and by these means and other pressures to wring from the central government whatever concessions in regard to oil or political control the Russians desired. This would have meant the end of the independence and integrity of Iran. Perceiving this, the Majlis passed a law in October 1945 forbidding elections for the new Majlis (the term of the old was to expire in March 1946) until after all foreign troops had left the country.

The plot was launched. The Communist-controlled Tudeh party in Azerbaijan dissolved itself, its membership was transferred to a so-called Democratic party under the leadership of the well-known Communist by the name of Ja'afar Pishehvari, and agitation for provincial autonomy began on a grand scale. Late in October 1945 news spread that additional Red Army divisions had entered Tabriz and that arms were being distributed to the Democratic partisans and the peasants. The revolt broke out in November in provincial centers surrounding Tabriz, and communications with Teheran were cut. The Red Army prevented the Iranian government from quelling the revolt, first by denying exit to the Tabriz garrison, and a few days later by denying Iranian troops sent from the south entry into the Soviet zone. In this situation, delegates were "elected"—all "Democrats"—to the Provincial Assembly of an Autonomous Azerbaijan. On December 12, 1946, the Assembly met and formed a government under Pishehvari, and rebel troops entered and took over Tabriz. The revolution was accomplished. Still, there was no demand for independence, only provincial autonomy. The Soviets wanted not just Azerbaijan, but control over the central government in Teheran, which they might attain through Azerbaijan.

These developments catapulted the Iranian situation onto the international stage. Protests to Moscow having accomplished nothing, the Iranian delegate attending the initial, organizing meeting of the United Nations in London, on January 19, 1946, formally accused the Soviet Union of interference in the internal affairs of Iran and requested the Security Council to investigate the situation. Andrei Vishinsky, the Russian delegate, spiritedly denied the allegations. After several days of acrimonious debate the Security Council referred the matter to direct negotiations between Russia and Iran, following the suggestion of Vishinsky, but kept it under the spotlight. Negotiations *à deux!* That is what the Russians had wanted all along. But the spotlight was decidedly inconvenient.

Even while the Security Council in London was considering the Iranian complaint, despair and economic and political strain caused by Russian pressure and the cutting off of Azerbaijan brought about the fall of the Iranian government and the replacement of Premier Hakimi by Qavam-es-Saltaneh, who was known to be considerably less anti-Communist than Hakimi and to have intrigued with the Tudeh party. Taking his cue from the Security Council, Qavam went to Moscow on February 19 for negotiations, saw Stalin and Molotov several times, and received demands that included indefinite retention of Soviet troops in some parts of Iran, recognition of the autonomy of Azerbaijan, and the formation of a Russian-Iranian joint stock company, in which the Russians were to hold 51 per cent of the shares, to exploit oil in the northern provinces. Qavam did not agree, and on March 11 he returned to Teheran. The March 2 evacuation date had passed, and not only had Russian troops not departed, but more were pouring in with heavy equipment and approaching Teheran. An armed coup by Tudeh and Soviet agents was momentarily expected in the capital. Qavam therefore instructed the Iranian Ambassador in Washington to reopen Iran's complaint before the Security Council, which he did on March 18, adding that "negotiations have failed." The Security Council took up the matter on March 25.

Why did not the Russians carry through the coup in Teheran in March 1946? Why, on March 24, did the Soviet Ambassador in Teheran reopen negotiations with Qavam on the basis of modified demands? Why, on March 26, did Andrei Gromyko, Soviet representative on the Security Council, announce that within five or six weeks Soviet troops would be withdrawn from Iran "unless unforeseen circumstances arise"? The most likely reasons are that the Kremlin was finally convinced by mid-March that it could not get away with an immediate and bold puppetization of Iran without a showdown with Western powers, and that, given the political situation it had created in Iran, it could probably achieve its ends over a somewhat longer period by promising to withdraw its troops, removing the case from the purview of the Security Council, and exerting continued, steady, but somewhat more reasonable pressure on Qavam.

Beginning in late February, Western leaders had publicly dug in their heels in resistance to further Soviet advances. The British Foreign Minister, Ernest Bevin, made Britain's position clear on that point in the House of Commons on February 21. Secretary of State Byrnes on February 28 made a speech before the Overseas Press Club in New York that laid the American position bluntly and unequivocally on the line. In the context of the developing Soviet threat in Iran it was virtually an ultimatum. It received no extraordinary attention in the United States, but its significance was appreciated in Moscow.

We have joined with our allies in the United Nations to put an end to war. We have covenanted not to use force except in the defense of law as embodied in the purposes and principles of the Charter. We intend to live up to that covenant.

But as a great power and as a permanent member of the Security Council *we have a responsibility to use our influence to see that other powers live up to their covenant.*[1] And that responsibility we also intend to meet. . . .

I am convinced that there is no reason for war between any of the great powers. . . . It is not enough for nations to declare they do not want to make war. Hitler said that. . . . To banish war, nations must refrain from doing the things that lead to war. . . . Though the *status quo* is not sacred and unchangeable, we cannot overlook a unilateral gnawing away at the *status quo*. The Charter forbids aggression, and we cannot allow aggression to be accomplished by coercion or pressure or by subterfuge such as political infiltration.

The similarities with certain passages in the Truman Doctrine are striking. It is no accident. The Byrnes speech was used in drafting the Truman speech more than a year later.

Mr. Byrnes continued:

We have openly, gladly, and whole-heartedly welcomed our Soviet ally as a great power, second to none in the family of nations. We have approved many adjustments in her favor. . . . only an inexcusable tragedy of errors could cause serious conflict between us in the future. . . . But in the interest of world peace and in the interest of our common and traditional friendship we must make it plain that the United States intends to defend the Charter.

We will not and we cannot stand aloof if force or threat of force is used contrary to the purposes and principles of the Charter. We have no right to hold our troops in the territories of other sovereign states without their approval and consent freely given. . . . We must not conduct a war of nerves to achieve strategic ends. We do not want to stumble or stagger into situations where no power intends war but no power will be able to avert war.

These were strong words indeed. Sixteen days later Byrnes followed them up with another speech in New York before the Society

---

[1] Italics the author's.

of the Friendly Sons of St. Patrick, in which he urged the immediate extension of the Selective Service Act, due to expire on May 15, and the long-run adoption of universal military training. Tragic experience, he said, had made us realize that weakness invites aggression and "causes others to act as they would not act if they thought that our words were backed by strength." To what use would continuing American military strength be put? Byrnes put the question and answered it. "The answer is simple. The United States is committed to support the Charter of the United Nations. Should the occasion arise, our military strength will be used to support the purposes and principles of the Charter."

On March 16 this clearly meant Iran. Sandwiched between these two public speeches of Secretary Byrnes was the formal United States protest of March 6 against the retention of Soviet troops in Iran past the March 2 evacuation date, pointing out that such action was against the principles of the United Nations, and the sharp, public inquiry on March 12 about reports that additional Soviet troops were pouring into Iran. Moreover Winston Churchill, on March 5 at Fulton, Missouri, with President Truman sitting on the platform, had startled the world with his famous "Iron Curtain" speech, in which, after describing vividly and in detail the methods and continuing expansionist efforts of the Soviet Union, he concluded that the Soviet Union respected only force and called for a close and strong political and military union of Great Britain and the United States.

Soviet leaders apparently concluded at the last moment, from the mounting evidence that the United States and Great Britain meant business, that the talk about defending the Charter really meant a determination to use force if necessary to defend Iran, and that the latter's reopened complaint of March 18 to the Security Council would be acted upon with vigor. There was some rapid gearshifting. Gromyko tried desperately to get a postponement past March 25 of the Security Council's consideration of the case. Failing, the Russians hurriedly reopened negotiations with Iran and took a great deal of the wind out of the Iranian complaint by announcing the fact on March 26 with an ambiguous statement about an "understanding" with Iran that Soviet troops would be evacuated within five or six weeks "unless unforeseen circumstances arise." What they were obviously hoping to do was to continue using troop evacuation as a bargaining point to wring from Qavam the other concessions they desired.

For ten hectic days, during which the Iranian representative to the United Nations persistently and devastatingly exposed the true situation before a session of the Security Council in New York and its members mercilessly spotlighted and probed, while Gromyko writhed in embarrassment and at one point walked out of the Council chamber, Qavam negotiated in Teheran under the pressure of the impatient Russians, with the American and British ambassadors calling upon him frequently to exert counterpressures. In the end the Russians appeared to have got a great deal of what they wanted in return for troop evacuation. The agreement announced on April 5 provided for the evacuation of the Red Army within a month and a half after March 24; for a joint Russian-controlled Russian-Iranian oil company to be established and ratified by the Majlis within seven months after March 24; and with regard to Azerbaijan, "since it is an internal Iranian affair, peaceful arrangements will be made between the government and the people of Azerbaijan for carrying out of improvements in accordance with existing laws and in a benevolent spirit toward the people of Azerbaijan." The Security Council kept the matter under scrutiny until May 22, when it was apparent that Red troops had in fact evacuated Iran. On that date discussion of the Iranian matter was formally adjourned, but the matter was kept on the agenda. There was great rejoicing over the bloodless United Nations victory, and Iran slipped to the back pages of the newspapers. The Iranian government was left to get an extorted oil agreement ratified and to work out a deal with a revolutionary Communist regime left by the Russians in Azerbaijan as a lever for further operations.

Hardly had the sustaining arm of the Security Council been withdrawn than Iran began to slip behind the Iron Curtain. Qavam sent a pro-Soviet official to Tabriz, where an agreement was concluded, giving Azerbaijan much of the autonomy that Pishehvari insisted upon and opening the way for greatly increased electoral weight of Azerbaijan representatives in the Majlis. Qavam then appointed as governor general in Azerbaijan one of the Cabinet ministers in the Pishehvari regime; and on August 2 he admitted three Tudeh members to his Cabinet, one as vice-premier. Things were going well indeed for the Russians.

Then occurred one of those unexpected counterstrokes that are as instructive in the art of dealing with Russian imperialism as the proceedings of the Security Council. In mid-July a well-known Tudeh leader and trade unionist by the name of Reza Rusta led a general strike, accompanied by widespread riots, death, and sabotage, in Abadan and other oil centers in that part of southwest Iran controlled by the Anglo-Iranian Oil Company. This violent extension of Communist power from Azerbaijan to the Persian Gulf brought British Indian troops in a hurry to Basra, in Iraq, just across the border from Abadan—with express Iraqi consent. Coincidentally, several tribal chieftains in the south announced their opposition to the increased influence of the Tudeh party in Teheran, and the Iraqi Independence party demanded the return of Khuzistan to Iraq. In September a number of tribes in the southern region revolted, formed a coalition, captured a wide area, and demanded of Teheran the ousting of Tudeh members from the Cabinet, local self-government in the southern provinces, and an increase in parliamentary representation—the latter to offset in the Majlis the increased weight of the Communists from Azerbaijan.

From them on Qavam was able to play both ends against the middle, and he did it skillfully. He protested the landing of British troops at Basra, demanded the recall of the British consul general at Ahwaz—one of the three British officials whom the Russians openly accused of having instigated the revolt—and asked the British to investigate charges against the other two. At the same time he arrested some Tudeh troublemakers in Teheran. Then he negotiated with the southern rebels and accepted most of their demands. On October 17 he resigned and re-formed his government, dropping the three Tudeh ministers.

Emboldened by success, by southern Iranian and British counter-pressure, and encouraged by the active diplomacy of the new American ambassador, George V. Allen, Qavam then moved to re-establish his authority in Azerbaijan. On November 24 he ordered central government troops into Azerbaijan to supervise the forthcoming elections to the Majlis. Pishehvari vowed to fight and called for resistance, but there was none to speak of. Government troops entered Tabriz on December 14, and the puppet regime collapsed. Pishehvari escaped to the Soviet Union and other officials were arrested or dispersed. The Iranian government was once more master of its entire house.

By the beginning of the Fifteen Weeks on February 21, 1947, parliamentary elections had been held. Qavam's party captured a substantial majority of the seats, the Communists but two. Political temperatures were nevertheless high, as the oil agreement with the Russians was to be debated when the Majlis should convene. And nobody knew from day to day what the Russians and their agents in Iran would do next to assuage their defeat.

This was an essential element in the wider situation that the President referred to on March 12. If Greece and Turkey should fall under Soviet control, Iran would undoubtedly slip back into the Soviet orbit.

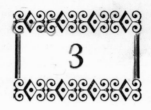

3

SOVIET PRESSURES ON TURKEY

THERE was a meeting at the White House on August 15, 1946, at which a decision was made to take a firm position against Soviet efforts to gain control of the Dardanelles and to hold that position at all costs. With the President in his office were Dean Acheson, James Forrestal, Secretary of the Navy, Kenneth C. Royall, Undersecretary of War, the Chiefs of Staff, including General Dwight D. Eisenhower, and several assistants. Eight days earlier, on August 7, the Soviet government had proposed to Turkey a "new regime" for the Straits—on the same day sending copies of its proposals to the United States and Great Britain—which would have meant the establishment of Soviet naval and air bases in Turkey, physical control of the vital waterways, and the end of Turkey's independence.

This was not the beginning of the Soviet campaign to bring Turkey under control. In fact, in August 1946, the campaign seemed to be nearing the end. As was known from captured German documents, during the period of the Nazi-Soviet alliance in 1940 Stalin had renewed historical Russian efforts to secure control of the Straits. In world-dividing negotiations with Hitler and Ribbentrop, Molotov had insisted, as the price of cooperation, that Soviet security be guaranteed by a mutual assistance pact with Bulgaria and the establishment of bases for Soviet land and sea forces in the Turkish Straits. Molotov also demanded specific recognition of

Soviet aspirations in the area south of Baku and Batum in the general direction of Iran and the Persian Gulf. The indignant Nazis did not even reply, and thus began the end of the Russo-German alliance.

On March 19, 1945, the Soviet Union had announced that it would abandon its twenty-year-old Treaty of Friendship and Neutrality with the Turks, in which each party undertook not to participate in alliances, coalitions, or hostile actions of any kind directed at the other. On June 7, 1945, Selim Sarper, Turkish Ambassador in Moscow, paid a courtesy call on Molotov before returning to Ankara for a visit. To his astonishment, the Foreign Minister suggested out of a blue sky that if Turkey wanted a treaty with the USSR along the lines of one signed with Poland, it could have it, but the price would be:

1. Cession to the Soviet Union of the Turkish districts of Kars, Ardahan, and Artvin, near the Russo-Turkish border in the Caucasus. These had been acquired by the Russians in 1878 and returned to the Turks after World War I.

2. Revision of the Montreux Convention governing the Straits. The Russians wanted a new regime administered by the Black Sea powers (meaning in effect Russia and Turkey) with third-nation or international interest eliminated.

3. Lease to the Soviet Union of strategic bases for naval and land forces in the Straits for "joint defense" purposes.

4. Abandonment by Turkey of her British associations and the conclusion of a treaty similar to those the Soviets were concluding with their Balkan satellites.

Selim Sarper rejected the proposition on the spot and said there was no use even discussing it. Two days later his government sent him back to say the same things to Molotov under official instruction.

Then the Soviet screw began to turn. A violent press and radio campaign was unleashed against Turkey in Bulgaria, Yugoslavia, Albania, and the Communist press of Greece, spreading to the Soviet press itself: Turkey was an eastern power who had no right to be in Europe! Western Thrace should be ceded to Bulgaria to give the latter an outlet to the Aegean Sea at Alexandroúpolis!

Turkish leaders had been pro-Nazi during the war! The Turkish government was fascist, capitalistic, imperialistic! In December 1945 agitation for a separate Armenia was started; and two Georgian professors from Tiflis laid historical claim, which was given enormous publicity in Moscow and throughout the Soviet Union, not only to Kars, Ardahan, and Artvin, but to several other Turkish districts extending westward along the Black Sea to Trebizond. Soviet troop movements, diplomatic pressure, and propaganda were well orchestrated. The reaction of the Turks was national solidarity, unanimous defiance, and a strengthening of the Turkish Army, which had been mobilized since 1939 and was already a serious economic strain. This was the setting in which the Soviet Union made its second bid for control of the Straits, this time in formal notes addressed to Turkey, the United States, and Great Britain.

It was a tense, dangerous month, August of 1946. The "Peace Conference" in Paris, where Secretary Byrnes was heading the American delegation, had degenerated into a bitter wrangle. Molotov, joined in chorus by his Communist puppets from the satellite states, was daily casting aspersions upon the American role in the war, impugning our aims and methods, railing against capitalism and British-American imperialism. Demands for the return of Trieste to the Yugoslavs were accompanied by Tito's provocations along the Morgan Line and threats to take the territory by force. Bulgaria, an ex-enemy, was being supported in its demands upon Greece for Western Thrace. British troops had been hurried to Basra, and the fate of Iran was in the balance. The Russians had massed twenty-five divisions, many motorized, on the southern border of the Caucasus, where they were equally useful as pressure on Turkey and on Iran. Violence was daily succeeded by violence in Palestine. General Marshall's mission to China had failed, and the Reds were on the verge of launching an all-out attack upon the Nanking government. And this was the month Tito's Air Force chose to shoot down two official U.S. transport planes on regular flights from Austria to Italy. The passengers of the first were miraculously spared death but were held incommunicado by the Yugoslavs. The passengers of the second were all killed.

One of the first things that was done in Washington upon receipt of the Soviet note of August 7 on the Turkish Straits was to order a respectable U.S. naval task force to the Mediterranean. Forrestal had earnestly advanced this suggestion in February. Byrnes had first accepted it and then vetoed it, settling for sending the battleship *Missouri* to Turkey—it arrived in the Bosporus on April 5 and stayed several weeks—for the publicly stated purpose of returning the ashes of the Turkish Ambassador in Washington, who had died during the war. Now the matter of a task force was revived. The new aircraft carrier *Franklin D. Roosevelt* and two destroyers weighed anchor promptly, made a rendezvous off Lisbon with two cruisers and three destroyers ordered from British waters, and shortly proceeded to the Mediterranean.

The next and more important step, in Acheson's view, was to get a firm, coordinated government position on standing resolutely with the Turks, regardless of the consequences. This was a more difficult thing to do in August 1946 than might be supposed, for in those days before the creation of the National Security Council there was no formalized machinery for achieving an agreed government position in foreign affairs committing all the Services. But the Secretaries of State, War, and Navy had established the habit of meeting together informally at a fixed time each week to discuss problems. At the next meeting the principals were joined by the Chiefs of Staff and flanked by their Mediterranean and Middle East experts. Acheson said that a grave matter had arisen affecting the foreign policy and future defense of the United States and that it was important to do an orderly job. All the Services should therefore jointly canvass their policies and capabilities and recommend to the President a coordinated view and program. It was clear to him that the Russians were trying to take over the Straits and establish a naval and air beachhead there, which would inevitably lead, according to the plain pattern of Russian behavior, to Turkey's loss of sovereignty. The question was simple. Could we and would we stand with the Turks? If we decided we could and would, regardless of the consequences, then we could afford to reply to the

Soviet note gently but firmly. But we must be prepared to follow it up.

There was general agreement with this view, and a working party representing the State Department and the Services was appointed to draw up and clear the necessary background and position papers. A few days later, there was a second meeting of the whole group and formal agreement was reached. On August 15 the principals and the Chiefs of Staff went to see the President. At that meeting Acheson laid out the facts as agreed to by all. The Russian demands on Turkey reflected a desire to control and dominate that country. Accession to these demands would be followed by Communist domination of Greece. The consequences of the loss of Greece and Turkey throughout the Middle East and upon communications in the Mediterranean would be disastrous. It was recommended that we tell the Russians firmly that the Straits were a matter of international concern and that we could not agree to their proposals, with the full realization that if we maintained our attitude it might lead to armed conflict.

The President listened, asked a few questions, solicited the views of others present, and then said that it was perfectly clear in his own mind that we should take a firm position, that we might as well find out now as in five or ten years whether the Russians were bent on world conquest. He authorized and directed the State Department and the Services to carry out the recommended program.

At this point General Eisenhower, who was seated beside Acheson, confided in whispers his concern that the President might be making his decision without fully understanding its importance and possible consequences. Then Eisenhower addressed the President and, emphasizing the gravity of the matter, suggested that Acheson be permitted to go over again the facts and implications of the Straits situation and the possible consequences of the decision that was being made. The President agreed, and Acheson did so. When this second analysis was finished the President opened a convenient desk drawer and drew out a large map of the eastern Mediterranean, the Middle East, and Central and South Asia. It was made in sections, covered for protection with transparent plastic, the sections held together with black tape permitting them to be folded and opened readily. The whole was well worn and had the air of long and frequent handling. Unfolding the map, Truman proceeded to give a ten- to fifteen-minute dissertation on the historical importance and present-day strategic significance of the area, which at least one person present described later as "masterful." Concluding, he turned good-humoredly to Eisenhower and asked whether he was satisfied now that the situation was understood. Eisenhower joined in the general laughter and admitted that he was.

Four days later, on August 19, Acheson handed to the Soviet Chargé d'Affaires in Washington a short and polite note accepting three of five Soviet principles to govern the revision of the Montreux Convention. But it rejected one which would establish a new regime for the Straits confined to Turkey and the other Black Sea powers and exclude all other countries. With regard to still another, in which it had been suggested that the Soviet Union and Turkey should organize jointly the defenses of the Straits, the United States government had this to say:

> It is the firm opinion of this government that Turkey should continue to be primarily responsible for the defense of the Straits. Should the Straits become the object of attack or threat of attack by an aggressor the resulting situation would constitute a threat to international security and could clearly be a matter for action on the part of the Security Council of the United Nations.

This did not sound like a world-shaking document. The decision behind it was nevertheless highly significant.

As it happened, this note was handed to the Russians the same day Yugoslav fighter planes shot down the second official U.S. transport plane within ten days. Although the occupants of the second plane were all killed, that fact was not known because the Yugoslavs refused U.S. authorities permission to investigate; the passengers of the first plane were still held incommunicado. Official restraint gave way to official indignation. The U.S. note on Turkey was released to the press at the same time as an ultimatum to Tito as furious and blunt as any in our history. The *New York Times* of August 22 carried a three-line banner reading: "U.S. Gives Belgrade 48 Hours To Free Fliers or Face Action before U.N. Security Council; Rejects Russian Share in Straits Defense." Tito backed down in a hurry, complied with our demands, permitted official U.S. investigation, and gave strict orders to the Yugoslav military forces not to fire on foreign planes, civil or military. Tension abated rapidly. The European Air Transport Service, which, after the second incident, had suspended all Vienna-Rome flights while the question was debated in Washington whether to give U.S. transport planes fighter escorts, resumed its service after a few days without escorts but in reconditioned and armed B-17s, whose crews had orders to shoot back if attacked. The U.S. naval task force paid leisurely courtesy calls in the Mediterranean, in Greece, Istanbul, and all the way to Jedda.[1]

In this context the American note of August 19, regarding the Straits, the similar British note of August 21, and the long, strong, and documented Turkish rebuttal of August 22 were read in Moscow. About a month later the Soviet government sent another round of notes substantially reiterating its position, and got another round of replies in opposition. The Turks, with government, opposition, and people united, stood firm as a rock and made no secret of their intention to maintain their army in full readiness as long as might be necessary and to fight to the last soldier and citizen to defend Turkish sovereignty. The steam seemed to escape a little from the Soviet roller. There the matter rested in uneasy inconclusiveness at the beginning of the Fifteen Weeks.

Several years later, in October 1949, when Acheson was Secretary of State, he and Mrs. Acheson were dining with President Truman in his private car on the way back from the dedication of the new UN building in New York. Sparked by some incident of the day, the President began to talk about the Middle East and Central Asia. As he spoke he became engrossed in the subject and,

---

[1] A U.S. naval task force was permanently assigned to the Mediterranean according to an official announcement of September 30.

pushing back the coffee cups, drew with his spoon on the tablecloth outline maps to illustrate his points. He described the travels of Marco Polo, the fabulous conquests of Genghis Khan, the rise and decline of the Moguls in India and Persia. Mrs. Acheson, fascinated, encouraged him to go on. He painted in broad strokes a picture of the rise of the Ottoman Empire, its check in Europe, its decline. He traced the growth of the power of European Russia, the irresistible spread of Russian control over Northern and Central Asia, the persistent historical drive of Russia to obtain southern outlets, including control of the Dardanelles, the frustration of Russian aims by British and French power and diplomacy.

Acheson was interested but not surprised at the President's knowledge of the Middle East and Central Asia, for he had had several occasions in previous years to discover it for himself. But it was a startling discovery for Mrs. Acheson.

"How does it happen, Mr. President," she asked, "that you are so versed in the history of an area that to most of us is only a great stretch on a map?"

The President laughed and told her. As a boy in Independence, Missouri, he had had to wear thick-lensed glasses, which limited his participation in the rough-and-tumble games of the neighborhood boys. His glasses were always getting in the way, or broken, and because of his vision sandlot sports were out. But with glasses he could read, and he read. He recalled that he must have begun with the letter A in the local public library and read through Z. His reading interests were varied, but, for some reason he cannot explain, the history of the Middle East and Central Asia held a particular fascination for him. Through his reading he had become something of a specialist in that area, and his interest in it had continued throughout his life.

Thus when the problems of Iran, Turkey, and Greece came before President Truman for decision in 1946–47 he did not have to be convinced of the importance of action. He already knew.

4

THE WINNING HAND—GREECE

THE Istanbul correspondent of the London *Times* reported on August 19, 1946, that according to "most reliable" information a secret meeting was held at the end of May 1946 at Gorni, in southern Bulgaria, of Yugoslav, Bulgarian, and Greek Communists under the chairmanship of a Russian agent, to draw plans for a general rising in Greek Macedonia with the object of creating an autonomous Macedonia under Yugoslav hegemony. After that meeting, he said, arms and agents had been smuggled into Greece, resulting in the outbreak of disturbances in Greek Macedonia and Thessaly. He drew attention to Yugoslavia's official backing of an autonomous Macedonia with an outlet to the Aegean at Salonika, and also to the coincidence between the outbreaks in Greek Macedonia and the Soviet move on the Turkish Straits. Apparently the same "reliable information" on the Gorni meeting was conveyed to Mallory Browne, of the *New York Times,* in London, who reported it to his paper.

There can be no question, on the basis of events as they unfolded from August 1946 onward, that there was a well-organized plot to bring part or all of Greece under Communist domination. The plot showed itself, in the not uncommon Communist manner, at Lake Success, New York, where the Ukrainian delegate to the United Nations Security Council, Dmitri Manuilsky, on August 25 brought unsubstantiated charges, which were dismissed shortly by the Council, that the Greeks were provoking border incidents with Albania, planning to wrest a portion of southern Albania by force, and persecuting minorities in Macedonia, Thrace, and Epirus—all these crimes aided and abetted, he charged, by British troops stationed in Greece. The plot was evident simultaneously at the Peace Conference in Paris, where Bulgarians pressed a claim for western Thrace, Yugoslavia demanded an independent Macedonia, and Molotov and his Balkan satellites loosed salvoes against the "monarcho-fascist" government of Greece, charging it with border provocations, territorial designs on Greece's neighbors, and internal terror and oppression. In the Soviet Union and the Communist-dominated Balkans the press and radio opened up a virulent campaign against Greece on these same points. And in Greece itself minor disturbances in the northern regions developed in August 1946 into organized, sustained, and well-supplied guerrilla activities, which prevented economic recovery and rapidly undermined what was left of the authority of the state. The guerrillas, numbering some 13,000, were armed, trained, and given border protection and guidance by the authorities in Yugoslavia, Bulgaria, and Albania. The poorly equipped and demoralized Greek Army was powerless to check their depredations.

This situation grew worse during the fall and winter. The Greek government repeatedly exposed it, the world press freely reported it, and the American Embassy in Athens kept it under close scrutiny. On December 19, 1946, following a request from the Greek government that cited chapter and verse of outside aid to Greek guerrillas, the Security Council of the United Nations appointed a Commission of Investigation and ordered it to Greece to report on the facts.[1]

This was of course only a new phase, now with the covert help of foreign allies, of an armed effort to dominate Greece that had been carried on for several years by veteran Greek Communists. Had it not been for the understanding, farsightedness, and diplomacy of Prime Minister Winston Churchill and his intervention in Greek affairs in the face of widespread criticism, Greece's future

[1] The formal report of the Commission to the Security Council on May 27 substantiated Greece's charges.

would have been foreclosed well before the end of the war in Europe.

During the enemy occupation of Greece many guerrilla groups had been organized to harass the Germans, but bitter personal and political rivalries, which the Nazi occupiers encouraged, had led to a dissipation of much of their strength in fighting among themselves. The two groups which had finally aborbed or destroyed the weaker guerrilla organizations were the Communist-dominated EAM (National Liberation Front), with its army of about twenty thousand, known as ELAS (Peoples' National Army of Liberation), and its smaller rightist rival known as EDES, with about five thousand men, bitterly anti-Communist, under the leadership of General Zervas. For a period the two guerrilla groups had cooperated with each other, and with British agents, to carry out sabotage operations, but by the middle of 1943 they had fallen apart and, making no further significant contribution to the war effort, had resumed their fight for political power to be exercised at war's end. To Churchill it was obvious that these two contending groups of men, organized and with guns in their hands, would be in a position to move in when the Nazis retreated and that one or the other would determine the kind of government under which 7,500,000 Greeks would live for a long time to come.

The only other contender for Greek power was the Greek King in London, with the royalist politicians that composed his government in exile in Cairo and his Greek Brigade assembled in Egypt. To the King, as the head and symbol of a state that had fought as Britain's ally during the war, Churchill felt a very strong obligation, though he appears to have had a thinly veiled contempt for the "royalist politicians" who surrounded him. But Churchill's foremost loyalty was to Greece and its people. His position was precisely and eloquently expressed in a telegram (April 9, 1944), to Mr. Leeper, British Ambassador to the Greek government in exile:

"Our relations are definitely established with the lawfully constituted Greek government headed by the King, who is the ally of Britain and cannot be discarded to suit the momentary surge of appetite among ambitious émigré nonentities. Neither can Greece find constitutional expression in particular sets of guerrillas, in many cases indistinguishable from banditti, who are masquerading as the saviours of their country while living on the local villagers. . . . Our only desire and interest is to see Greece a glorious, free nation. . . . The King is the servant of his people. He makes no claim to rule them. He submits himself freely to the judgment of the people as soon as normal conditions are restored. He places himself and his Royal House entirely at the disposition of the Greek nation. Once the German invader has been driven out, Greece can be a republic or a monarchy, entirely as the people wish. . . ." [2]

The Communist-dominated EAM, recognizing the probable role the King and his government in exile, backed by the British, would play in the liberation, in 1943 began a campaign, consisting of political maneuvering and propaganda, to prevent the return of the King and to destroy the authority of the Greek government in exile, or join and dominate it. In August 1944, on the eve of liberation, EAM finally joined the Greek government in exile, securing six ministerial posts.

Prime Minister Churchill and Foreign Secretary Eden had it in mind as early as September 1943 that British troops might have to land in Greece when the Germans left "to give support to the restored lawful Greek government" and to discourage trouble between contending guerrilla groups. In July 1944, with German evacuation impending and with the Greeks at one another's throats, Churchill began actively to lay military and political plans for such a course; these plans were completed during his trip to Italy in August. He knew with fair certainty by then what the EAM would try to do, and he was determined to forestall it by a lightning parachute occupation of Athens and naval entry into Piraeus. By these maneuvers he would gain time in which to bring the Greek Brigade from Italy and install the Greek government. This was accomplished as planned, closely timed and adjusted to German withdrawal, between the 4th and 17th of October 1944.[3]

[2] Winston Churchill, *Triumph and Tragedy* (Boston: Houghton Mifflin Company, 1953).

[3] Churchill took the precaution of bargaining with Stalin in Moscow on

The smoothness of the operation was due in considerable measure to an agreement reached at Caserta on September 26 between the Greek Prime Minister and the commanders of the two leading guerrilla armies in Greece, General Saraphis of the Communist ELAS, and General Zervas of the Rightist EDES, the latter two summoned by General Sir Henry Maitland Wilson, British Supreme Commander in the Mediterranean. The guerrilla leaders agreed to place themselves and their forces under the orders of the Greek government, who in turn placed them under the command of the British General Scobie. The Greek generals declared that none of their men would take the law into his own hands and agreed that in Athens any action would be taken only on the direct orders of the British commander.

Even before the last German troops crossed the northern frontier on November 10, with ELAS armed bands taking over and showing no respect for central authority, it was apparent in Athens that ELAS and EAM were going to try to seize power by force, and on November 15, General Scobie was directed to make preparations accordingly. Following two weeks of Cabinet consideration of proposals for demobilizing and disarming the guerrilla forces in order to avert civil war, the six EAM ministers resigned from the government, a general strike was called, and the Communist party moved its headquarters from Athens. Shots were fired on December 3 when police collided with Communists engaged in a banned demonstration, and the next day civil war began.

A concerted attack was made by ELAS and armed civilians to capture Athens. Churchill sent General Scobie the most stringent orders to intervene and hold Athens, but this was easier said than done, and all but the very center of Athens was soon lost. Bloody street fighting went on for several weeks, marked by extreme cruelty, wanton destruction, and reprisal, Greek against Greek. Toward the

---

October 9, even as British troops were landing in Greece, for a free hand for Britain in Greece without Soviet intervention or criticism. The price he paid was a free hand for the Soviet Union in Romania, already occupied by the Red Army. Churchill claims that Stalin lived up to his agreement during the critical months of December and January following, when the EAM-ELAS launched a bloody attack to seize power.

latter part of the month the arrival of strong British reinforcements turned the tide. By month's end the rebels were driven from Athens, and by mid-January British troops controlled all Attica. A truce was signed with the insurgents on January 11, 1945, and a peace agreement at Varkiza on February 12, stipulating ELAS disarmament, a plebiscite on the king, and national elections under Allied supervision. Already the King of Greece, giving in to Churchill's persuasion, had on December 30 appointed Archbishop Damaskinos as regent and announced that he would not return to Greece until called by a vote of the people.

The horrors perpetrated by the Communists during the civil war of 1944–45 so revolted public opinion in faction-ridden Greece that a measure of cohesiveness was brought about, not in affirmation of a positive program but at least in opposition to Communism and its exponents in Greece. In the general election held on March 31, 1946, under the watchful eyes of fifteen hundred American, British, French, and South African official observers, who pronounced it on the whole a fair expression of opinion, the parties of the Right won a large majority, and on September 1, 1946, the King was recalled to Greece by a plebiscite. The EAM nevertheless remained exceedingly active and vocal, and whatever may have been its relations with Moscow before and during the civil war, as the wartime alliance of the powers disintegrated after the cessation of hostilities in Europe, it became the clearly recognized instrument of Soviet policy in Greece and the Balkans.

The upsurge of Communist guerrilla activities in Greece in the fall of 1946 and the following winter thus had a substantial, violent, and confused history, one that was little known or appreciated in true perspective. The prevailing impression of what had been going on in Greece from 1943 onward was a distorted one. Public opinion in the United States had never therefore looked favorably upon Churchill's Greek operations. During the brief civil war in Greece it was powerfully hostile, and continued to look askance in 1945 and 1946 at the gyrations of the incompetent and often corrupt Greek politicians who were protected and sustained by British troops and by British financial aid. When on March 12, 1947,

President Truman proposed to assume the burden in Greece theretofore borne by the British there was considerable public concern in the United States over aiding a corrupt, monarchical, "fascist" regime in Greece, and about "pulling British chestnuts out of the fire." Nevertheless, confronted with the brute consequences of not doing so, the American people faced up to realities.

Years later, in the concluding volume of his history of the Second World War, *Triumph and Tragedy,* Churchill, writing about British intervention in Greece, had this to say:

> It is odd, looking back on these events, now that some years have passed, to see how completely the policy for which I and my colleagues fought so stubbornly has been justified by events. Myself, I never had any doubts about it, for I saw quite plainly that Communism would be the peril civilization would have to face after the defeat of Nazism and Fascism. It did not fall to us to end the task in Greece. I little thought, however, at the end of 1944 that the State Department, supported by overwhelming American public opinion, would in a little more than two years not only adopt and carry on the course we had opened, but would make vehement and costly exertions, even of a military character, to bring it to fruition.

Notwithstanding $700 million in direct foreign aid (from UNRRA, Great Britain, the United States, and organized charities), Greece in 1945 and 1946 managed merely to survive, and the country's ability to sustain itself economically was scarcely better in early 1947 than when German troops had evacuated the country in late 1944. Greece had always had a hard time making ends meet, the poverty of its natural resources being such that it had always needed more imports than could be paid for with exports. A large part of the exports had always gone to Central European markets, especially Germany, which after the war were closed. The Italian invasion, the German invasion, four years of cruel enemy occupation, and the scorched-earth policy of the retreating Germans had left Greece the most thoroughly destroyed, disorganized, and demoralized country in Europe.

In the first two years after liberation seven changes in government did little to improve things. Some progress was made in restoring emergency communications and in reviving agriculture, but industrial production and export trade had hardly done more than start a comeback. Foreign aid kept the country from starvation, but while most people were barely subsisting, profiteers, speculators, and black marketeers throve in ostentatious wealth and luxury, causing inevitable embitterment among the masses, and none of the seven Greek governments dealt effectively with the problem.

The end of the civil war in February 1945 and the nominal disarming and disbanding of the guerrillas brought a cessation of large-scale violence, but no peace and security. Widespread lawlessness and the uncertain intentions of Greece's neighbors to the north made necessary the maintenance of an army of 100,000 and police forces of half that number, far more than Greece had ever supported, with crushing, intolerable effects upon the budget. Notwithstanding, people lived in a perpetual state of fear. This, plus bitter social and political tensions that had grown out of civil strife, created a climate in which governments could hardly govern at all, much less engage in rational planning, develop an effective economic policy, or inaugurate and enforce the controls necessary to bring order out of economic and financial chaos. A psychology of helplessness and inertia prevailed, a feeling that individual efforts were futile, that Greece because of her sufferings was entitled, without determination and effort on the part of Greeks themselves, to be taken care of by Greece's rich allies.

This was the situation in the fall of 1946 when the heat was turned up under Greece by her Communist neighbors. Well-supplied guerrilla bands spread terror and devastation. Refugees from the rural districts streamed into Athens and other cities. Communications were disrupted. A bad psychological, administrative, and economic situation rapidly turned worse. UNRRA was scheduled to end March 31, 1947, and the flow of life-sustaining supplies was already slowing down. Foreign exchange reserves were gone, and minimum import needs could not be financed. There was a prospect for a 1947 budget *deficit,* including provision for an expanded military establishment, of nearly $300 million, or three times the currency in circulation. By February 1947 prices were moving up steadily, threatening to skyrocket, and wage demands and social discontent were accumulating at a rapid rate.

The British had been the chief stabilizing and sustaining element in this chaotic situation. Not only had they helped finance the Greek Army, but 16,000 British troops, landed in Greece in October 1944 to aid in taking over control from the defeated Germans, had remained to help stabilize the country and organize and equip the Greek Army and police forces. British troops were not engaged in combat against the guerrillas in the north; nevertheless, concentrated in and around Athens, they were an important factor in maintaining order. But on February 3 the British government announced that for reasons of economy it was immediately withdrawing half its troops. The British Cabinet, confronted with financial disaster, had been debating for many weeks the matter of withdrawing all its forces, had decided upon such a course, to be effected in two stages, and although no date had been set for departure of the last contingent of 8000, it was expected to be soon. The Greeks felt abandoned and feared the worst.

Several times in 1946 the Greek government had asked the United States for increased financial aid, and Washington had done all it could under existing appropriations and authority, which were limited. Prime Minister Constantin Tsaldaris spoke to Secretary Byrnes early in October about Greece's need for financial assistance and military equipment. He raised the question with Byrnes again in December in New York, where he had come to request the United Nations to send a commission to Greece to investigate his charges of foreign aid to the Greek guerrillas. Secretary Byrnes and President Truman took the matter up with the Export-Import Bank, but as there was no reasonable assurance of repayment nothing further could be done under the law. In conversations between Tsaldaris and Undersecretaries of State Acheson and Clayton, it became apparent that the Greek economic and financial and administrative system was in complete chaos, that the Greeks had no documented case for loans but just wanted money and arms on a large scale, and that if granted they would probably be wasted.

Accordingly, it was decided to send an American Economic Mission to Greece to make a thorough survey of the situation, and Paul A. Porter was selected to head the mission. He and his party arrived in Greece on January 18, 1947, approximately the same time as the commission appointed by the United Nations to investigate Greek frontier incidents. The United States representative on that commission was Mark Ethridge, editor and publisher of the *Louisville Courier-Journal* and the *Louisville Times*.

Porter, Ethridge, and the American Ambassador in Athens, Lincoln McVeagh, operated more or less as a team. By the latter part of February it was their combined judgment that unless Greece received immediate assurance of large-scale military and financial aid, the last vestiges of the authority of the Greek government would disappear within a matter of weeks in a skyrocketing inflation, strikes, riots, and public panic, leaving the field clear for the increasingly bold and successful Communist guerrillas to take over. One thing more was clear to them: aid in the old pattern, no matter how extensive, would not save the situation. Large-scale economic aid was necessary over a period of years, but it was equally important that this should be administered on the spot by an American mission large enough, expert enough, and exercising sufficiently direct participation in and sanctions over the Greek government to bring about a thorough reorganization of the Greek economy and administrative system. Otherwise the money would be lost, the supplies wasted, the errors of the past compounded.

There was never any doubt in Washington that aid to Greece would have to be accompanied by intervention in the country's internal affairs. When on March 3, 1947, the Prime Minister and the Foreign Minister of Greece addressed another urgent, formal appeal to the United States for financial and military aid, they also asked for "the aid of experienced American administrative, economic, and technical personnel to assure the utilization in an effective and up-to-date manner of the financial and other assistance given to Greece, to help to restore a healthy condition in the domestic economy and public administration and to train the young people of Greece to assume their responsibilities in a reconstructed economy." This was no accident. The message was drafted in the State Department and suggested to the Greek government.

To Americans in 1947 intervention was an ugly word. But in the long and turbulent history of Greece since the Golden Age mere foreign intervention had been among the nicer things that had happened to the Greek people. The more usual pattern had been, for more than two thousand years, foreign invasion, occupation, and indescribable oppression and exploitation. On the other hand, it had been the concerted, armed intervention of the British, French, and Russians in 1827–32 that had saved the Greek revolution started in 1821 against the centuries-old rule of the Ottoman Turks, and had resulted in the establishment of an independent monarchy under the protection of the three powers. Thereafter throughout most of the nineteenth century all three had intervened briefly but often, singly or jointly, in Greek affairs, but the net result of their rivalry and competitive intervention had been the maintenance, as a matter of common interest, of an independent Greece. The Nazi invasion and occupation of Greece in 1940–41 and the Soviet effort in 1946–47 to seize control were throwbacks to a much earlier pattern of conquest, rule, and oppression. Both sought the disappearance of an independent Greece, previously sustained by agreement for the common good.

The word intervention was never used by Will Clayton, Paul Porter, and others in explaining to the congressional committees how American aid to Greece would be administered. But their administrative plans, fully described, added up to intervention on a massive scale, upon the request of the Greek government, to make Greece a strong, independent, self-supporting, democratic state. The alternative was to sit by and allow an armed Communist minority, aided by foreign Communist countries, to exploit weakness and fasten upon Greece an irrevocable Communist control at the service of the Soviet Union's drive toward world domination. It is not likely that history will judge either Mr. Churchill or Mr. Truman harshly for their interventions in Greece.

WESTERN EUROPE ON THE BRINK

THAT Great Britain was running into trouble of an alarming
character began to be reported to the State Department early in
January 1947 and was publicly confirmed by the British government on January 20, in a White Paper on the problems of economic
recovery. "The position of Britain is extremely serious," the government frankly admitted. Britain, which had during the war sold at
least half her external assets and piled up huge debts abroad, was
month by month going still further into debt abroad as imports
exceeded imports, and the American and Canadian loans of $5
billion granted the previous year were being used up at a rapid rate.
Production and exports were being hampered by shortage of manpower and low productivity. It was imperative, the government said,
that production and exports be increased if, within the "short breath-
ing space" allowed by the American and Canadian loans, Britain
was to become self-supporting. Even if Britain increased exports by
75 per cent she could live only at the prewar level. The implications
of the White Paper were that in order to do this Britain would
have to cut her military commitments at home and abroad (there
were a million and a half men in the armed services, and the work
of another half million men was required to keep them supplied)
and further reduce the standard of living. The national accounts
were inexorable, Britain was living beyond her means, and the time
was extremely short.

Looking forward to the budget for the next fiscal year beginning April 1, the British Cabinet, deeply conscious of maintaining as far as possible Britain's world position, resumed with heavy hearts consideration of further reductions in Britain's overseas. commitments. British troops around the world—in Germany, in Greece, in Egypt, in Palestine, in Korea, in Japan, in Malaya—and British loans and grants to foreign countries in support of political commitments, were a heavy drain on the balance of payments and took manpower from the critical job of production. Decisions were made to reduce the armed forces from 1,427,000 to less than 1,100,000 during the following fiscal year.

There was no mention in the White Paper of the alarming, immediate problem of coal, which in reality merited a White Paper all its own. Even though exports had ceased, the nation's stockpile of mined coal had fallen far below what was admitted to be the danger point. Reviving industry was using it faster than it could be mined. A number of factories important to the export drive had already suffered temporary shut-downs when coal failed to arrive. On January 13 the government had reduced coal allocations to all industries by half on the grounds that deliveries were consistently falling short of previous allocations by that amount and it was only realistic to cut down. There had also been localized but annoying temporary cut-offs of electricty in some areas because of lack of coal. Not only was not enough coal being mined, but there were not railway wagons to assure smooth delivery of what was available at the mines.

The coal shortage was already therefore being called "calamitous," and the nation had been alerted to a grave economic crisis, when on January 25 there descended on the usually temperate British Isles a succession of blizzards, such as no Briton had ever experienced on home soil, interspersed with bitter, unrelenting, unprecedented cold. Roads and railways were blocked, rivers were frozen solid, ships were held in port, hundreds of communities were isolated, coal pits were closed, and winter wheat was killed. Utility companies began to cut down immediately on electricity and gas supplies, and factories began closing in droves: they had been living hand to mouth as far as fuel was concerned, and now the hand was frozen. The British economic machine ground more and more slowly for ten days and then on February 7, following new blizzards, more than half of British industry came to a complete standstill. On that day Mr. Shinwell, Minister of Fuel and Power, announced to a shocked an incredulous House of Commons that for at least three or four days all electricity would be cut off to industrial consumers in London, Southeast England, the Midlands, and all northeast England except Yorkshire and perhaps Lancashire. Domestic electricity would be cut off during the daytime hours of nine to twelve and two to four. Five million workers were immediately without jobs, confined to heatless homes. Intemperate weather lasted for a month, and was followed by floods. It would take months to dig out, acquire stocks of fuel, open factories, and restore orderly production and trade.

Suddenly the whole world recognized the weakness-unto-death of the British Empire. "Dunkirk" was on the lips of all—it was the most meaningful comparison available. Commentators found it hard to summon words to describe the disaster adequately. The financial editor of Reuter's wrote, "The biggest crash since the fall of Constantinople—the collapse of the heart of an Empire—impends. This is not the story of a couple of snowstorms. It is the story of the awful debility in which a couple of snowstorms could have such effects." The New York Times was "shocked" by the situation: "It has projected before our imagination the picture of a world without Britain. The consequences to us of such a void in the economic and political universe are alarming."

Britain's export drive had bogged down completely and would chin the gutter only several months hence. The probable loss in exports was conservatively estimated at the time at between $200 million and $400 million; actually it proved to be nearly $800 million. It was absurd that this could make the difference between the life and death of a great nation, but it was recognized that this was the straw that would break the camel's back. Even with superhuman effort, even with extreme and painful belt-tightening, even with the most severe and humiliating abandonment of overseas political and military commitments, Britain would fall far short of her export and financial targets for the year, would have to dig even more deeply into meager and irreplaceable reserves, would not, with the "breathing space" allowed by the American and Canadian loans, come anywhere near becoming self-supporting.

This was only part of the revelation, the lesser part. Great Britain was finished as a world power![1] Suddenly the steady, pounding, daily news reports of the previous year and a half formed a pattern: the strongest bastions of the imperial system had collapsed —India, Burma, Egypt, Palestine; elsewhere Britain's authority was being reduced to a shadow because of troop withdrawals and reductions in financial and political aid; and now the citadel of the Empire, Great Britain, heavily in debt and unable to sustain itself even with generous foreign aid, faced collapse. The Foreign Minister of Great Britain was reduced to bemoaning in the House of Commons on February 15, that if he had forty million tons of coal— and they were there in England under the ground—he would be three times more powerful in European councils. With manufactured goods for export, he said, he could do a better job of peacemaking; if he had credits to extend abroad, he could do an "enormous amount."

On February 21, the day that opened the Fifteen Weeks, the British government issued a new White Paper, "Economic Survey for 1947," which *The Times* of London described as "the most disturbing statement ever made by a British government." The deficit for 1946 had not been £328 million as previously estimated, but £450 million. Revising its estimates for 1947 in view of the industrial paralysis of preceding weeks, the government set new export targets that were lower, but still so high as to be considered by many as wholly unrealistic; even so, a 1947 deficit of £350 million in the balance of payments was forecast by the government. But this was not all. The dollar deficit would probably be larger than the £350 million over-all deficit, the government said, because

[1] In 1955, with Britain prosperous and playing a major if diminished role in world affairs, it is easy to recognize these conclusions as exaggerated. It was not so easy in 1947.

of two things: (1) Britain was obliged to buy 42 per cent of her food and raw materials in the Western Hemisphere and pay for them in dollars, but she was selling there only 14 per cent of her exports. In the Eastern Hemisphere she was selling much more than she bought, but many of those countries had no gold or dollars or essential goods in which to pay, with the result that Britain had to accept inconvertible currencies or allow sales to cancel out Britain's wartime sterling debts to them. The Eastern surplus could not be used to pay the colossal Western (dollar) deficit. (2) Britain was obliged by the terms of the United States loan of 1946 to institute free convertibility of sterling by July 15, 1947, and this, it was admitted, "may result in some loss of dollars."

The British government, according to American and British observers, was greatly understating the case in order to avoid panic. The dollar trade deficit would more likely be in the neighborhood of $2 billion (£500 million). As for convertibility, *The Times* said it might prove "impossible or disastrous," with "incalculable, even catastrophic consequences"; *The Observer* predicted that it would "seal our bankruptcy." The more likely prospects were that of the £955 million ($3820 million) remaining of the American and Canadian loans on January 1, 1947, the loss during the year would run, not to £350 million, but nearer twice that; and that Britain would still be a long way from self-support and with very little remaining from the loans to finance the continuing large deficits in 1948. Privately British officials discussed the possibility that Britain might have to give up completely the job of maintaining order in the Middle East, withdraw from the occupation of Germany, pull out of the International Trade Organization, and Food and Agriculture Organization, the World Bank, the Monetary Fund, forgo all contributions to foreign relief, institute rigid trade restrictions, and default on foreign debts.

Winter severity did not of course stop at the English Channel. It swept over all Central and Western Europe. On the Continent it caused no such sudden economic breakdown and financial crisis as in Great Britain, but it intensified the misery of peoples already hungry and cold. It catalyzed despair and hopelessness to such a degree that it created highly dangerous political situations which could no longer be ignored.

There was no confidence to spare. *World Report* published on January 21 a survey of the state of European recovery. It concluded that industrial recovery was beginning to stall in Europe. Lack of confidence on the part of businessmen and shortage of productive labor were partly responsible, but even more so was the growing feeling of hopelessness and frustration, which reduced and undermined government authority. Consumer supplies originating on the Continent were about half what they were before the war. Lack of things to buy reduced the incentive to work hard and earn more. "What Europe finds is that disorganizations in normal life are proving much harder to overcome than the physical distruction caused by the war. Consequently the goals of Europe's planners appear to be far ahead of reality. The difficulties . . . may stall industrial rehabilitation for a long time."

"Food, give us food!"—that was the cry the world around. In the International Emergency Food Council and in the Food and Agriculture Organization desperate nations were clamoring for food. The *New York Times* published on February 3 a lengthy survey of the food situation, made by its correspondents abroad, country by country. The conclusion was that famine or severe food shortages confronted victor nations and vanquished alike. With UNRRA ending on March 31, Poland, Hungary, Greece, Italy, Austria, and Yugoslavia, already in a very bad way, would find themselves desperate. Everywhere in Europe people were hungry. Severe drought had killed most of the 1946 wheat crop, and now the cold cut back sharply the prospects for 1947. In France an estimated 3,200,000 to 3,800,000 acres of wheat planted in the autumn were destroyed in January and February, confronting the nation with the probable necessity of importing two to three million tons of wheat at a hundred dollars a ton. Both in France and Italy farmers were not sending supplies to the markets, and the cities were slowly starving. The underfed, freezing people were reaching a point where they would accept any system that fed them and kept them warm.

The situation was not overlooked by the Communists. In France and Italy their voting strength was about one-third the total and they occupied prominent posts in the Cabinets. General strikes, led by powerful Communist-dominated unions, were daily threatening to break out. From seizures previously made, arms were known to be in the hands of the militant party men. And all the way from the Elbe to the Atlantic there was nothing to stop a military drive by the Red Army for more than a few days.

The awful implications of Europe's weakness as revealed in January and February were known to at least some in the United States. On February 17, Anne O'Hare McCormick wrote in the *New York Times:*

> Last week it was suddenly brought home to us that we are now in the front line. . . . The crisis in Britain and France pointed up a truth the United States knows but shrinks from facing. They are primarily economic crises, signs of the difficulty of treating post-war breakdown by democratic means. They reveal how battered and shaken are the old strongholds of democracy in Europe, and how few these strongholds are. Most of all they throw the ball to us, giving notice that if freedom as we understand it is to survive it's up to the United States to save it. . . .
>
> Everywhere the pressures to give up the fight for freedom are almost irresistible. The fight for survival is so primitive, the submergence of the middle class so general, the individual so helpless, the sense of human dignity so blunted by inhuman transfers of people, the desire for change, and the feeling that any change must be for the better so overwhelming, that it is harder to stand fast than to follow the easier path—toward a Communist dictatorship or reaction. It cannot be said too often that the greatest danger to democracy . . . is the weariness and faltering spirit of democrats. . . . The extent to which democratic government survives on that Continent depends on how far this country is willing to help it survive.

Hanson Baldwin was moved to eloquence in the *New York Times* of March 2. He reviewed the "plague and pestilence, suffering and disaster, famine and hardship, the complete economic and political dislocation of the world." We knew, he said, that this would follow the titanic eruption of the world's greatest war, and here it was. Germany was divided and broken. The Netherlands, with the Empire nearly gone, was in a bad condition, everybody wanting to emigrate. Belgium was weak and confused. France and Italy could be taken over by the Communists at any time. But, most important, Great Britain, whose "Pax Britannica" was maintained for decades past by the power of the British pound and the power of the British fleet, supplemented by allies and a small but efficient army scattered over the world—Britain was in desperate plight, and could no longer back up the forces of Western civilization. And nature abhors vacuums. Baldwin continued:

> Heavy are the responsibilities of power. . . . Today the torrent of history is seeking a new channel. The forces of the surging waters . . . tear at the past and undermine the ramparts of tradition. They will not be stayed, but they can be guided. The United States today lies squarely in that stream of history; it can guide that stream or be swept away by it. . . . The United States is the key to the destiny of tomorrow; we alone may be able to avert the decline of Western civilization, and a reversion to nihilism and the Dark Ages.

Such, then, was the situation in Western Europe at the beginning of the Fifteen Weeks. But it would be erroneous to assume that it was fully and widely appreciated in Washington. The alarming public and official reports from Europe during the first three weeks of February made a profound impression on certain government officials, congressional leaders, and commentators, and convinced them of the need for the boldest kind of action. On the whole, however, the contrast between political reality in Washington, and the reality of human misery, physical wreckage, national debility, and mounting Communist menace in Europe and Asia, was so great in early 1947 that the spectrum barely accommodated it. Perhaps the most remarkable and encouraging thing about the national conversion of United States policy and attitude during the Fifteen Weeks is that it took place, as we shall see in the next chapter, in a political setting that could scarcely have been less favorable.

PART III

THE IMMEDIATE SETTING

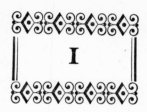

I

THE POLITICAL SCENE IN WASHINGTON

NOTHING appeared farther removed from the realities of American political life at the opening of the year 1947 than that the United States would shortly assume the responsibilities of its power and embark upon a vigorous, expensive, and sustained course of action designed to help create in the world the essential conditions of freedom and orderly progress. The facts of the situation were available in what Theodore H. White calls "the obscurity of total detail," but their implications were blinding, overwhelming, and therefore largely ignored by people, who, after years of war, sacrifice, and confusion, sought only to readjust their lives to normalcy.

The authority of the executive branch of the government was about as low as it was possible to be. President Truman had not been elected to his office. Catapulted into it by the death of President Franklin D. Roosevelt, he inherited not only a mantle that was ill fitting, but also the bitter resentments against the Democratic party that had accumulated during four unprecedented Roosevelt elections and more than twelve years of continuous and revolutionary Democratic administration. Truman lacked confidence in his ability to perform acceptably the functions of his high office, and freely admitted it. Moreover his performance during the first year and a half, as he learned the ropes, was not distinguished. The impression conveyed almost unanimously by the press and radio was that he would remain in office only until the voters had a chance to replace

89

him. Through most of the critical year of 1946 the shadow of the congressional elections in the fall hung over Washington. And in November, true to prediction, the Republicans, for the first time in fourteen years, captured both Houses of Congress.

When the 80th Congress of the United States convened in Washington on January 3, 1947, there were 51 Republicans and 45 Democrats in the Senate; 245 Republicans and 118 Democrats in the House. Not only had the President and his party been repudiated at the polls, but a situation had been created—a Republican Congress and a Democratic executive—which is the classic formula for national frustration and inaction. The all-absorbing question of the day was not whether the President would or could lead the United states to accept heavy world responsibilities, but how far the new Congress would roll back New Deal legislation, cut appropriations for the armed services and foreign relief, and carry us back to the political isolation of the 1920s and the economic isolation of the Smoot-Hawley Tariff.

Speaker Joseph Martin of Massachusetts, in his opening address to the House on January 3, 1947, sounded the keynote of Republican intentions, which was promptly echoed by other leaders of the majority party in both Houses: an across-the-board reduction in income taxes by 20 per cent and sufficient reduction in government spending to make it possible. It was rumored that President Truman would submit a budget of $41 billion; Republican leaders immediately suggested a maximum of $34 billion. When President Truman on January 10 submitted a budget of $37.5 billion, Republican leaders called the President's request "astounding." Throughout January and February, as if the press and radio were not bringing daily frightening stories of the world's hunger, hopelessness, despair, and drift to Communism, of the breakdown of the world's economic machine, controversy raged among Republican leaders as to whether the President's budget should be cut by $6 billion, to allow the 20 per cent tax reduction, or by $4.5 billion, which would allow a lesser tax reduction. On February 14 the Joint Congressional Committee on the Legislative Budget recommended a cut of $6 billion, reducing the President's budget to $31.5 billion, and reported a measure to that effect to the Senate and House floor. A cut of $1750 million was proposed in the operating budgets of the Army and Navy plus a cut of 50 per cent in the $1 billion requested by the War Department for preventing starvation, disease, and unrest in occupied Germany and Japan. Secretary Forrestal promptly announced that the proposed reduction in the Navy budget "would so greatly reduce the effectiveness of the Navy as to render it practically immobile and impotent as an instrument of national policy." Secretary Patterson said it would result in starvation, unrest and bloodshed, would leave the Army too weak to carry out its duties, and "might compel abandonment of the occupation of Germany and Japan." Secretary Marshall commented that if the Army could not feed people in the occupied countries "a practically impossible situation is created for our troops and our government's position in its international commitments." Nevertheless on February 20 the House voted the $31.5 billion budget. On February 26 the Senate voted a $33 billion budget, and a few days later a payment on the national debt of $2.6 billion. Republican Senator Henry Cabot Lodge commented that the Republican approach to budget cutting was "like a man wielding a meat ax in a dark room" who "might cut off his own head.'"

Aside from the budget, the entire structure of United States foreign economic policy built up since 1934 was in jeopardy of nullification by Congress. This was designed for a different world than that of 1947, and was pathetically inadequate to support American aims for a world economically and politically free. But it was a substantial step toward the assumption of American responsibilities as economic giant of the free world. And yet, in early 1947, this irreducible minimum of a foreign economic policy was under heavy congressional attack and the administration was on the defensive.

From the beginning of the war in Europe in 1939 the administration had realized that the physical destruction of war, the economic dislocation, the wastage of human, material, and financial assets, would widen the enormous disparity between production and productivity in the United States and that in Europe, which had existed, had increased, and had plagued world economy and international relations ever since World War I. The Lend-Lease program adopted in 1941 had of course as its main object aid to countries fighting the Nazis, but an important collateral consideration in Roosevelt's idea was to prevent a mass of unpayable war debts from weighing upon the postwar world, stultifying its economy and poisoning political relations. Postwar planners in the State Department were virtually obsessed with the difficulties of creating a balanced world economy that would provide for man's need when the most destructive war in history should end. Government and private studies converged upon a few solutions that were simple— if politics would allow: (1) the United States should take the steps necessary to maintain a high level of business activity at home; (2) the United States should reduce drastically its trade barriers and greatly increase its imports (few said *remove* trade barriers—it was too shocking to say so—but that is what most of them meant); (3) the United States and other countries able to do so should prevent starvation and alleviate misery and unrest in devastated countries in the period immediately following the war through large-scale grants for direct relief; and (4) the United States should engage in huge and continuing lending operations after the war for reconstruction and development, the government granting or guaranteeing the loans to the extent necessary.

The anxiety of the administration for the economic viability of the postwar world grew out of an acute consciousness of the mistakes made after World War I, which had laid the basis for twenty years of economic and political troubles. The United States had emerged from that war as a full-fledged industrial and creditor nation but had continued to act in its world economic relations like an adolescent debtor. Mountainous war debts had been serviced for many years in an atmosphere of growing recrimination, until the debts were, by agreement or otherwise, defaulted through sheer inability to pay. The wild boom in the United States beginning in 1919 had yielded in late 1920 and 1921 to a severe business recession, followed by a period of abnormal and unbalanced economic expansion that had ended in the great depression of 1929–33, which, in turn, had been succeeded by seven years of economic lameness. Tariffs, which by all economic accounts should have been lowered, had been raised in 1921, again in 1922, and again, to extreme heights, in the Smoot-Hawley Tariff of 1931; and while imports had been restricted, exports had been vastly promoted by the government. In effect, the huge flow of private investment abroad during the twenties, most of which was defaulted, paid for the large U.S. export surplus. For ten years after 1929, with high tariffs and low business activity in the United States and with American foreign investments only a trickle, foreign countries had been starved for dollars with which to buy our goods and pay their debts to us. At least partly, if not chiefly, as a consequence of this situation, the liberal world trade and payments system was radically altered during the 1930s. Fluctuating and unstable currencies, all-around tariff increases, preferential tariff and commercial arrangements, direct trade and exchange controls through quotas and licensing arrangements—these had become the rule. The reciprocal trade agreements patiently negotiated by Secretary of State Cordell Hull, from 1934 onward, with great care not to arouse opposition by going too fast, alleviated only slightly the world's starvation for dollars, and little impact was made upon the new commercial practices that held trade down to low levels and lessened every man's wealth and opportunity.

This bit of history was as well known in Cordell Hull's State Department as the Bible's account of the Fall in the Garden of Eden. History must not be repeated! The State Department therefore took the lead in planning, negotiating, and putting into operation economic and financial institutions on a scale that seemed vast, in the fervent hope and expectation that the leading trading nations of the world could re-establish the liberal world trading system that had existed before 1930.

A central aim of our policies in early 1947 was the establishment of convertible currencies the world over, the ending of quantitative restrictions upon trade, and the cessation of bulk purchases and barter by governments. Only if these barriers were removed could private enterprise tackle successfully the vast job of reconstruction, production, and trade. The chief instrument for accomplishing the reduction of trade barriers was the Trade Agreements program, originally authorized by an act passed in 1934, and renewed each three years thereafter, by Democratic majorities. The State Department announced late in 1946 that it would undertake simultaneous negotiations with eighteen foreign countries for the reciprocal lowering of trade barriers at a conference that would open in Geneva early in April. The conference would also complete the drafting of a World Trade Charter and an International Trade Organization designed to aid the restoration of liberal, multilateral trading practices and to bring order and responsibility into the conduct of trade relations. At the Geneva negotiations a number of countries made plain that United States tariff cuts were essential to their agreement to adopt the liberal trade practice provided in the charter and ITO.

The other pillar of United States foreign economic policy after the war was loans for reconstruction and development, which were intended to fill on a sound and continuing basis the gap in foreign supply left by the termination of Lend-Lease and the approaching end of the mammoth relief activities carried on through the United Nations (for which most of the funds had been supplied by the United States). Repayment of these loans was of course dependent upon the revival of production and trade, upon the ability of foreign countries ultimately to repay in goods they produced, so that the reduction of trade barriers was essential to the soundness of the loan program. The lending authority of the United States Export-Import Bank had been increased by Congress in 1945, from $700 million to $3.5 billion. The International Bank for Reconstruction and Development, a United Nations agency, had been authorized with a capital of $7.6 billion and a lending power twice that, a large part of which was expected to be obtained from private investors in the United States; subscription to the capital of the bank was $3175 million. A special loan of $3.75 billion to Great Britain had been authorized by Congress on July 15, 1946, to permit that key trading nation to import essential machinery and raw materials, revive production for export, and re-establish convertibility of the pound sterling by July 15, 1947. And a variety of other loans and credits had been made available, totaling several billions of dollars.

Moreover the International Monetary Fund had been created, as a consequence of United States initiative, with a United States contribution of $2750 million as part of its working capital. The object of the Fund was to aid countries to maintain reasonably stable exchange rates. All these measures added up to a more than respectable plan, backed by authorized funds, to aid the postwar world in reestablishing itself.

The postwar economic planners nevertheless made enormous miscalculations. For these they can hardly be held accountable, since there were no precedents. They had not greatly underestimated the extent to which factories, transportation facilities, mines, and farms had been destroyed and what it would take to get them in working order; but they had not reckoned on such a complete breakdown in the basic economic and commercial motivation and organization by which food and raw materials are produced on the farms and exchanged for manufactured goods produced in the towns and cities, or produced in one country and exchanged for necessities produced in another. They had not taken into account the demoralization that followed the war in Europe—the loss of hope and confidence of the people in themselves, in their governments, in their countries, in the future. They had not bargained for a series of unprecedented natural disasters—such as two successive years of crop failure due to drought, blizzards, extreme prolonged cold, and floods, or for man-made disasters in the form of strikes, absenteeism, and unrest—which made necessary the use of financial reserves, not for reconstruction, but for the importation of sufficient food and fuel merely to keep people alive. They had assumed that the governments of Europe would be able without too much delay to exert their authority over the vital elements of national economies and use their financial reserves and actual or available loans from the outside to bring about a fairly prompt reconstruction and self-sustaining recovery. They assumed that governments and industries would be able to qualify for loans that, according to generous and reasonable standards, had a chance of being repaid.

The extent of these miscalculations began to be realized in official Washington only in January of 1947. It was revealed more fully, and dramatically, in February. During the same two months, Ramadier formed the first government of France's Fourth Republic and took four Communists into his Cabinet, one as Vice-Premier and another as Minister of Defense. (Communists had been in the Italian Cabinet since 1945.) It began to be apparent that Greece, France, and Italy, and to a lesser degree other countries in Western Europe, were in imminent danger of being taken over from the inside by well-organized, armed Communist minorities.

It was precisely at this time of approaching calamity that the Republican-controlled 80th Congress threatened to limit the inadequate means available to the administration for dealing with the situation. In the House of Representatives only two Republicans had voted for the three-year Reciprocal Trade Agreements Act in 1934, three in 1937, five in 1940, 145 in 1943 (because we were at war and the program was inoperative anyway), and 33 in 1946; in the Senate, five Republicans had voted for it in 1934, none in 1937 and 1940, 18 in 1943, and 15 in 1946. Hardly had the 80th Congress convened than loud and persistent noises began to be heard in both Houses of Congress, especially among powerful members of the House Ways and Means Committee, against the entire Trade Agreements program and in favor of higher tariffs. A resolution was introduced into the House designed to prevent the administration from making further tariff cuts or attending further international trade conferences until the Tariff Commission had made a study of the needs of American industry for protection.

A great majority of Republicans in Congress had also voted against the Export-Import Bank Act of 1945, against the British loan, and against the Bretton Woods Agreements that established the International Bank and the International Monetary Fund. The British loan was already made and partly spent, and the International Bank and Fund were not yet going concerns, so there was little that could be done about these. But in February 1947 Republican leaders called in William McChesney Martin, chairman of the Board of Directors of the Export-Import Bank, and Dean Acheson, who as Undersecretary of State was an influential member of the board, and made it clear that the bank's lending policies should be tightened up and loans restricted to gilt-edged, self-liquidating projects that directly promoted American exports. It was plain to the administration that the period of easy lending was over.

The world, the nation, and the administration in Washington had awaited with great anxiety the answer to the question whether the Republican Congress would accept the economic responsibilities of America's new role in the world. Through its power over the purse Congress controlled economic policies; the United States, with more than half the industrial capacity, gold, investment capital, and shipping of the world, could determine the world's economic future; and it was becoming increasingly clear that the future political pattern of the world—indeed, the survival of human freedom itself—would depend upon the early revival of production and trade. The Republican party had abandoned political isolationism during the war, had accepted the role of the United States in the United Nations, and Republicans by and large supported the world political aims of the Truman administration. But would they now face up to the economic realities of our world position; would they support the specific economic measures necessary to make a reality of our foreign policies? The question was one of intense and widespread debate in January and February of 1947.

The voting record of Republicans in previous Congresses suggested an answer. The "meat-ax" performance on the budget in the early weeks of the 80th Congress tended to confirm it, as did the threats about tariffs and loans coming from extremists such as Senator Hugh Butler of Nebraska and Representatives Harold Knutson of Minnesota, Bertrand Gearhart of California, Thomas A. Jenkins of Ohio, and Daniel Reed of New York. Nevertheless it was apparent that the Republicans in Congress were by no means unanimous in their approach to foreign economic policies, that a number were willing to accept fully the economic implications of our world position, and that more were undecided and reasonable. The unknown quantity was how far the most influential Republican in Congress, Senator Arthur H. Vandenberg, President *pro tempore* of the Senate, chairman of the Senate Committee on Foreign Relations, would go in leading his colleagues toward support of the specific appropriations and other economic measures required by our foreign policy. He had broken with isolationism during the war and had played a powerful and continuing role since 1943, surpassed in effectiveness by none, in leading his party and his colleagues in Congress to support full United States participation in world affairs. Would he repeat his performance now with respect to economic measures needed to make that participation effective? His record on economic matters was mixed and offered no certain grounds for hope.

Senator Vandenberg, appearing on the same program with Secretary of State Byrnes at the Cleveland Council on World Affairs on January 11, strongly affirmed continuation of a bipartisan foreign policy and strong support for the United Nations. As to economic policies, he gave assurances that relief appropriations would continue and that "reasonable rehabilitation credits" would be extended. Reciprocal trade agreements would be continued "in one form or another," but he cast doubts upon whether they would continue on a multilateral basis. In a radio broadcast on January 20 the Senator said that Republicans were going to "ask more questions" in matters dealing with international trade. The United States, he said, would cooperate through the United Nations for collective security and do its part in "legitimate economic cooperation," but that we must make sure we do not jeopardize our national economy. Zealous protection of our own economy, he added, is no threat to peace.

What did all this about economic policies mean? In succeeding days Senator Vandenberg showed what he meant. He began a series of behind-the-scenes moves to head off the drive rolling in Congress to nullify the Trade Agreements program and prevent the completion of negotiations for the World Trade Charter and the International Trade Organization. With his close friend Senator Eugene D. Millikin of Colorado, he summoned Undersecretaries of State Dean Acheson and Will Clayton and worked out with them a compromise, according to which congressional action on tariffs and trade would be deferred until the next session. In return the administration would insert in any reciprocal trade agreement thereafter negotiated an "escape" clause permitting any country to modify or withdraw a tariff concession if it should result, or threaten to result, in serious injury to a domestic industry, any such action by the United States to be preceded, however, by a hearing before the Tariff Commission, a public recommendation by the commission to the President, and final decision by the President. This agreement was reached early in February and confirmed in an executive order issued by the President on February 25. With this agreement in his pocket, Senator Vandenberg then persuaded a number of influential and uncommitted Republican leaders to come out publicly in support of the Trade Agreements program (not including Senator Taft, who broke with Vandenberg openly on the question). Thus was the wind temporarily taken out of the protectionists sails, and the irreducible minimum of our foreign economic policy, the Trade Agreements program, was reduced only partially.

Such was the political reality in Washington as the Fifteen Weeks began.

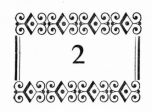

2

THE CHIEF ACTORS

WGA+

THE question is often raised as to who was primarily responsible for the precision and scope of the decisions of the Fifteen Weeks. It is a question that deserves an answer. The situation itself, gigantic, inexorable, was crushing in its compulsiveness. But as is evident from history, men in authority may act to deal with compelling situations, or they may just rock along and see what happens; they may act boldly and decisively, or they may act timidly, partially, ineffectively. In positions of authority in Washington in 1947 there were men of courage who knew history, who knew and had faith in the American people, who worked together in mutual confidence and in a disciplined manner, and who were therefore able, in spite of a most discouraging political climate, to make bold decisions that fixed a new course for the United States in the world and swung the Congress and the country behind them in support.

President Truman, Secretary Marshall, and Undersecretary Acheson—and the extraordinary relationship that existed among them, based upon a precise knowledge of their powers, obligations, and limitations—made possible the achievements of the Fifteen Weeks. In world affairs the President had the judgment of a widely read student of history and the courage of an Army sergeant. Secretary Marshall, as a matter of training, met and solved problems instead of fighting them and insisted that his staff do the same. When he gave Dean Acheson, under his command, full authority over

100

policy, administration, and operations, the Department of State for
the first time in years became an integrated institution subject to
the authority of the President, capable of conducting foreign relations in an orderly manner. Acheson, rather than competing with
members of his staff, knew how to draw from them wise counsel,
harmony, and constructive effort. The relations of Marshall and
Acheson with Senator Vandenberg were based upon mutual respect
and confidence; and Secretaries Forrestal and Patterson were men
of breadth and decisiveness, deeply conscious of the strength and
responsibilities of the United States. The sum total of these facts
and conditions was a combination for responsible action on the
world stage.

Disorder had prevailed in the conduct of foreign relations for so
long that it had come to be accepted as normal and inevitable. President Roosevelt, from 1939 onward, had been in effect his own
Secretary of State. With supreme self-confidence and with genuine
ability, he had to a very large degree conducted foreign relations
from the White House. Secretary of State Cordell Hull was valuable
to him because of his prestige in Congress and his veneration in the
country. He was also useful as a conservative sounding board for
the President's own ideas; he could always be counted upon to
exercise a corrective, stabilizing, frequently retarding influence upon
policy. But as has been confirmed by the records and memoirs
published since the war at home and abroad, Secretary Hull had
amazingly little to do with most major aspects of foreign policy after
1939. Other Presidents before and since have depended upon their
Secretaries of State to draw upon the combined knowledge of the
State Department staff at home and abroad, brief them on problems,
and recommend alternative courses of action. Not F.D.R. He called
upon the Secretary of State for advice and information; but in a
personal and irregular manner, he also called upon the Undersecretary of State, or on any Assistant Secretary of State or Department officer he happened to know and trust, or on other Cabinet
members, or on generals and admirals, or on members of his inner
circle of advisers scattered throughout the government, or on any
number of Barney Baruchs. And Roosevelt usually ran with the

ball. The result was sometimes brilliant, improvised performance, sometimes appalling, egregious error; and at most times it meant frustration in the State Department, where the staff felt that a more disciplined and orderly procedure could have avoided the worst mistakes.

It is more than possible that in a world convulsed by war the gains from Roosevelt's personal diplomacy outweighed the losses: the unconditional surrender of our enemies was achieved. It is not intended here either to condemn or praise President Roosevelt's manner of operating in foreign affairs—in any case it was the only way he knew how to operate—but to try to throw some light, by way of contrast, upon President Truman's manner of operating.

There was one aspect of Roosevelt's administration of foreign affairs, however, that can only be judged as unfortunate: it failed to educate the Congress and the American people fully on the responsibilities of the United States in the postwar period. It is a major irony that this should be true. Roosevelt, as Assistant Secretary of the Navy in the administration of President Wilson, had been deeply affected by Wilson's failure to lead the country into the League of Nations following World War I. He was determined that Wilson's mistake in failing to keep the country with him should not be repeated. The United Nations was planned even before Pearl Harbor, was brought almost to fruition before Roosevelt's death, and as it developed there was never any serious question of the American people's rejecting a role in it. But, fearing a repetition of 1920, Roosevelt actually retarded the genuine, informed acceptance by the people of the very thing he so fervently desired—our full participation in world affairs. He failed to speak fully and frankly about the risks and burdens of a world role, failed to suggest that blood, sweat, and tears might be involved in postwar order-keeping. Engaging all the while in personal, behind-the-scenes diplomacy, he charmed the public with talk of advantages rather than responsibilities, appealed to idealism rather than practicality, exploited the loyalty of a personal following rather than the informed judgment of a nation. There was scarcely a whisper about the organization and use of power in the world. Roosevelt moved toward his goals by indirection, by an occasional dramatic stratagem rather than by steady progress accompanied by full and logical exposition. Perhaps his approach was necessary. But the fact remains that although the American people supported our participation in a whole array of United Nations organs, it was more or less with the idea that somebody else, some other nations, or that abstract concept, the collectivity of nations—not the United States—would do the job of keeping the world peaceful and prosperous. In February 1947 they were not particularly interested in who did it, or how.

General Marshall summed up the American attitude in his first public address as Secretary of State, delivered at Princeton University on February 22, 1947:

Now that an immediate peril is not plainly visible, there is a natural tendency to relax and return to business as usual, politics as usual, pleasure as usual. Many of our people have become indifferent to what I might term the long-time dangers to the national security. It is natural and necessary that there should be a relaxation of wartime tensions. *But I feel that we are seriously failing in our attitude toward international problems whose solution will largely determine our future. The public appears generally in the attitude of a spectator* [1]—interested, yes, but whose serious thinking is directed to local immediate matters. Spectators of life are not those who will retain their liberties, nor are they likely to contribute to their country's security. There are many who are willing to deplore, but few who are willing to act. . . . Action depends upon conviction, and conviction in turn depends upon understanding—a general understanding both of the history of many on this globe and an understanding that action is a basic necessity of man's nature.

The situation that confronted Harry S. Truman when suddenly he found himself President on April 12, 1945, was complex and overpowering. The war in Europe was drawing to a close, the war in the Pacific was approaching a climax, peace throughout a devastated world remained to be won, the nation would soon require conversion to the continuing requirements of peace, and the man who for twelve years had held and maneuvered the threads of American

[1] Italics the author's.

policy and power was gone. The amiable but wholly ungrounded Edward J. Stettinius was Secretary of State. He had never been more than one of many assistants to the President in the conduct of foreign relations, and he was in technical charge of a Department that had long since ceased to deal in major policy. Truman, Vice-President for only a few weeks, had not been made privy to the world problems of state or even acquainted with the machinery for the conduct of foreign relations.

His first act, therefore—on the train returning from Roosevelt's funeral—was to ask his old Senate colleague, James F. Byrnes, to become Secretary of State as soon as the San Francisco Conference (which was to open within a matter of days with Stettinius as head of the American delegation) should end. Byrnes, a sound man of great ability, had worked in the White House, had been at Yalta with Roosevelt, and was greatly respected on Capitol Hill. He was a natural choice. Overwhelmed by the mountain of sudden responsibility, Truman's idea was to select trusted men for Cabinet posts and leave them free to run the affairs of their Departments. It was only with time, as Jonathan Daniels has pointed out in his book *The Man of Independence,* that Truman learned that "while he could delegate every duty he could escape no responsibility. . . . Truman was to discover that whether he wished it or not the President is the whole executive and above his subordinates, must bear the weight. He must be the chief in actual command of the government or the clerk of a contentious Cabinet. Above all, what Truman found was that with many assistants but with no equals the President himself must make the policy of his administration in the United States. And in no field did he find that to be so true as in that of foreign policy about which he was so little informed when he became President of the United States. It took him many papers and more time than a few months to discover that."

Regardless of what Byrnes' shortcomings as Secretary of State may have been, the nation owes him a great debt, for it was his hide, his nerves, and his patience that for a year and a half bore the brunt of the insistent, wearying, exasperating, often insulting cold-war assault of the Russians upon their wartime allies at a time when it had not been determined that friendly relations were impossible. There was nothing theoretical about the punishment Byrnes took: of his 562 days in office he spent 350 days away from his desk, and most of those days he was face to face with the Russians in international conferences. His patience endured while the Russians fully exposed their hand; and in the end the Russians took as the spoils of war in Europe what they physically controlled, and very little more.

Byrnes nevertheless failed to establish, either with the President or with the staff of the State Department, those procedural and personal relationships necessary to a positive, constructive course in world affairs. By the very nature of things the United States and the West were on the defensive in 1945 and 1946, and Byrnes' role was a defensive role. But it is highly doubtful that, given his relations with the President and the State Department staff, he could have played any other.

Jonathan Daniels has analyzed more fully and probably more accurately than anyone else the complex and difficult situation that developed between Truman and Byrnes. Byrnes had wanted to be President; he had wanted to be Vice-President when Truman was chosen; he felt himself far better qualified than Truman; he felt that he, a cheated man, was doing Truman a favor by taking on the difficult job of Secretary of State. The result of this attitude, combined with Truman's initial lack of confidence in himself and, indeed, his early conception of what he wanted Byrnes to do, was that Byrnes failed to supply the President with complete analyses of important problems and then to trust to his decisions; instead, he sometimes committed the United States without authority. As the President became more sure of himself and more aware of his responsibility for foreign policy, an estrangement inevitably grew between them. An open row occurred in late December of 1945, as a result of Byrnes' concessions to the Russians at the Moscow Conference without consulting or reporting to the President, and in April 1946 Byrnes, "on the advice of a physician," handed in his resignation. It was agreed that he would remain until the completion of the preliminary peace treaties, a process which, as it turned out, required the remainder of the year.

Byrnes' relations with his staff were hardly more satisfactory. Dean Acheson was Undersecretary of State. He had been earnestly intent upon resigning immediately after the war, but had succumbed to the pressure exerted by Secretary Byrnes and President Truman and had accepted the new post. From many years of close observation he knew very well the condition of the State Department and especially the uncertain authority exercised by the Undersecretary; but, cynic though he was, he entertained some hope that orderly procedures could be established. Even Acheson was dismayed. Byrnes appointed as Assistant Secretary of State in charge of administration his friend Donald Russell and made him directly responsible, not to the Undersecretary, but to himself. As far as operations and policy were concerned, political advisers, chiefs of offices, and even division chiefs continued the practice, hallowed by years, of playing sometimes with the Undersecretary and sometimes, as far as occasion would allow, with the Secretary, with little cross-referencing. The Undersecretary, who for more than half of Byrnes' tenure had to assume the responsibilities of Acting Secretary of State, had normal authority over neither policy nor operations. As for Byrnes, though he was no Roosevelt, he tried the same kind of personal (as opposed to institutional) operations and diplomacy, drawing advice and assistance in a disorderly manner, not necessarily from the chosen chiefs of established offices but from a few men he happened to know and like. The Department was not run, it just jerked along.

George Catlett Marshall brought order to the conduct of foreign relations. A good soldier, he possessed instinctively the highest degree of loyalty to his Commander-in-Chief, a loyalty which, with close contact, developed into respect and friendship beyond the call of duty. A good general, he immediately straightened out the lines of authority in the State Department, placed them in the hands of the man best qualified to be his chief of staff, Undersecretary Acheson, and insisted upon orderly staff procedure. His splendid presence, his enormous prestige, commanded respect on Capitol Hill. In a stroke, the authority, participation, and responsibility of the President in the conduct of foreign relations was restored; and the Department of State as an institution was put in business again. The change was felt from top to bottom and called forth a great surge of ideas and constructive effort. This is not to say that Marshall would necessarily have been at all times, for any President, or working with any Undersecretary, the perfect Secretary of State. He might have been outstanding under any circumstances. But in the circumstances of January 1947 he brought to the conduct of foreign relations precisely what it most needed.

Under the command of Marshall, Acheson ran the State Department, with authority over policy formulation, operations, and administration. The Undersecretary discussed matters with "the man on the bridge" and sought his decisions on important questions, but the orders that went down through the ship were those of the Undersecretary. Marshall required that each problem be analyzed in writing, with alternative solutions proposed and argued in writing. He would accept, reject, or revise. Moreover he would do so with enormous comprehension of the problems involved. According to those most closely associated with him, nothing could be further from the truth than that he had what is pejoratively referred to as "the military mind." The military mind in Secretary of State Marshall extended only to orderly procedures; the compassionate, comprehending, history-informed mind took over from there, and his decisions usually had every appearance of being right in their political, social, and economic contexts.

The breadth and depth of Marshall's thinking stands out clearly in his remarks addressed to the graduating class of Princeton University on February 22, 1947:

> We are living today in a most difficult period. The war years were critical, at times alarmingly so. But I think that the present period is in many respects more critical. . . . We have had a cessation of hostilities, but we have no genuine peace. Here at home we are in a state of transition between a war and peace economy. In Europe and Asia fear and famine still prevail. Power relation-

ships are in a state of flux. Order has yet to be brought out of con-fusion. Peace has yet to be secured. And how this is accomplished will depend very much upon the American people.

Most of the other countries of the world find themselves ex-hausted economically, financially, physically. If the world is to get on its feet, if the productive facilities of the world are to be re-stored, if democratic processes in many countries are to resume their functioning, a strong lead and definite assistance from the United States will be necessary.

This is George C. Marshall speaking, fifteen weeks before his historic speech at Harvard, foreshadowing the necessity for Ameri-can leadership and American aid.

Twenty-five years ago the people of this country, and of the world, for that matter, had the opportunity to make vital decisions regarding their future welfare. I think we must agree that the nega-tive course of action followed by the United States after the First World War did not achieve order or security, and that it had a di-rect bearing upon the recent war and its endless tragedies. There were people in those days who understood the lessons of history, who knew well what should be done in order to minimize the danger of another world disaster, but their combined voice was a feeble one, and their proposals were ignored. . . .

In order to take a full part in the life which is before you, I think you must in effect relive the past so that you may turn to the present with deep convictions and an understanding of what man-ner of country this is for which men for many generations have laid down their lives. Therefore, a deep understanding of history is necessary . . . an understanding of that history that records the main currents of the past activities of men and which leads to an understanding of what has created and what has destroyed great civilizations.

You should have an understanding of what course of action has created power and security, and of the mistakes which have under-mined the power and security of many nations, and above all, a clear understanding of the institutions upon which human liberty and individual freedom have depended, and the struggles to gain and maintain them. . . . One usually emerges from an intimate understanding of the past, with its lessons and its wisdom, with convictions which put fire in the soul. I doubt seriously whether a man can think with full wisdom and with deep convictions regarding certain of the basic international issues today who has not at least reviewed in his mind the period of the Peloponnesian War and the fall of Athens.

I am therefore greatly concerned that the young men and women of this country . . . shall acquire a genuine understanding of lessons of history as they relate to governments of the peoples, and life and progress. You should fully understand the special position that the United States now occupies in the world, geographically, financially, militarily, and scientifically, and the implications involved. The development of a sense of responsibility for world order and security, the development of a sense of overwhelming importance of this country's acts, the failures to act, in relation to world order and security—these, in my opinion, are great "musts" for your generation.

"Gentlemen, don't fight the problem, solve it!" was one of Marshall's favorite expressions. Only those who have worked under Cordell Hull can possibly appreciate what that attitude at the top meant to the Department of State. The endless, exasperating, fruitless conferences in his office during the eleven years of his tenure have become legendary—conferences in which problems were wrestled with until all concerned were exhausted and what emerged as a solution was the lowest common denominator of opinion that no one had further energy to oppose. The attitude that had made such problem-fighting possible had permeated the Department, had become deeply imbedded. It often appeared that the central object of procedure and conference was to prove any suggested solution impossible. Marshall's attitude swept through the Department like a fresh, invigorating breeze.

Another of Marshall's outstanding qualities, and one that was of great consequence, was his ability to judge what was important and what was less so, a quality that had a great deal to do with his rise to the top of the military profession. When the Greece-Turkey crisis arose in late February 1947, Marshall was being intensively briefed in preparation for his first international conference as Secretary of State, the meeting in Moscow of the Council of Foreign Ministers at which the extremely important question of the future of Germany and Austria was to be considered and perhaps decided.

It was clear that aid to Greece and Turkey would greatly offend the Russians and that the President's message to Congress would explode in Moscow shortly after the conference opened. A lesser man would easily have reckoned that the negotiations regarding Germany and his position at the conference were more important than taking a stand against the Russians in connection with aid to Greece and Turkey. Not Secretary Marshall. He participated in the decision to aid Greece and Turkey, and before he left sent orders to the staff through Acheson that they were to draw up the Greece-Turkey program and draft the President's message to Congress without any regard for the effect it might have on his personal or official position at the Moscow Conference. It is also worthy of note that while recognizing the supreme importance of the Greece-Turkey matter, Marshall did not seek to have the Moscow Conference postponed, on the ground that his presence in Washington was indispensable. The decision made, he left it in the hands of his chief of staff and departed for Moscow.

Whatever shortcomings Marshall may have had as Secretary of State, they were made up for by his Undersecretary. A distinguished lawyer, Dean Gooderham Acheson had entered the State Department in February 1941 as Assistant Secretary of State for Economic Affairs, had later served as Assistant Secretary for Congressional Relations and as Undersecretary, and knew the Department and its staff as few men before or since have known it. A man with a profound philosophy and a highly logical mind, he had learned the hard way how the Department should be run if it were to be an effective instrument for the conduct of foreign relations. He felt that the Secretary should call together groups working on particular problems, and through participation in their consideration at an early stage lend character and direction to discussions. This was the method Acheson himself later employed as Secretary of State. He usually had four or five or more such groups in operation on important problems, and he found time to meet with them frequently, get the feel of problems, and bring his logic to bear upon the formulation of possible courses. Acheson tried several times to persuade Marshall to adopt some such method, but Marshall declined. Most discussions were largely "hot air" anyway, he thought, and no way for a Secretary to spend his time. He wanted complete analysis and alternatives placed before him. Thus it was Acheson who worked with the staff in his chosen manner, with great rewards for the Secretary and for the staff and for the country.

Nor was Marshall as careful as Acheson to make certain that the President had an opportunity to influence policy before it congealed into flat alternatives. Truman, regarding Marshall as a man and public servant as nearly perfect as can be found on this earth, had complete confidence in him, was awed by him, and was never relaxed in his relations with him. Marshall, for his part, was correct and loyal and courteous, but, as with everyone, dry and brief. Acheson, on the other hand, had a comfortable and relaxed relationship with the President, one which was nevertheless based upon a profound respect for the office of the Presidency and a definite view of the proper accommodations between an adviser and his chief. As he told the Senate Foreign Relations Committee, the adviser should be "frank, forthright, and vigorous in counsel" and "energetic and loyal in accepting decisions and carrying them out." Having drawn information and ideas from his staff, and having added the corrective of his own logical mind, Acheson was able to go to the President with his briefing book and, enjoying the President's confidence and friendship, impart not only facts and reasoning but the warmth and feel of the problems coming up for decision.

Meeting with members of his own staff, Acheson never stated an opinion or conclusion until everyone present had an opportunity to give his own ideas about the subject and suggest a remedy. By questions he stimulated others to talk, while he listened and took occasional notes. When every aspect of the matter had been carefully and fully considered, he would summarize what he had heard, point out conflicts in points of view, attempt to reconcile them, introduce facts and reasoning that might not have appeared, and finally suggest a solution. It was as though he were aware that his own logic and facility for expression might, if brought into play too early, intimidate full expression. Doubts usually fell away at the close of Acheson's meetings and ended in agreement, each person present feeling that his view had made a major contribution.

Similarly, in talking with the President, Acheson was careful not to push a policy, not to prejudice a conclusion in advance. Rather, he expounded a problem, and in the end the answer was usually clear. If not, and the President asked him his opinion, he would give it directly.

While Acheson was Marshall's Undersecretary the question of who would brief the President scarcely had occasion to arise. In the early weeks of his office, which began on January 20, 1947, Marshall naturally left it to Acheson, who already had the problems in tow, or would ask Acheson to accompany him to meetings with the President. Marshall consciously refrained from getting involved in all but decisions on the most important policy matters, as he was preparing himself intensively for the Moscow Conference. He left for Moscow on March 4, returned April 28, and after May 2 took a few days leave. About June 1 Acheson began withdrawing from active policy consideration preparatory to his departure from the government on June 30.

Acheson's attitude and working methods enabled President Truman to carry with serenity and assurance his responsibility for the foreign policies of the United States. Truman and Acheson saw each other at least four or five times a week, often more, and they were in frequent telephone conversation. According to Acheson, by 1947 Truman had developed a profound, disciplined conception of the Presidential office. Moreover he had the kind of character that, given recognition of the dignity and prerogatives of the Presidency, invited the closest and warmest working relationship. Both men clearly recognized at all times their respective roles: there was no doubt as to who was President, and there was none as to who was Secretary or Acting Secretary of State. Truman would modify and change policies and actions proposed by Acheson; he would consult others on foreign policy; but he always informed Acheson of these talks with others, he never committed himself in foreign affairs except through or with the knowledge and concurrence of the

Secretary of State, and he always left the ball in the hands of the State Department. On the other hand, there was only one point of view communicated to the State Department staff. *"We* have decided," Acheson would say, or, "It is going to be done this way." There were no divergences between State Department and White House, for policy had been worked out together; even if there had been, they would not have been expressed in the Department by Acheson. The result was to give the President assurance, to bring out his extraordinary courage, common sense, and decisiveness in dealing with foreign affairs; and it led in the State Department to an *esprit de corps* that has never been surpassed, encouraging the full, creative contribution each officer had to offer. To those who knew of this relationship when Acheson was Undersecretary there was no doubt, when Truman was re-elected in 1948 and Marshall expressed his desire to retire, as to who would be appointed Secretary of State.

There were things about Harry S. Truman that never ceased to amaze even his closest associates—the wealth of his knowledge derived from wide reading, the deeply driven historical and philosophical pegs on which he hung his thinking, his common-sense judgment that mixed idealism and practicality in workable proportions, and above all his courage in the face of politics and other risks when he knew or thought he knew he was right. There is no question that he floundered often during his first year and a half in office, although his 1946 decisions with regard to Iran, Turkey, and Yugoslavia must be remembered. However, once he had the ground beneath his feet there may have been mistakes but no floundering. He adopted and sustained, beginning with the Truman Doctrine, a courageous and responsible course for the United States in world affairs, which in fact, not in slogans, checked and rolled back Soviet-Communist aggression and influence in large parts of the world, increased immeasurably the nation's security, and raised American prestige in the world to a high pinnacle. The Truman Doctrine, the Marshall Plan, the Atlantic Pact, the Military Defense Assistance Program, the Berlin Airlift, the NATO army in Europe, the Mutual Security Program, the Point IV Program, the resistance

to Communist aggression in Korea—these were only the main decisions he made in foreign affairs; lesser ones similar in quality would
fill pages. Truman recognized that the main, the colossal danger to
the United States was Communist aggression and subversion abroad,
not under the bed at home. He also had the wisdom and common
sense to recognize that the President has the duty, under the Consti-
tution, of protecting the dignity and rights of citizens, the integrity
of his government and the morale of its servants, and the prestige
of the nation abroad; and he saw that they must be protected against
those who sought to exploit fear of communism at home for personal and political gain.

No one who has read Tolstoi's *War and Peace* conceives of
history wholly in terms of what emperors and foreign ministers and
commanding generals, or even Presidents and Secretaries of State,
think or decide. They have the power and responsibility for decision, and if their attitudes and decisions and commands are wrong,
it makes little difference what the individual members of the army
or the bureaucracy do, for the campaign will inevitably be badly
conducted or lost. But given the correct relations and decisions at
the top, what the members of the bureaucracy or army do or fail
to do can have an enormous, perhaps decisive, influence in any
situation. Under the conditions created by Truman, Marshall, and
Acheson, the staff of the State Department was able to make its
fullest possible contribution. As the record will show, it had a
powerful influence upon the character of the decisions and developments of the Fifteen Weeks. That this is so does not detract from,
but enhances, the stature of their chiefs, who, recognizing their
powers and limitations, were able to draw out and use the talents
of those they commanded.

Because of the importance and fascination of its activities, the
State Department normally attracts some of the finest talent in the
country—from the student bodies and faculties of the universities,
from the legal and writing professions, from business. It not only
attracts good people, but under reasonable conditions the nature
of its operations so continuously informs them, instructs them, re-
fines and disciplines their thinking, as to create an extraordinary

competence and sense of responsibility. The political scientist or economist or historian coming to the Department brings a needed richness of knowledge and theory, but he is obliged to park theory in some convenient place and develop his capacity for dealing with the world in a practical way. The writer brings a useful talent, but glibness and mere facility for expression must yield to profundity and responsibility. The businessman coming to an executive post in the Department finds that mere efficiency unrelated to the aims of foreign policy is self-defeating, and he must develop a knowledge of and sensitivity toward those aims. The young man on the bottom rung of the State Department service, at home or abroad, quickly learns that the business of the State Department and its Foreign Service revolves about the question, What do I do today, with this action paper, this idea, this function, to protect and promote the interests of the United States today, tomorrow, six months, several years hence? The competence that is attracted to or developed in the State Department is therefore of an exceptionally practical variety.

It should not require saying, but in the context of 1955 it seems to require saying, that diversity of talent, diversity of personality, diversity of view among the staff, are essential to the protection and advancement of the interests of the United States in a dangerous world. The State Department not only directs the relations of the government of the United States with other governments, but determines the conditions in which the infinitely varied relations of the American people with other people take place. Its work is as varied, as complex, as subtle, as the world itself. There is seldom any single answer to any foreign-relations problem, and unless all possible answers can be suggested freely without fear of reprisal, the State Department is put into a strait jacket and the security of the nation is impaired. Within each office there is room for—indeed, there is need for—the practical executive, the dissenter, the advanced idea man, the critic, the traditionalist, all bringing different backgrounds and approaches to the consideration of a single set of problems. "Unity in diversity" is more than a phrase; it is a necessary condition in an effective State Department staff.

Just as in the relations between the Secretary and the President, so the subordinate officer in the State Department should be "frank, forthright, and vigorous in counsel" and "energetic and loyal in accepting decisions and carrying them out." There is a tendency in the State Department, as in most organizations, to follow the latter half of this formula and neglect the first. It is the exceptional administrator who, even in normal circumstances, is able to encourage both in proper proportions and make the Department hit on all cylinders. It becomes impossible for even the best administrator to achieve this when conditions conspire to bring about uniformity in the types retained or selected for service or to enforce through fear conformity of view. Foreign policy, the "first line of defense of the United States," becomes paralyzed, immobilized, when the State Department officer must make each comment or decision with the congressional investigator looking over his shoulder, with the security gumshoe listening at the door or on his wire, with the dissatisfied secretary spying on him, with every opinion and idea stripped and searched by immature minds for evidence of "disloyalty," with the knowledge that a congressional claque may break out against him personally at any moment and that his chiefs will not protect him in the honest and impartial performance of his functions. Both counsel and action are perforce reduced to what is gauged to be safe, acceptable not only to all the chiefs but to the most retarded among the security officers. The massacre that has been committed in recent years on the personnel, morale, and intellectual vigor of the Department of State is one of the greatest crimes of this generation and cannot fail to have dire consequences for the security and well-being of this country.

The 1947 staff of the State Department had for a very long time suffered restraint, but not the restraint of fear. It was the restraint of policy lag. Educated or professionally active in the interwar period, its members were acutely conscious each day of the role the United States could be playing to assure greater prosperity at home and help prevent a new war, and yet they had almost invariably seen United States action fall far short of the need. The retreat into political isolation and economic nationalism after World

War I had been so complete that it remained without significant challenge in Congress or the country at large, except as it was mildly tempered in 1934 and after by the Trade Agreements program, and slowly after 1937 as a consequence of growing fears of Japanese ambitions in Asia and German ambitions in Europe. By and large it had been necessary to accept the restraints imposed by the political context, but the State Department staff had never ceased to strain and press against them. It had not been comfortable to see war approaching from two directions, and yet to be acutely aware, from daily experience, that the power and influence of the United States was tied on short leash by public and congressional unawareness. Even after Pearl Harbor, with political restraint largely removed, with a *tabula rasa* in Europe and Asia, with a whole world to be remade with American initiative, it had not been comfortable to witness at close range, daily, the great emphasis placed upon "unconditional surrender" and the little emphasis upon building, in the white heat of war, new patterns of international life that would have a better chance of assuring the peace. And then, even before the war was over, the new danger had arisen—Soviet imperialism—and new restraints in dealing with it: always the policy lag! Throughout these years of restraint the State Department staff had nevertheless been in ferment, a largely uncultivated but fertile source of ideas, pushing, ever-pushing toward more effective policy, toward greater United States assumption of world responsibility commensurate with its power.

The Truman Doctrine decision unleashed for the first time the creative effort of the State Department staff. At last the political and economic power of the United States would be used fully to create world conditions in which the United States and other free nations would have a chance to live in freedom, peace, and well-being. In succeeding weeks emotion quivered near the surface as ideas surged forth. The responsible leaders made the breakthrough; but it was the State Department staff that swept through the breach made by the Truman Doctrine and was to a very important degree responsible for the advance to the Marshall Plan.

The President was not lonely in the decisions he made during the Fifteen Weeks. Not a single voice in his entire Cabinet was raised in opposition. Even more important than lack of opposition was the active support of Forrestal, Patterson, and Averell Harriman, then Secretary of Commerce. Will Clayton, Undersecretary of State for Economic Affairs, deserves mention in the Cabinet class because of his great prestige in and out of the government.

Forrestal, as Undersecretary of the Navy, had initiated in 1944 a project for a course on "The Foundations of National Power" to be incorporated in the Navy's V-12 educational program. It rested upon the proposition that "in order to understand the world position and responsibilities of our own country, it is necessary to know as much as possible concerning the strengths, aims, and policies of other countries. . . . The nature and distribution of political power among nations are matters of basic importance in any discussion of international relations or American foreign policy." One of the notes for a talk Forrestal was to have delivered as part of the course ran as follows: "Our problem—to achieve accommodation between the power we now possess, our reluctance to use it positively, the realistic necessity for such use, and our national ideals." Walter Millis, editor of *The Forrestal Diaries,* comments that "In one shape or another this was to Forrestal the fundamental problem, and it was never far from his mind throughout the rest of his career."

The Forrestal quotations indicate what the *Diaries* prove and his colleagues attest, that throughout his career as Undersecretary of the Navy, as Secretary of the Navy, and as Secretary of Defense, Forrestal consistently encouraged and promoted, in Cabinet meetings and out of them, the assumption by the United States of the responsibilities of its great power. Moreover he early recognized the possibility that the Soviet Union would not cooperate with us on reasonable terms, would, in fact, become a menace to our security. The practical expression of these two ideas was his prolonged effort to combine the defense services and bring them together with the State Department and other vital agencies, under the President, for the orderly projection of foreign and defense policies. When the matter of aid to Greece and Turkey, with its larger implications, came up for decision in February–March of 1947, there was no question as to where he would stand; in fact, it was his attitude for some time back that contributed importantly to the intellectual climate in which the decision was made.

Robert P. Patterson, Secretary of War, was a New York Republican judge whom Henry L. Stimson brought into the government as Assistant Secretary of War in July 1940 and made Undersecretary in December of that same year. When Stimson retired as Secretary in 1945 there was no doubt as to whom the President would appoint as his successor: "Judge" Patterson had during the war earned such universal respect for his dependability, industry, and wisdom that he had become almost indispensable. He was not a flashy man, nor a particularly subtle one. But quiet confidence and strength radiated from him, for he was completely fearless, and faced up to problems directly and thoroughly. Trained in the law, he made himself an authority on military history through wide and continued reading. Strongly imbued with a sense of the importance of military affairs, he nevertheless believed even more profoundly that they should be under firm civilian control. As for his views of the world and the role of the United States, he was a true disciple of Henry L. Stimson: he felt deeply the world responsibilities of American power. In the many hard and dangerous decisions the President had to make in 1946 and 1947 involving the commitment of American power abroad, he could always count on courageous, informed, and sound advice from "Judge" Patterson.

When W. Averell Harriman joined the President's Cabinet in October 1946 he had just returned from six years of residence in Great Britain and the Soviet Union, in each of which he had served first as special representative of the President in charge of Lend-Lease and shipping matters, and later as ambassador. He knew the political leaders and basic economic and political conditions in both countries as well as any living man. He had accompanied Roosevelt to most of the top-level wartime conferences, and Truman to Potsdam. He had lived on intimate terms with the British during the dark days of 1941 and 1942, the brighter days of early 1943, and the days of mounting, desperate trouble in 1946; and as Ambassador in Moscow he had spanned the period from the peak of Soviet-American cooperation and friendship in 1943 to the virtual break of late 1945 and early 1946. Very early Harriman had hoisted the warning signals about Soviet postwar intentions and had continually urged measures to strengthen our Western allies and check the spread of Soviet influence. With great prestige, with factual information at hand, he had a powerful influence upon the trend of thinking in the highest official circles of Washington. His direct participation in the developments of the Fifteen Weeks was limited to support in the Cabinet of action proposals which his attitudes and wider influence had helped to inspire. After the Marshall speech at Harvard on June 5, the President made Harriman chairman of the Advisory Council, which worked so prodigiously to translate the Marshall idea into a practical plan and to secure its passage in Congress, and he administered the Marshall Plan in Europe during its first two years.

William L. Clayton, Undersecretary of State for Economic Affairs, was ill in Arizona in late February and early March of 1947, when the decisions were made to aid Greece and Turkey. There was no doubt whatever where he stood. His fervent internationalism had come partly from an extraordinary native idealism and partly from his business experience. For many years he had headed the largest firm of cotton brokers in the world, Anderson, Clayton Company, of Houston, Texas, and he knew the value—indeed, the necessity—of foreign trade and therefore of liberal, cooperative trading policies. As Assistant Secretary of Commerce from 1942 to 1945, and as Assistant Secretary and Undersecretary of State for Economic Affairs, he had become even more impressed with the fact that the free world economy would cease to exist, so preponderant had become the productive and financial power of the United States and so weakened and destroyed were the other main countries of the trading world, unless the United States took the most radical and sacrificial steps to restore a balance. He was also deeply aware that democracy and freedom and the security of the United States were at stake in the restoration of a viable world economy.

Clayton's prestige in the business community and in Congress was unequaled, and he had made full use of it in putting over, almost personally, the $3.75 billion postwar loan to Great Britain. He had sent the Porter Mission to Greece. He had worn himself out in the year and a half after the war trying to find ways, within the limits of existing authority, to bolster our friends abroad.

Clayton returned to Washington on March 10 and took charge of preparing, and presenting to the Senate Committee on Foreign Relations and the House Committee on Foreign Affairs, the economic side of the administration's case for aid to Greece and Turkey, following which he left for Geneva to head the United States delegation in negotiating trade agreements with eighteen nations and in concluding negotiations for the World Trade Charter and the International Trade Organization. In Geneva, Clayton heard from the economic chieftains gathered there what was happening in Europe, and from Geneva, Clayton traveled to the principal countries of Western Europe, talked to their leaders, saw at first hand that recovery had stalled and that Europe was sliding into chaos. His reports to the Department and his letters to Washington officials played an important part in the development of official thinking during the Fifteen Weeks. His role in connection with the specific developments of that period will be related elsewhere.

There remains to be mentioned the role played by the senior Senator from Michigan, Arthur H. Vandenberg, chairman of the Senate Committee on Foreign Relations. Had it not been for his powerful support for administration foreign policies during the Fifteen Weeks and after, that period would probably not be worth writing a book about. In a very real sense the epic of Vandenberg's intellectual development after December 7, 1941, was the epic of the United States. No senator was more effectively isolationist than he before Pearl Harbor; in fact, he was the leader of the noninterventionist bloc in Congress. But the day the Japanese attacked

Pearl Harbor, as Vandenberg wrote later, "ended isolationism for any realist." His son, Arthur H. Vandenberg, Jr., who edited *The Private Papers of Senator Vandenberg,* suggests this remark may have been hindsight. At any rate, Vandenberg immediately cooperated completely, in a non-partisan manner as far as the war effort was concerned, and started along the long, slow approach toward internationalism. By August 3, 1943, he was able to write to Thomas Lamont: "I am hunting for a middle ground between those extremists at one end of the line who would cheerfully give America away and those extremists at the other end of the line who would attempt total isolation which has come to be an impossibility." Later in the month, at a meeting of Republican leaders on Mackinac Island, Michigan, Vandenberg was instrumental in bringing about a compromise declaration on foreign policy, known as the Mackinac Charter, that for the first time united Republicans in favor of "responsible participation by the United States in post-war cooperative organization among sovereign nations to prevent military aggression and to attain permanent peace with organized justice in a free world." The Mackinac Charter, which became the basis of the foreign-policy plank of the Republican party's 1944 platform, was one of the most important non-military developments of the entire war period: it removed isolationism *per se* from the American scene and brought the minimum level of public debate up to the question of what kind of world participation, and how much.

Senator Vandenberg's development continued at an accelerated pace. By April of 1944 he was meeting periodically, as a member of a bipartisan Committee of Eight, with Secretary Hull, to discuss postwar plans and particularly the kind of postwar organization that would be created. And on January 10, 1945, in a dramatic, well-timed, and carefully prepared speech delivered in the Senate, he in effect confessed that he had been an isolationist once but that he had changed:

> I do not believe that any nation hereafter can immunize itself by its own exclusive action. Since Pearl Harbor, World War II has

put the gory science of mass murder into new and sinister perspectives. Our oceans have ceased to be moats which automatically protect our ramparts. Flesh and blood now compete equally with winged steel. War has become an all-consuming juggernaut. If World War III ever unhappily arrives, it will open new laboratories of death too horrible to contemplate. I propose to do everything within my power to keep those laboratories closed for keeps. I want the maximum American cooperation, consistent with legitimate self-interest, with constitutional process, and with collateral events which warrant it, to make the basic idea of Dumbarton Oaks succeed. I want a new dignity and a new authority for international law. I think American self-interest requires it. But, Mr. President, this also requires whole-hearted reciprocity. . . .

The Senator went on to say that the Soviet Union appeared to be more interested in surrounding itself with completely dominated buffer states than in a just peace maintained by collective security. He urged strongly that the President speak out convincingly on postwar aims and make certain that all unilateral decisions made in consequence of military need should be subject to postwar agreement and revision.

The speech was a sensation, and the public response to it throughout the country was even more so. Arthur H. Vandenberg, Jr., has written that "it was the over-all impact of the Senator's declaration that made the speech a turning point, that brought his sudden and tremendous surge of popular support and led to the emergence of a new and unique figure in the history of American foreign policy." As James Reston later wrote in *Life,* (May 24, 1948): "The important thing about that speech . . . was not that Vandenberg made it but that the American people responded to it with such enthusiasm. He did not change the American people. He made a tentative public confession . . . and the American people, by their response to his speech, changed him. What he did was merely to express and symbolize their change and then stick single-mindedly to the *action* necessary to implement their will. Since then, however, his record is unprecedented."

By February 1947 Vandenberg had become a veteran in bipartisan internationalism—strong, dependable, indispensable to the conduct of foreign relations. He had helped frame the United Nations Charter in San Francisco and secure its ratification in the Senate. He had attended a whole series of postwar international conferences as a member of Secretary Byrnes' delegation and had offered steady support. He had become disillusioned, and then alarmed, somewhat earlier than some of his colleagues, at the behavior and apparent intentions of the Russians, and was becoming increasingly critical in private of the administration for not taking a stronger stand. He was at least partially in the frame of mind to welcome the Truman Doctrine.

Partially, but not wholly. For by then the Republicans controlled Congress; a stand against the Russians meant money, and a great deal of it, to aid Russia's intended victims; and Vandenberg had never faced up fully to the economic realities of American responsibilities in the postwar world, in terms of tariffs, commercial policies, foreign aid, and taxation. Moreover he could not be certain how far his party, having accepted international cooperation in principle, would follow him in economic internationalism. Nevertheless he accepted and supported the specific measure of aid to Greece and Turkey. As projects for large-scale aid elsewhere began to burgeon in the administration during the Fifteen Weeks, he drew back in initial alarm, but later accepted the necessity for the Marshall Plan and supported it to the hilt.

It is not unfair to say that Vandenberg, had he been in a position of executive power, would probably never have conceived in time the measures of the Fifteen Weeks, or any of the remarkable steps that were taken in succeeding years to assure the security of the United States through cooperative effort with our allies. His genius was rather as leader of the "loyal opposition." His first reaction to a new proposal made by the administration was usually either noncommittal or negative (although this was not true of the proposal to aid Greece and Turkey). But he had that most uncommon quality of being able to be convinced by facts and reasoned argument.

To mention Senator Vandenberg here and to fail to mention the other senators and congressmen, both Democrats and Republicans, who lent valiant support and constant encouragement to the basic foreign policies of the Truman administration, is not to underrate the contribution of the larger number. It is only to recognize the key position Vandenberg occupied in the Congress and in the country. It was necessary to negotiate with Vandenberg. Once his support was forthcoming, success for radical advances in the foreign policy of the United States was assured.

PART IV

THE FIFTEEN WEEKS

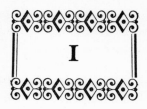

I

A WEEK OF DECISION

NEARLY three days of the Fifteen Weeks had already elapsed when the British ambassador met with Secretary Marshall at 10 a.m. on Monday, February 24.[1] His call was something of an anticlimax, for, as we have seen, the First Secretary of the Embassy, Mr. Sichel, had brought copies of the British notes over to Henderson the previous Friday afternoon. When the Ambassador arrived, Secretary Marshall had already read the notes, as well as the memorandum that Henderson and his staff had prepared over the weekend. Moreover he had already had a long session with Acheson, who had brought him up to date on what had happened since he left his office early Friday afternoon.

Lord Inverchapel delivered his messages orally, referring to the texts of the notes, and added a few comments of his own. There was little discussion. Secretary Marshall assured the Ambassador that the Greece-Turkey matter seemed to be of the utmost importance and that he would give it his immediate attention. He promised to discuss it at once with the President and the Chief of Staff and give answer promptly.

Two hours later, while the Cabinet was assembling for luncheon with the President, Secretary Marshall told Forrestal of the Ambassador's call, the serious problem it dumped in our lap, and remarked that it was tantamount to British abdication from the

[1] H. M. Sichel and Loy Henderson were also present.

Middle East with obvious implications as to their successor. At that moment Lord Inverchapel was leaving Washington for New Haven, Connecticut, where he spent a convivial evening as guest of the Yale Whiffenpoofs.

Marshall's reaction was similar to that of all the others in the Department who had heard the news. Without any exception known to the writer, everyone in the executive branch recognized what this meant, and saw that if Russian expansion was to be checked, the United States must move into the defaulted position in the Middle East.

The instant recognition of this, the virtual unanimity of view, made it possible, within a single week beginning February 21, for the staff of the State Department to prepare a documented statement of position and recommendations, for this to be approved by Acheson, Marshall, the Secretaries of War and of the Navy, and the President, for it to be cleared by the President with congressional leaders, and for a State Department working party to start preparing a detailed program of action. The singleness of reaction grew from accumulating facts that had been shouting for recognition for a long time. One more fact was added, and the situation no longer shouted, but commanded, and was obeyed. History took a new course.

For reasons of high policy and good manners the United States did not during the Fifteen Weeks, or thereafter, dramatize the takeover of leadership of the free world from Great Britain. It was not to our national interest at that critical moment to emphasize Britain's weakness in the Mediterranean and the Middle East, and good sportsmanship forbade noticing more than was necessary the exhaustion of a team mate. But during the Fifteen Weeks the consciousness that a chapter in world history had come to an end was so real and ever-present as to seem almost tangible. During those weeks of tough decision and hard-headed thinking, emotion—proceeding from a realization that world power was at that moment changing hands—was not far from the surface. And even while the eyes observed the new spectacle with pride, the memory persistently called up the gallant role Great Britain had for so long played as world leader.

There were no officers in the Department of State who appreciated that role more than Loy Henderson and Jack Hickerson, the two who first received the news of Britain's decision. Henderson, born in Arkansas, had been in the Foreign Service for twenty-five years, nine of them spent in the Soviet Union or countries on its periphery, and had served many years as assistant chief of the State Department's Division of European Affairs. He was regarded as one of the Department's experts on the Soviet Union. Hickerson, born in Texas, had entered the Foreign Service in 1920 and had served some years abroad; then for nearly twenty years he had held top posts in the Department's offices dealing with European Affairs and had a wide knowledge of the affairs of the British Commonwealth. Both were vigorous, hard-hitting, responsible men, aware that order in international relations is not a natural condition but one that can at times be created by the full and wise and systematic organization of power. Perhaps more important, their initiative had not been eroded by sycophancy or intimidated by public attack.

Dean Acheson was thoroughly familiar with the situation in Greece. Only the day before, Ambassador MacVeagh, Mark Ethridge, and Paul Porter had climaxed a series of alarming cables from Athens with a message, concurred in by all three, that could only be characterized as frantic: Greece was on the point of panic, in danger of complete collapse, economically, psychologically, and militarily, within a matter of weeks, and if it collapsed the armed Communist bands would take over. That very morning, February 21, before leaving for Princeton, Secretary Marshall had sent Acheson a memorandum recommending that a bill be drawn up for congressional approval providing for a direct loan to Greece, and that a decision be cleared through the executive branch to transfer military equipment to Greece. But reports from Athens and the Secretary's decision had not taken into account the towering new fact of which Acheson was now apprised: the imminent cessation of British support. The probability of Greece's early fall was now transformed into a certainty unless the United States should act to prevent it. Not just part of the responsibility for saving the situation, but most of it, was now ours. Moreover urgency would have to be measured on an entirely new scale; likewise the kinds and amounts of aid that would have to be provided. Stopgap measures would no longer suffice. The problem had to be faced fully and frontally. For not just the fate of Greece was at stake. Greece was the key to a much wider situation: the freedom and security of a large part of the world.

Acheson, Henderson, and Hickerson knew the problem well, and they were in general agreement: the discussion among them was therefore brief that Friday afternoon. The most important thing was to work out an orderly procedure and get things moving fast. Acheson suggested that Henderson call a staff meeting for that evening to consider the problem and prepare a paper summarizing the most pertinent facts and estimates of the situation in Greece and Turkey as reported by United States representatives. It was also necessary to list the funds and authority available to the executive branch (they were known to be wholly inadequate) for extending military, technical, and economic assistance, and to analyze the significance of Greece and Turkey to the defense of the free world. This memorandum would be handed to Secretary Marshall before he received Lord Inverchapel on Monday morning. Acheson also asked Henderson and Hickerson to confer the next day with Vice-Admiral Forrest P. Sherman, Deputy Chief of Naval Operations, and Major General Lauris Norstad, Director of Plans and Operations of the War Department General Staff, giving them full information on the situation and the new problem that had arisen, so that they might brief the Secretary of the Navy and the Secretary of War for a meeting with Marshall and Acheson on Monday. Then, as Hickerson and Henderson hastened back to their offices to begin a weekend of heavy labor, Acheson telephoned President Truman at the White House and Secretary Marshall in Princeton to tell them of what had happened and the arrangements he had made.

George F. Kennan chaired the staff meeting in the Department that evening. Henderson, Hickerson, the senior members of their

offices, and a few others were there. Kennan, then lecturing at the
War College in Washington, had acquired great prestige in the
Department and in the upper echelons of the government generally
as a consequence of the realism and incisiveness of his reports from
Moscow. In one notable cable (it ran to eight thousand words)
submitted a year earlier when he was chargé in the Moscow Embassy, he had so impressively analyzed Soviet motivations and designs as to contribute markedly to the stiffening of United States
policy toward Soviet expansionism. Kennan had recommended that
the American public be told the full truth about the realities of the
Russian situation, that the Western world develop cohesion, firmness,
and vigor in its dealing with the Soviet Union, that we proceed with
courage and self-confidence and put before the free peoples of the
world a "much more positive and constructive picture of the sort
of world we would like to see than we have put forward in the past." [2]
Henderson and Hickerson, realizing that large-scale United States
aid to Greece and Turkey involved at its core our relations with
the Soviet Union, and aware also that Secretary Marshall had asked
Kennan to create and head a Policy Planning Staff in the Department when his assignment at the War College ended in May, thought
it fitting to invite him to the first staff meeting on the Greek crisis
and offered him the chair.

There is apparently nothing that is recorded and little that is
remembered about that meeting except that all present agreed that
the United States would have to give extraordinary economic and
military aid to Greece. The problem of aid to Turkey, being of
secondary urgency, was hardly discussed. Everyone was aware that
what was involved was the commitment of American power in
Greece and the Middle East. The members of the Office of Near
Eastern and African Affairs were quite openly elated over the possibility that the United States might now take action on a broad
enough scale to prevent the Soviet Union from breaking through
the Greece-Turkey-Iran barrier into the Middle East, South Asia,

[2] Kennan's report is described at length, with quotations, in *The Forrestal
Diaries*. Kennan published his views in the July 1947 issue of *Foreign Affairs*
under the signature of "Mr. X," an anonymity that was soon pierced, and
Kennan became publicly labeled as the author of the policy of "containment."

and North Africa. They had long felt themselves virtually unarmed in trying to deal with this problem, which was to them as real as the walls about them and held frightful potentialities for the security of the United States and the future of the world.

After the discussion ended Henderson made assignments, and by midnight the first draft of a factual paper on the situation in Greece was completed. Thus, eight hours after the transmission of the first spark from the British Embassy, ended the first day of the Fifteen Weeks. Kennan recalls driving home with a sense of great developments impending. Nevertheless, occupied with another job, he had nothing further to do with the Greece-Turkey matter except for an intervention that will be described later.

Saturday, February 22, was a busy day in the State Department. Hickerson and Henderson had a long session with Admiral Sherman and General Norstad in Hickerson's office, in which all aspects of the Greece-Turkey problem were considered. Acheson conferred throughout the day with his staff, initiating studies and giving guidance. The Near Eastern Affairs staff worked furiously; by late Sunday afternoon they had revised, expanded, and refined the paper that had been hastily drafted on Friday evening, had buttressed it with supporting studies, and Henderson had delivered the end-product to Acheson at his Georgetown home.

Secretary Marshall's induction Monday morning into the Greece-Turkey crisis has already been related. Shortly before noon he crossed Executive Avenue to confer with the President, as was customary, before the regular weekly luncheon of the Cabinet. Marshall told the President of the British Ambassador's call and the problem it posed for the United States. He also told him of the steps that were being taken to bring about a coordinated recommendation by State, War, and Navy for the President's early decision.

Secretary Marshall, busy preparing for the Moscow Conference only a few days away, deliberately left the Greece-Turkey ball with Acheson, who had first caught it and who would have to run with it when Marshall left. Marshall therefore attended only the meetings where his presence was absolutely required. Acheson of course kept him fully informed and sought his approval on important decisions.

Monday afternoon, February 24, Acheson, assisted by Henderson and Hickerson, presided over a conference with Forrestal, who was accompanied by Admiral Sherman, and Patterson, who was accompanied by General Norstad. This was an important meeting, for the problem of aid to Greece and Turkey was considered on a high level in its wider world setting, and a broad government position began to grow. Forrestal and Patterson showed themselves to be well informed on the details of the Greece-Turkey problem. The discussion was long, and many questions were asked and answered all around. At the end Acheson summed up the conclusions, and all found themselves in agreement that it was vital to the security of the United States that Greece and Turkey be strengthened; that only the United States was in a position to do this; and that the President should therefore ask Congress for the necessary funds and authority. Acheson told Forrestal and Patterson that a formal statement of position and recommendations would be drawn up and submitted to them for approval on Wednesday. Later Acheson told Marshall of the conclusions reached, and Marshall concurred.

Were it not that the subordinate staff of the State Department contributed so markedly to the policy development of this period it would not be important to record here a meeting of key political, economic, legal, and information officers that Acheson held Tuesday afternoon, February 25. In a judicial manner Acheson laid out the problem posed by the withdrawal of the British from Greece and Turkey and outlined alternate courses of action the United States might follow. He refrained until near the end of the meeting from expressing any conclusions: instead, in the characteristic manner described before, he stimulated all present to express their views, to raise questions, to voice doubts. Some were concerned over the responsibility involved in challenging the Soviet Union at a time when our military strength was at a low ebb and no one knew what the Soviet reaction would be. Some were elated over the possibility that the United States might at last stand out boldly against Soviet expansion. Others offered ideas as to how the matter ought to be presented to the public or pointed out obstacles that would have to be overcome. All were to some degree filled with awe at the turning point that the United States had reached in its history.

When all had spoken, Acheson made his summation, in the process allaying doubts, resolving conflicts, incorporating ideas presented to him, pointing up the logic of the discussion. Thus Acheson broadened his own conception of the problem and fortified his staff for creative work on the project ahead. Chief and staff were as one. There was only one point of view, and that was growing, evolving, from a free flow of ideas. After this meeting Acheson, Henderson, and the staff of NEA worked late, writing the final version of the "Position and Recommendations of the Department of State Regarding Immediate Aid to Greece and Turkey."

The general position taken in that document was that the political and territorial integrity of Greece and Turkey should be maintained and that every effort should be made to extend the aid necessary to assure the development of those countries as democratic states with sound economies. It was recommended that the British be so informed, and be asked to give assurances that they would continue to do all possible to achieve the same ends. There were a number of specific recommendations for action:

That the administration propose to Congress, first, immediate legislation authorizing the Export-Import Bank to extend credits free from the restrictions that normally hamper the Bank's lending activities, and, second, legislation authorizing longer-range financial aid;

That all available military supplies that could be transferred under existing legislation be sent to Greece and Turkey, and that legislation be prepared and proposed to Congress authorizing the furnishing of supplies and equipment needed to restore order and maintain independence;

That legislation be prepared and proposed to Congress which would authorize the sending of United States government personnel for administrative, economic, and financial work with the Greek government;

That plans be worked out for an American administrative organization in Greece that would control the Greek economic program in order to assure proper use of the funds and supplies furnished by the United States (it was recognized that a program of several years would probably be required);

That Greece be given precedence in the matter of military requirements and that discussions be inaugurated at once with British representatives in Washington on Greece's military needs and how the furnishing of military supplies might be expedited;

And, finally, that measures be taken to inform the public of the urgent need of aid to Greece.

Forrestal and Patterson met with Marshall and Acheson on Wednesday morning, February 26, to consider the State Department's "Position and Recommendations." The question was discussed at this meeting, as it had been two days earlier at the meeting of Acheson with Forrestal and Patterson, of the probable needs of other countries for aid similar to that proposed for Greece and Turkey. The necessity for large-scale aid to South Korea was looming at that moment. It had become clear that the Soviet Union was not going to agree to a unification of the northern and southern zones, and the American-held southern portion required vast economic reconstruction and delevopment if it was to exist as an independent country. China also might require further aid. When, therefore, the Greece-Turkey crisis arose, General Eisenhower, Chief of Staff of the Army, addressed a memorandum to the Secretary of War in which he called attention to the various problems of foreign aid that were arising and suggested that a study be made of the prospective needs of all foreign countries for United States aid, with a view to asking for an appropriation to cover the whole.

This point of view was considered at the meeting on February 26, but it was recognized that the suggested study would take a long time to prepare, that getting a general aid bill approved by Congress would be extremely difficult and in any event would take a very long time, and that the Greek crisis required the fastest possible action. The Secretary of War and the Secretary of the Navy therefore endorsed the State Department's "Position and Recommendations" regarding immediate aid to Greece and Turkey, but it was understood that a comprehensive study should be made of other situations that might require our aid.

That afternoon Marshall and Acheson met with President Truman and fully explained the recommendations of the three Departments. Truman required no convincing. He had already discussed the matter in a preliminary way with Marshall, and several times with Acheson over the telephone, and, as we have seen, he knew the problems of the Middle East intimately. He accepted and approved the joint State-War-Navy recommendations. The problem was not what should be done, but how to get authorizing legislation through Congress. There was no time to be lost, and Marshall would be leaving soon for Moscow. The President decided to invite congressional leaders to the White House the next day to hear Marshall and Acheson put the case and to get their reaction to the proposed program. The White House telephoned the invitations.

That February 27 meeting at the White House is of great importance in this chronicle. Present from Capitol Hill were Senator Vandenberg; Speaker Martin; Representative Sam Rayburn, Democrat, House Minority Leader; Representative Charles A. Eaton, Republican, chairman of the House Committee on Foreign Affairs; Senator Styles Bridges, Republican, chairman of the Senate Appropriations Committee; Senator Tom Connally, ranking Democrat on the Senate Foreign Relations Committee; and Representative Sol Bloom, ranking Democrat on the House Foreign Affairs Committee. Representative John Taber, Republican, chairman of the House Appropriations Committee, was invited but could not attend; nevertheless he hastened to the White House in the afternoon and was informed in detail on what had happened.[3]

At the request of the President, Secretary Marshall led off in the

[3] Senator Taft was not invited, an error that Senator Vandenburg pointed out to President Truman the next day in a brief note: "If another congressional conference on any matter of *fundamental* and *far-reaching* importance (as yesterday), I respectfully suggest that the representation of the congressional majority include Senator Taft because of his position as chairman of the Republican Senate Policy Committee." Taft was thereafter invited; notably, he attended the second meeting on the Greece-Turkey subject at the White House on March 10.

presentation of the problem. In dry and economical terms he gave the congressional leaders the facts about the imminent withdrawal of British support from Greece and Turkey, the situation those countries were left in, vulnerable to Soviet domination, and the recommendations for aid that had been agreed upon the executive branch.

There is no question that the Secretary understood thoroughly the strategic importance of Greece and Turkey, but somehow his summary and cryptic presentation failed to put it across to his listeners. In fact he conveyed the over-all impression that aid should be extended to Greece on grounds of loyalty and humanitarianism, and to Turkey to strengthen Britain's position in the Middle East. This did not go down well with some of the congressional leaders, whose major preoccupation at that moment was reducing aid abroad and taxes at home. Their initial reaction was later described as "rather trivial" and "adverse." The immediate questions asked were: "Isn't this pulling British chestnuts out of the fire?" "What are we letting ourselves in for?" "How much is this going to cost?" Answers only took the discussion farther off the main track.

Things were going very badly indeed, and Acheson was greatly disturbed. Leaning over to Secretary Marshall, who sat beside him, Acheson asked in a low voice, "Is this a private fight or can anyone get into it?" Whereupon Marshall addressed the President and suggested that Acheson had something to say. Acheson was given the floor. Many of the things he said are already known to us, but in view of the impact upon his listeners it is worth following his argument.

In the past eighteen months, Acheson began, the position of the democracies in the world had seriously deteriorated. While Secretary Byrnes and Senator Vandenberg and Senator Connally had gone from conference to conference trying to negotiate peace settlements that would save certain countries of Central Europe from Soviet control, the Soviet Union had been busy elsewhere, and with greater success than was generally realized. It was clear they were making the most persistent and ambitious efforts to encircle Turkey and Germany and thus lay three continents open to Soviet domination.

Acheson described the direct pressures of the Soviet Union on Turkey during the preceding year and a half for territorial cessions and for military and naval bases in the Turkish Straits that would mean the end of Turkish independence. These had been accompanied, he said, by a vicious and prolonged propaganda campaign and, more important, by encircling movements aimed at Iran and Greece. The Turks, with British and American diplomatic support, had stood firm against Soviet pressures, and the move against Iran had for the time being failed. Now Communist pressure was concentrated on Greece, and there was every likelihood that unless Greece received prompt and large-scale aid from the outside the Communists would succeed in seizing control. Reports from Greece indicated that complete collapse might occur within a matter of weeks.

The Russians had any number of bets, Acheson went on. If they won any one of them, they won all. If they could seize control of Turkey, they would almost inevitably extend their control over Greece and Iran. If they controlled Greece, Turkey would sooner or later succumb, with or without a war, and then Iran. If they dominated Italy, where Communist pressures were increasing, they could probably take Greece, Turkey, and the Middle East. Their aim, Acheson emphasized, was control of the eastern Mediterranean and the Middle East. From there the possibilities for penetration of South Asia and Africa were limitless.

As for Europe, Acheson continued, it was clear that the Soviet Union, employing the instruments of Communist infiltration and subversion, was trying to complete the encirclement of Germany. In France, with four Communists in the Cabinet, one of them Minister of Defense, with Communists controlling the largest trade union and infiltrating government offices, factories, and the armed services, with nearly a third of the electorate voting Communist, and with economic conditions worsening, the Russians could pull the plug any time they chose. In Italy a similar if less immediately dangerous situation existed, but it was growing worse. In Hungary and Austria the Communists were tightening the noose on democratic governments. If Greece and the eastern Mediterranean should fall to Soviet control, the material and psychological effects in the countries that were so precariously maintaining their freedoms and democratic institutions would be devastating, and probably conclusive.

It had been remarked, Acheson observed, that in aiding Greece and Turkey we would only be "pulling British chestnuts out of the fire." Britain's world power was shattered, he said, just as was that of every other democratic country except the United States. Great Britain was in grave financial trouble. He mentioned the two recent White Papers and their dark outlook for national survival, and explained that for financial reasons Britain was now obliged to withdraw troops and economic support from still other positions upon which her world power was based.

Only two great powers remained in the world, Acheson continued, the United States and the Soviet Union. We had arrived at a situation unparalleled since ancient times. Not since Rome and Carthage had there been such a polarization of power on this earth. Moreover the two great powers were divided by an unbridgeable ideological chasm. For us, democracy and individual liberty were basic; for them, dictatorship and absolute conformity. And it was clear that the Soviet Union was aggressive and expanding. For the United States to take steps to strengthen countries threatened with Soviet aggression or Communist subversion was not to pull British chestnuts out of the fire; it was to protect the security of the United States—it was to protect freedom itself. For if the Soviet Union succeeded in extending its control over two-thirds of the world's surface and three-fourths of its population, there could be no security for the United States, and freedom anywhere in the world would have only a poor chance of survival. The proposed aid to Greece and Turkey was not therefore a matter of bailing out the British, or even of responding on humanitarian grounds to the need of a loyal ally. It was a matter of building our own security and safeguarding freedom by strengthening free peoples against Communist aggression and subversion. We had the choice, he concluded, of acting with energy to meet this situation or of losing by default.

Acheson had abandoned the manner of a judge and for ten or fifteen minutes had spoken as a fervent advocate. When he finished a profound silence ensued that lasted perhaps ten seconds. It was broken by the voice of Senator Vandenberg. Slowly and with gravity, Vandenberg said that he had been greatly impressed, even shaken, by what he had heard. It was clear that the country was faced by an extremely serious situation, of which aid to Greece and Turkey, although of great importance, was only a part. He felt that it was absolutely necessary that any request of Congress for funds and authority to aid Greece and Turkey should be accompanied by a message to Congress, and an explanation to the American people, in which the grim facts of the larger situation should be laid publicly on the line as they had been at their meeting there that day.

The President went around the circle, inviting the comments of everyone present. Not one registered opposition. Not one asked trivial questions or raised side issues. All had apparently been deeply impressed. Vandenberg wrote some time later that no commitments were made at this meeting. That is true. None had been asked. But the very definite impression was gained, and was conveyed to the State Department staff the next day as a working hypothesis, that the congressional leaders would support whatever measures were necessary to save Greece and Turkey, *on the condition,* made by Senator Vandenberg and supported by others present, that the President should, in a message to Congress and in a radio address to the American people, explain the issue in the same frank terms and broad context in which it had been laid before them. What Vandenberg meant by the broad context may be indicated by something he wrote six days later to a congressional colleague:

> I am frank in saying that I do not know the answer to the latest Greek challenge because I do not know all the facts. I am waiting for all the facts before I say anything. . . . But I sense enough of the facts to realize that the problem in Greece cannot be isolated by itself. On the contrary, it is probably symbolic of the world-wide ideological clash between Eastern communism and Western democracy; and it may easily be the thing which requires us to make some very fateful and far-reaching decisions.[4]

[4] Arthur H. Vandenberg, Jr., ed., *The Private Papers of Senator Vandenberg* (Boston: Houghton Mifflin Company, 1952).

The question has often been raised as to why the matter of aid to Greece and Turkey was presented to Congress and the American people enveloped in a statement of global policy that picked up the ideological challenge of communism. The February 27 meeting at the White House holds part of the answer. The explicit reaction of all in the government, from the President down, who were concerned with the decision to aid Greece and Turkey was that a historical turning point had been reached, that the United States must now stand forth as leader of the free world in place of the flagging British and use its power directly and vigorously to strengthen free nations. But there is a great difference between thinking or determining this and announcing it as the policy of the United States to a questionable Congress and an apathetic electorate. Because of the searing political lessons of the previous twenty-eight years, beginning with rejection of membership in the League of Nations and continuing through the isolationism of the twenties, the neutrality of the thirties, and the reaction against President Roosevelt's "quarantine" speech in Chicago in October 1937, the cautious, limited, backdoor approach to involvement in world affairs had become almost a reflex in successive administrations, notwithstanding support of the United Nations and vigorous participation in the negotiation of peace treaties. At the meeting with congressional leaders Acheson discovered that he had to pull out all the stops and speak in the frankest, boldest, widest terms to attract their support for a matter which in parliamentary democracies without a tradition of isolationism would have been undertaken quietly and without fanfare. This time the frank and bold approach, far from shocking congressional leaders into timorousness, paid off. They were deeply impressed and felt that on that basis they could go before their constituents. It was Vandenberg's "condition" that made it possible, even necessary, to launch the global policy that broke through the remaining barriers of American isolationism.

President Truman promised the congressional leaders to have a detailed program prepared for a second meeting with them, which he would call for Friday, March 7 (actually it was not held until Monday, March 10). He agreed that the matter of aid to Greece and Turkey should be presented by him to Congress in its broadest context and in the frankest terms, and promised that a message would be prepared along these lines. The question was raised as to whether the British could be persuaded to keep their remaining troops in Greece, and Marshall replied that the matter was under discussion with the British. Neither the President nor Secretary Marshall could give any assurances that the situation in Greece and Turkey could be saved by American assistance, but only that it was clear it could *not* be saved *without* American assistance. The meeting came to an end.

The evening of February 27 Acheson held an off-the-record background conference with about twenty newspaper correspondents who regularly covered the State Department. The press had got wind of momentous happenings, had begun to speculate on them, and knew of the morning's meeting at the White House. Acheson thought it important to give the correspondents the correct pitch at the beginning, even though at this early stage it was not possible to issue a release, talk particulars, or authorize quotation. He told them of the British notes regarding Greece (Turkey was not mentioned at this stage), of the situation in Greece and its relation to the security of the eastern Mediterranean, of the decision to ask Congress to authorize aid for Greece, and of the morning's meeting with congressional leaders at the White House. More important, he pitched the problem of aid to Greece in its broad context. During the succeeding days Acheson met with other small groups of radio commentators, columnists, and newsmen in similar off-the-record conferences.

Following the first of these conferences, James Reston, in the *New York Times* of March 1, posed the problem of aid to Greece in terms of three questions:

Is the United States prepared to take specific action in Greece in opposition to the expansion of Soviet influence in the eastern Mediterranean?

Is the United States prepared to assume the risks and expense of bolstering world stability as Britain did in the ninteenth century?

Can the two major political parties, one in control of the Executive and the other in control of Congress, agree on a policy of aid to a government supported by the British and violently opposed by the Soviet Union?

A great deal of the radio, editorial, and columnist comment during the early days of March was in this same vein. It encouraged those engaged in articulating and implementing policy and performed an invaluable service as advance agent to Congress and the public for the President's message of March 12.

The morning of February 28 was a memorable one in the Department of State. At 10:30 in the Secretary's conference room Acheson met with those departmental officers who would have the chief responsibility for working out all aspects of the program.[5] The meetings of the preceding seven days had been devoted to probing, discussing, sizing up the problem. This one was different. The scope of the problem had been determined, decisions made and approved. At this meeting no suggestions were invited, no questions asked. The problem, the solution, the pitch, were set forth fully and concisely. The show was put on the road.

Acheson, revealing his awareness of the epochal importance of what he was saying only by an unusual gravity of manner, reviewed briefly the events of the preceding week, told of the decisions that had been made by the Secretary and the President, and then proceeded to a detailed description of the previous day's meeting with the congressional leaders. Tenseness and controlled excitement grew by the moment in the large room as Acheson launched into a full statement of the larger issues, repeating the exposition that had so impressed the legislators. And when he described their generally favorable reaction and the indications they had given of support, and told of Vandenberg's "condition," which the President had

[5] Present were:

Office of Near Eastern and African Affairs: Loy Henderson, Henry Villard, Gordan Merriam, John Jernegan, and William Baxter.

Office of European Affairs: Jack Hickerson, Llewellyn Thompson, Tom Wailes, Harry Labouisse.

Economic Affairs: Tyler Wood, Norman Ness, Hubert Havlik

Public Affairs: Francis Russell, Joseph Jones

Legal Division: John Howard

Office of Assistant Secretary of State for Occupied Areas: Ernest Gross

Central Secretariat: John Gange

welcomed, it seemed to those present that a new chapter in world history had opened and that they were the most privileged of men, participants in a drama such as rarely occurs even in the long life of a great nation.

There was a great job to be done, Acheson said, and it would have to be done with great speed. Within a few days it was necessary to draw up in detail a program of economic, military, and technical aid to Greece and Turkey, to draft the necessary enabling legislation, the President's message to Congress, and a radio "fireside chat" to be delivered the day the message went to Congress, and to develop and get under way a program of public information. Acheson reported Secretary Marshall's injunction that the matter be presented to Congress and the public in the fullest and frankest terms. He also reported Marshall's instruction that the staff should go about their work vigorously without any regard to the effect that the Greece-Turkey program, or any public statement of it, might have on the Moscow Conference or upon his personal position there. The mind went back at this point to other Secretaries of State and the priorities they almost certainly would have established even under these circumstances. Had Secretary Marshall not seen what was important, and what was relatively less so, the history of recent years might have been far different. *All* barriers to bold action were indeed down.

Acheson advanced only one caution. Although we should be vigorous and forthright, we must not be belligerent or provocative. Our policy was not directed against any country or even any movement, but was a positive policy directed toward helping free nations strengthen their democracy and their independence and thereby protecting the liberties of the individual citizen.

The group there assembled, Acheson concluded, would have the responsibility for the program. Henderson would head up and coordinate the work, Hickerson would be his second, and Jack Jernegan would be the executive secretary of the coordinating committee. (Actually the group never functioned as a committee. There was so much to be done in so little time that there was no time for formal committee sessions. Henderson did direct and coordinate the staff work, however.)

At this point Acheson withdrew from the meeting and turned it over to Henderson, who began to make assignments. When, a few minutes thereafter, he was called away, Hickerson took the chair. John Gange of the Central Secretariat, in consultation with Acheson and his chief lieutenants, had prepared a document outlining the various parts of the work program and indicating those responsible for each part: economic and technical aid; military aid (this was left for Henderson and Hickerson to work out with the War and Navy Departments); public information; and the determination and drafting of needed legislation. The drafting of the President's message and his radio address were not assigned at this meeting; however, Joseph Jones assumed the assignment would fall to him and proceeded upon that assumption, which proved to be correct. These other specific tasks were assigned: the drafting of replies to the British notes, the drafting of the specific terms of a request for United States aid which would be suggested to the Greek government, the drawing up of an agenda of matters to be discussed with the British, and the preparation of more detailed background studies on Greece and Turkey that would be needed in everybody's work. In concluding, Hickerson said that we were dealing with the most important thing that had happened since Pearl Harbor, and counseled that each approach his job with humility. The meeting broke up; the members returned to their offices to undertake tasks in which they found release from the professional frustrations of years.

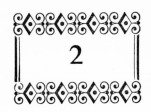

2

DRAFTING THE TRUMAN DOCTRINE

THE method by which the President's message was drafted was strikingly similar to that by which the decision to act was reached. The message was not the inspiration of any one mind but the product of many. Moreover it reflected a unanimity and spontaneity of view rare in the government even on matters of lesser import. Had it been otherwise, the drafting method employed would almost certainly have resulted in a mediocre, compromised message drained of statesmanship. Group drafting usually leads to the lowest common denominator of policy content. In this case there were no cautious voices raised. All concerned were agreed that the President should address Congress and the American people in bold policy terms.

The State Department drafted the message. The White House pointed it up and stylized it for presidential delivery. Acheson, using the contributions of many, selected the major lines of argument, phrased a number of parts, and edited the whole closely. In the interest of a homogeneous style a single hand, that of the writer of this book, held the pen and the master draft until the White House took over for editing. There was a moment at the end of a long drafting conference when Acheson almost repented of the drafting method he had chosen. But just as he thought that such a far-reaching decision on foreign policy should be a wide reflection of

148

the will of the Department and the government and had adopted a procedure to make it so, he felt that the public expression of a radical new policy should capture the inspiration and reflect the judgment of his staff.

Under other circumstances, and handled by one less adroit than Acheson, this would have been a risky thing to do. To a degree far greater than is healthy, each subordinate officer in the State Department operates and makes recommendations on the basis of a personal estimate of what Congress or the American people will accept, and usually there are enough low estimates along the line to keep policy and action flying low, if not grounded. But the circumstances of early March 1947 were so desperate, the need for United States action so compelling, and the apathy of the country so evident, that there was little dissent in the Department or anywhere in the government from the view that the boldest kind of confrontation was necessary.

The boundaries of the President's message were fairly well fixed during the week of February 21–28 before the drafting started. Moreover a great deal of doctrine and phaseology had come into common usage among the officials concerned during that week of decision. In alternating talks with his staff and with Secretary Marshall, the President, the Secretaries of War and Navy and their military and naval chiefs, and above all in his meeting with congressional leaders and his subsequent report on it in the Department, Acheson reflected within the Department the views of the nation's leaders, and reflected to these leaders the views of his staff, so that by February 28, many minds were running along parallel courses.

Nevertheless there is quite a difference between a policy decision with its general accompanying thought pattern and a finished policy declaration. It is the easiest thing in the world for statesmanship to get left behind in the transition: in drafting the President's message the State Department staff added highly important policy concepts.

From February 28 to March 8 the preparation of the President's message and a program of public information occupied the center of the stage in the State Department. Work proceeded concurrently on the substance of the aid program, but a longer time was allowed for it.

Although the drafting of the President's message was not assigned at Acheson's staff meeting on February 28, Francis Russell, Director of the State Department's Office of Public Affairs, was directed to start work immediately on a program of public information. Russell lost no time. Clearing the matter with Acheson, he immediately convoked for that very afternoon a meeting of the Subcommittee on Foreign Policy Information of SWNCC (State-War-Navy Coordinating Committee). Russell was chairman of this subcommittee; the other principal members were the information chiefs of the War and Navy Departments. At this meeting each of the three Departments was represented by a large delegation drawn not only from information staffs, but also from policy and operations. Russell himself brought a group that included a number of officers from the Office of Near Eastern and African Affairs and the Office of European Affairs. This point is emphasized because there is in the Department a seldom-bridged chasm, wide and deep, between policy-operations work and information activity. On this occasion the policy-operations officers were among the most effective in making suggestions on the tone and content of the public approach, and the information officers were equally effective in analyzing strategic and political considerations. There is a major lesson in public administration here, for there is no question that the information officers, with their sensibilities attuned to the public, made a powerful contribution to the Truman Doctrine.

The specific tasks of the subcommittee were to draw together background information from the three Departments relating to all aspects of the problem, to point out the main obstacles to public acceptance and suggest how to overcome them, to define the program of aid contemplated, to draft the themes to be used in the public approach, to consider what the lines of Soviet propaganda would be and how to counter them, and to prepare information programs for getting the story over to the press, radio, periodicals, and group leaders throughout the country. But at this meeting there was no distinction made between what might be said in the President's message and his then-contemplated radio address, and what might be said in supporting speeches and documents used before Congress and in institutional information programs. The President's message was not mentioned.

Russell gave a full account of the events and decisions of the preceding seven days, including Acheson's staff meeting that morning, and emphasized that Acheson was leaving it to the subcommittee to decide how far to go in public presentation. The most striking thing about the ensuing discussion was the unanimous view that the new policy of the United States should be presented to the public in terms of assistance to free governments everywhere that needed our aid to strengthen and defend themselves against Communist aggression or subversion. This was not a proposition that was stated by one and acquiesced in, committee fashion, by others. With gravity it was advanced in different words by representatives of each of the three Departments:

"We should couch it in terms of a new policy of this government to go to the assistance of free governments everywhere."

"We should say we are prepared to back any country that is a democracy."

"We should relate military aid to the principle of supporting democracy. We should say the United States will support free governments to the point where they can defend themselves."

"The only way we can sell the public on our new policy is by emphasizing the necessity of holding the line: communism *vs.* democracy should be the major theme."

"We should emphasize the idea of a common purpose with all democracies."

Two other points that were repeatedly emphasized deserve mention:

The new United States policy should be presented as an affirmative American policy in the interests of the United States, not as aid to Britain or a takeover of British responsibilities. Insofar as possible, mention of the British should be avoided.

Our new policy is not warlike, but on the contrary the best way we know of avoiding war.

The concrete result of this subcommittee meeting was a paper entitled "Public Information Program on United States Aid to Greece," based upon the discussion of the meeting, which was drawn up over the weekend by a working party appointed for the purpose. The title of this paper hardly suggested its contents, which are indicated by the subcommittee's statement of the "Problem":

1. "To make possible the formulation of intelligent opinions by the American people on the problems created by the present situation in Greece through the furnishing of full and frank information by the government.

2. "To portray the world conflict between free and totalitarian or imposed forms of government.

3. "To bring about an understanding by the American people of the world strategic situation."

The "Public Information Program" in fact phrased the new foreign policy of the United States and focused for the public Greece's problems, their importance as "key to a much wider situation," and their relation to the world interests of the United States. It was policy expression of so wide and sweeping a nature that it became far-reaching policy determination. In addition, it drew together a great deal of factual information in a way that made it of great use in the drafting, among other things, of the President's message. This Public Information Program was approved by the SWNCC subcommittee in a meeting on March 3, and after approval by Acheson was distributed to the three Departments for implementation. It became the most significant document used in the drafting of the Truman Doctrine.

The most important part of the document, an opening section entitled "Basic United States Policy," was drafted by Russell on Saturday, March 1, as being the consensus of the subcommittee meeting and of the subsequent discussions of the working party. The whole section in the President's message of March 12, beginning with "One of the primary objectives of the foreign policy of the United States . . . ," including the statement of the choice between two ways of life, and ending with "I believe it must be the policy of the United States to support free peoples who are resisting attempted subjugation by armed minorities or by outside pressures," was upon Acheson's direction virtually lifted word for word from the SWNCC document and incorporated in the first draft of the President's message. It survived all subsequent revisions almost intact, most of the few alterations being additions by Acheson.

It snowed heavily in Washington Saturday night, March 1, a heavy-flaked, wet snow that melted the next day in a bright sun. That Sunday three people, in anticipation of the job that was looming ahead, tried their hands at drafting the presidential message: Loy Henderson, Gordon Merriam, and Joseph Jones. None of these drafts was used as a framework but all contributed to focusing the problem. Late Monday afternoon Acheson called Jones to his office and asked him to undertake the task under his direction.

Acheson's first drafting conference, held Tuesday afternoon, March 4, attended by a dozen Department officers, largely fixed the tone and content of the message. From a number of papers before him Acheson read paragraphs or sentences he thought might be used, these were discussed, and the papers handed to Jones, who was taking notes on what was wanted.

The first paper considered was the SWNCC subcommittee's "Public Information Program." In addition, there was a section in Henderson's draft that was recommended, and several of his ideas were developed further in discussion. The official appeal of the Greek government for aid had been delivered to Acheson the day before by Paul Economou-Gouras, Greek Minister-Counselor in Washington. This note was now read, and it was decided to draw from it for the opening portions of the message, especially the part specifying the four kinds of aid required. There were several papers dealing with the economic, political, and military situation in Greece, and general suggestions were made as to what might be included on these subjects. There was a paragraph in the "Public Information Program" to the effect that the *status quo* was not sacred, but that we could not allow changes in the *status quo,* in violation of the Charter of the United Nations, by such methods as coercion and pressure or by subterfuges such as political infiltration. Acheson recalled that this was from a 1946 speech of Secretary Byrnes and suggested that Jones look it up and use it if it seemed appropriate. (This was used, attributed to Byrnes, in the first draft and remained in that form almost to the last, when Clark Clifford, Special Counsel to the President and his principal adviser on state papers and messages, reminded Jones that the President never quoted anyone in public addresses. The attribution was omitted but the statement was retained.) Relatively little was said about Turkey at this first drafting conference. Few indications were given as to how Turkey should be treated. In his first draft, therefore, Jones contrived a modest paragraph, more or less to flag the subject. The paragraph remained modest through to the final draft. Other ideas were advanced and discussed; most of them were dropped, a few were agreed to be acceptable. From the whole Jones got a fair idea of what was wanted. He worked late that night and turned out the first working draft of a message dated March 4, which, notwithstanding successive revisions, substantially retained its identity.

This draft was considered at Acheson's second drafting conference on March 5, at which he led a group in a line by line consideration. Many deletions and additions, mostly word and phrase changes, were suggested. Acheson wrote out several rephrasings on a memo pad, but for the most part Jones made changes directly on his master copy and took notes on additions suggested. That evening Jones produced a second draft, which was edited the next day in a meeting with Acheson and several assistants; few changes were made. The outcome of this meeting was a third draft, which Jones cleared with Henderson and Hickerson and took to Acheson's office before noon on March 6. Acheson promptly had the text cabled to Secretary Marshall, who had left Washington the day before and was then in Paris en route to Moscow. The Secretary went over the proposed message upon his return late in the evening from a state dinner as guest of the President of France, Vincent Auriol. He immediately cabled his approval, and the text was sent on March 7 to Clark Clifford.

A curiously ironic note should be added here in passing. George Kennan, often regarded as the master-mind of the policy of containment, came over to the State Department from the War College on the afternoon of March 6 to find out how things were going and was shown a copy of the message that had been drafted. To say that he found objections to it is to put it mildly. He objected strongly both to the tone of the message and the specific action proposed. He was in favor of economic aid to Greece, but he had hoped that military aid to Greece would be kept small, and he was opposed to aid of any kind to Turkey. It was nevertheless to the tone and ideological content of the message, the portraying of two opposing ways of life, and the open-end commitment to aid free peoples that he objected most. The Russians might even reply by declaring war! Kennan voiced his objections to a number of people, including, finally, Acheson. It was too late. The decisions had already been taken and widely approved.

On Saturday morning, March 8, Acheson asked Jones to go over to the White House to discuss the draft message with Clifford. Jones was accompanied by Carl Hummelsine, Director of the Executive Secretariat. Clifford made a number of useful suggestions. His main criticism was that the message did not build up steadily toward a climax: it opened with a mention of the British notes concerning Greece, described the nature of Greece's appeal for aid, mentioned the British note on Turkey, recommended aid to Greece and Turkey, proceeded to present the "broad implications" involved, and then returned to describe conditions in Greece and Turkey and their importance in a "much wider situation," ending with a request for legislation. Clifford thought the message would be more dramatic if the factual material on Greece and Turkey, somewhat compressed, were all concentrated in the first part, with the "broad implications," the statement of United States policy, and the "wider situation" following in a climatic build-up to the request for legislation.

Clifford also made several specific suggestions. He thought a paragraph should be added emphasizing the request of the Greek government for American administrators, economists, and technicians and the great importance of American supervision of the funds so that each dollar would count toward making Greece self-supporting. (Incidentally, this paragraph, which was added, brought one of the three bursts of applause that interrupted the President in the delivery of the message on March 12.)

He also thought a stronger peroration was needed and suggested the ideas that went into it, beginning with "This is a serious course upon which we embark. I would not recommend it except that the alternative is more serious."

He liked the statement in the draft, which Jones had written on his own motion, "I believe that our help [to free peoples] should be primarily through economic and financial aid which is essential to economic stability and orderly political processes," and himself added in the peroration, "The seeds of totalitarian regimes are nurtured by misery and want. They spread and grow in the evil soil of poverty and strife. They reach their full growth when the hope of a people for a better life has died."

Jones, returning to his office, in two hours revised the speech as suggested, making other rearrangements in the process, and after clearing it with Acheson took the revised draft dated March 8 over to Clifford's office in the early afternoon.

Late Monday afternoon, March 10, Clifford came over to show Acheson the revision he and the White House staff had made and which had been approved by the President. Acheson asked Jones to be present. Clifford had tightened up the message further and had adapted it slightly to suit the President's delivery. Except for three additions, he had made no material change in organization, content, or phraseology. The additions were all, upon Acheson's advice, deleted. One of these—in a single line—pointed out more sharply than Acheson thought desirable the strategic importance of Greece in relation to the Middle East. The second referred to the great natural resources of the Middle East which should not be under the exclusive control of any single nation. Acheson felt that this gave undue prominence to only one of several considerations, some of which were far more important. The third stated that there had been a world-wide trend away from the system of free enterprise toward state-controlled economies, that continued chaos in other countries and pressure exerted upon them from without would mean the end of free enterprise and democracy in those countries, and that the disappearance of free enterprise in other nations would threaten our economy and our democracy.

This third addition was a matter of considerable importance, and Acheson had definite views on it: it would become, he said, a dangerous limitation upon the new policy that was being proclaimed. The 1946 loan to Britain had been opposed by some in the United States, he continued, because a Labour government was in power in Britain and was asserting greater state control over the economy and narrowing the area of free enterprise. And yet what was happening in Britain was being done through democratic processes, and the free institutions and basic freedoms of the British people had not been impaired. It would be absurd to suggest, he said, that the trend of economic organization in Britain made that country's survival as a free and independent nation any less important to the security of the United States. Britain was in a very bad way financially, and we might very well be called upon to aid her further, in which case we might be seriously embarrassed by the free-enterprise argument. The important thing from the point of view of the United States, Acheson concluded, was not the form of economic organization in any foreign country, but whether the country was independent and wanted to remain so, whether its government was one of consent, whether individual liberties were protected, whether its government and people were free to work out their destinies in their own way.

Clifford did not argue this matter. He merely listened and agreed to its deletion. It seemed fairly clear that neither he nor the President had suggested this, but that it had been included at the behest of someone else.

Clifford returned to the White House, where he had a final meeting with the President and the staff. The deletions were agreed to. A few minor changes were made. The official text of the Truman Doctrine was thus cleared for mimeographing and release.

The way in which certain decisions of wide consequence were made during the process of drafting the President's message may be of considerable interest.

From the moment the British notes were first received, it was realized by all concerned that Greece and Turkey were only the crux of a world problem, and that, although they were in the most urgent need, they were only two of many countries that might require United States support in one form or another. This was specifically recognized in discussions within the Department of State, in talks of Marshall and Acheson with the President and with the Secretaries of War and of the Navy. But the State Department recommendation approved by the President was in terms of aid only to Greece and Turkey. And although Senator Vandenberg at the February 27 meeting suggested that the message be couched in broad policy terms, Acheson, in reporting upon that meeting to his staff the next morning, did not mention the possibility of asking Congress for wider authority. Nevertheless there is evidence that Acheson's mind was not wholly made up, and that he was considering the possibility of phrasing it so as to include other countries.

It is not clear how it happened, but it should be recorded here that at least three people concerned got the impression either that Congress was going to be asked or should be asked for funds and authority to aid not only Greece and Turkey but other countries also. Henderson had in his draft presidential message the following: "I, therefore, firmly believe that the United States must be prepared to give similar assistance to other democratic countries who may require our aid in order to preserve their independence. . . ." Gordon Merriam in his draft wrote: "I should be lacking in frankness, moreover, if the Congress should gain the impression that the problem is restricted to the two countries I have mentioned. Greece and Turkey, which are friendly to us and to each other, stand or fall together. The loss of one will lead to the fall of the other. But we cannot be sure what country or countries will also come under pressure in the future, and we must be in position to apply a suitable remedy or variety of remedies whenever and wherever the situation warrants." In his first working draft, Joseph Jones, without the subject having been specifically discussed at the drafting conference, included a request for funds and authority to aid Greece *and* funds and authority to aid Turkey "and such other country as may find itself in need of help in maintaining its independence and free institutions." The coincidence probably resulted from spontaneous and unrelated deductions from the tenor of current policy discussions, without any decision having ever been made or even indicated. Acheson underlined in pencil the clause quoted above from Jones' first draft message and put a question mark in the margin. The matter was nevertheless not discussed in the second drafting conference: consideration of the final section requesting legislation was deferred.

This troubled Jones very much from a drafting standpoint. It was clear that a specific sum would be asked for Greece. Was a specific sum to be asked for Turkey? Or for Turkey and "such other country . . ." ? The decision seemed unmade, or infirm; and yet the philosophy and policy content of the message as it was shaping up were of so wide and sweeping a nature as to lead up to an open authorization. Was this appropriate if the request was to be limited to Greece and Turkey?

Jones went to see Acheson on the morning of March 6 and put the questions to him. Acheson leaned back, looked over at the White House, thought a while, and said slowly, "If F.D.R. were alive I think I know what he'd do. He would make a statement of global policy but confine his request for money right now to Greece and Turkey." Jones revised his draft accordingly.

There is only one other thing to be added on this point. Jones did not then know that the day before Acheson had formally initiated a survey, which was to be carried on for many weeks, to determine which other countries might in the months ahead urgently require United States aid to preserve their integrity and independence.

In view of the extensive criticism that was leveled at the Truman Doctrine on the grounds that it by-passed the United Nations, it may be of interest to record that insofar as this writer has been able to discover, neither during the week of decision (February 21–28) nor during the drafting of the President's message was any suggestion made that a recommendation to Congress for aid to Greece and Turkey be delayed or circumscribed in any way on the grounds that it would by-pass the United Nations. It is possible that the officers in the State Department's Office of Special Political Affairs, which handled relations with the United Nations, might have suggested delay if their opinion had been asked, but even this is doubtful, and in any case they do not appear to have been brought into the decision-making. It was too clear that the United Nations had no funds and authority to extend military aid and that it would not conceivably extend economic aid of the kinds required, in the amounts required, and with the kind of supervision required, to save Greece, and above all that it could not act quickly. Senator Vandenberg, on March 5, wrote to a colleague: "I am frank to say I think Greece could collapse fifty times before the United Nations itself could even hope to handle a situation of this nature."

What should be said about the United Nations in the President's message was never a major issue. In none of the early drafts of the message, informal or official, were more than passing references made to the United Nations—references such as "Assistance of this kind is entirely in accord with the purposes and principles of the United Nations"—and most of these were deleted in the drafting process. In the "Public Information Program" a greater effort was made to square things with the United Nations, but the relevant portions of this document were not indicated for inclusion in the message at the drafting conferences. In the March 7 draft that went to the White House there was this reference: "The Charter of the United Nations presupposes a world of free nations. In helping such nations to maintain their freedom and independence, the United States would be giving effect to the purposes and principles of the Charter." Clifford suggested no change in this, but while Jones was in his office on March 8, revising the message in accordance with Clifford's suggestions, Acheson sent in a short statement for inclusion which had been drafted in the Office of Special Political Affairs. A number of its men had been unhappy over the short treatment given the United Nations in the draft message, and Dean Rusk, Director of that Office, had persuaded

Explanation of to U.N.

Acheson to amplify the reference quoted above by adding the following:

> We have considered how the United Nations might assist in this crisis. But the situation we must meet is an urgent one requiring immediate action, and the United Nations and its related organizations are not yet in a position to extend assistance of the kind that is required.
>
> The extension of direct aid by the United States to Greece and Turkey means that the United States is stepping into the breach in order to help maintain conditions in which the United Nations can grow in international confidence and authority. The United States has already taken a lead in the establishment of international agencies designed for the rehabilitation of devastated areas and for long-term economic reconstruction. We will continue to study ways and means through which the United Nations and related international agencies might undertake financial and economic responsibilities in such areas.

The White House adopted only the first paragraph of the proposed addition. Acheson raised no objection when Clifford brought the White House version over for clearance, and Jones did not even notice the omission. In view of the known attitudes of the time a speculation may be made as to why the larger reference to the United Nations was dropped. The President's message was to be a simple and unadorned statement of American policy, an incomparable assumption of responsibility, in the United States' own right, of a kind never assumed before, for strengthening free nations and protecting freedom in the world, and it was to contain no hint of ways of avoiding full and direct responsibility.

This may have been a mistake. Many people think so. The writer of this book thinks it was not. In 1947 the prestige of the United Nations was important, but there was one thing even more important, and that was a fearless confrontation of the American people with the responsibilities involved in the use of the tremendous and unique power of the United States to promote peace and well-being and preserve freedom, whether directly in relation with other countries or through the United Nations. It would probably

opinion on U.N.

be generally agreed now that the United Nations has been the gainer from that confrontation rather than the loser. The subject is considered later in this book.

It cannot be denied that the treatment of Turkey and the strategic importance of the Middle East in the President's message was something less than the "full and frank" presentation that Senator Vandenberg had wanted. Turkey was the key to the defense of the eastern Mediterranean and thus to the defense of three continents. Greece had great strategic importance in her own right, but even more in relation to Turkey, and Turkey was in a dilemma between financing her defenses and strengthening her economy, and both were sorely needed. It was therefore decided to supply military rather than economic aid to Turkey, in the knowledge that, if helped with the military burden, Turkey could probably qualify, with some delay, for large-scale economic reconstructions loans from the World Bank and the Export-Import Bank. The strategic importance of Turkey ranked high in discussions within the executive branch and in discussions with congressional leaders. They were, however, consciously played down in the President's message, in the public sessions of the congressional committees, and in the public approach generally. There were two main reasons for this. The American people were not accustomed to thinking then, as they are now, in strategic-military terms in time of peace, and too much emphasis upon supplying straight military aid to Turkey might have been alarming to the point of defeating the proposed action. The other was of course that supplying military aid to a country on the border of the Soviet Union, even though purely for defense against Soviet pressures, involved some danger of Soviet reaction, and at the very least there would be cries of "provocation" and "encirclement" which would be used in Soviet world-wide propaganda. It was therefore considered advisable to play down military aid to Turkey and to present that aid, as could be done with truthfulness, in the context of Turkey's over-all economic situation. Military aid to Turkey was not concealed; but it was not emphasized.

There was therefore a grain of truth in the remarks of one witness before the House Committee on Foreign Affairs:

. . . Administration and congressional spokesmen have themselves volunteered only the briefest discussion of the Turkish problem or of proposed United States aid to Turkey. Now, I do not mean to be ribald, but I really cannot help saying this: It almost appears that when the new dish was being prepared for American consumption, Turkey was slipped into the oven with Greece because that seemed to be the surest way to cook a tough bird.

While the President's message was being drafted, Acheson's background talks with representatives of the press and radio bore fruit in the shape of a formidable and generally well-informed public build-up for a major policy change. At the same time the congressional leaders who attended the White House meeting were quietly exerting their influence on their colleagues. News and radio men collected and spread the pollen of information and speculation among congressmen, government officials, and the public. On March 4 the State Department released the text of the appeal of the Greek government for aid, together with a brief statement by Secretary Marshall: "The problems involved are so far-reaching and of such transcendent importance that any announcement relating to them could only come from the President himself. The final decision will rest with the President and the Congress." These served to extend the horizons of expectation, and speculation ran riot.

On March 8 the *New York Times* reported a "growing excitement on Capitol Hill," with a generally favorable sentiment apparent. "Many hope the President's message will outline the horizons of the influence in the world that Mr. Truman believes now the United States should attempt to exercise." Leading publicists cast the expected policy change in the widest possible terms: the assumption by the United States of the responsibilities of world leadership. If the government was reluctant to speak publicly of the decline in British power and to suggest that the time had come when any hope for peace and well-being in the world required that the United States step into the role formerly played by Great Britain, public commentators and editorial writers were not. By March 12 a high degree of public expectancy prevailed, and when the President went to Capitol Hill the American people were prepared to hear a declaration on a situation that Representative Charles A. Eaton had publicly described as "the most fateful in the history of our country."

Meanwhile, during the first week of March, diplomatic exchanges went on between the United States and Great Britain. Lord Inverchapel called on Acheson on March 1 to receive replies to the British notes of February 24. The Ambassador was told that the executive branch was of the opinion that the political and territorial integrity of Greece and Turkey must be maintained, had decided to make every effort to that end, and would seek the necessary authority from Congress. Congressional action would take time, however, and it was important to have the fullest cooperation of the British in Greece and Turkey and to have assurances that the British government would continue support on an emergency basis to stave off collapse until United States aid could be authorized and become effective. It was also necessary to open talks at once on the specific military requirements of Greece and Turkey, as well as on their financial, economic, and administrative needs. Moreover it was the view of the United States that the maintenance of the political and territorial integrity of Greece and Turkey was closely related to problems of common concern involving other countries in Europe and Asia, and it was therefore important to open conversations at once on those problems to determine the respective intentions, capabilities, and responsibilities of the two governments. These matters were raised orally with the Ambassador and confirmed in two *aides-mémoires* handed to him.

Equally important was the question of whether the remaining contingent of British forces in Greece, numbering 8000, could be kept there until the United States should have a chance to strengthen the Greek Army and stabilize the financial and economic situation. The withdrawal of British troops in the situation of near-panic then existing would have been a profound psychological blow to the government and people of Greece, and might have precipitated collapse before United States aid could arrive. Secretary Marshall had discussed the matter informally with Lord Inverchapel on February 24, and Acheson raised the question again on March 1.

On March 5 the Ambassador called at the State Department, upon instructions from London, and assured Acheson that the British government would cooperate to the full extent of its ability and was prepared to enter into immediate discussions with the United States on the needs of Greece, which, being more urgent, should be given priority. On the assumption that the United States government would apply to Congress for authority to furnish assistance to Greece in such quantity that Great Britain would be relieved of that financial responsibility, the British government had decided to give Greece, in addition to the £2 million of military equipment they had already decided to offer, a further contribution of £2 million monthly in the form of a loan, for a period not exceeding three months, for the maintenance of the Greek armed forces. As regards the retention of British forces in Greece, the Ambassador reported that the British government intended to carry out a decision made earlier to reduce British troops in Greece to one brigade by March 31 and that the remaining brigade would be withdrawn during the summer. In this connection the Ambassador mentioned that his government had been embarrassed by questions raised in the House of Commons on March 3 in connection with press reports that United States aid to Greece was conditional upon the maintenance of British troops in that country. (Assurances had been requested of the government in the Commons that British troops would not be kept in Greece "in exchange for United States money.") The British government had therefore been obliged to make this statement to the press:

> With reference to reports that conversations with the United States are proceeding on the basis that British troops will be retained in Greece it is learnt in authoritative circles that there is no change in present arrangements for the reduction of British forces in Greece nor in the government's decision to withdraw the remainder as soon as practicable." [1]

The only thing to be added on this point is that the British did not find it "practicable" to withdraw the last contingent of British troops from Greece until 1950.

[1] Major C. P. Mayhew, Parliamentary Undersecretary for Foreign Affairs, gave assurances in virtually the same words in the House of Commons on March 5.

President Truman left Washington on March 2 to pay a long-planned visit of state to President Alemán of Mexico. Returning on March 6, he stopped over in Waco, Texas, to accept an honorary degree from Baylor University and to deliver a speech on United States foreign economic policy. The press speculated that the President might deal in this speech with aid to Greece and unveil the major change in United States foreign policy then in the wind. He did not do so. His speech, drafted in the State Department's Office of International Trade Policy, had been conceived and largely completed before the Greece-Turkey crisis arose. At least one effort was made at the last moment to get it opened up to foreshadow the grim realities that were closing in, but it did not get very far. For a pre-crisis world it was a hard-hitting speech and was well received by the press. The President declared:

> We are the giant of the economic world. Whether we like it or not, the future pattern of economic relations depends upon us. The world is waiting and watching to see what we will do. The choice is ours. We can lead the nations to economic peace or we can plunge them into economic war.

As for particulars, the President discussed the aims of United States foreign economic policy in terms of reducing trade barriers through reciprocal agreements and otherwise, the re-establishment of liberal trading policies, the negotiation of a World Trade Charter, and the establishment of an International Trade Organization. These matters were the irreducible minimum of United States economic responsibility, but even these were under heavy attack in Congress. The President said nothing about the need of foreign countries for emergency aid, and nothing even about the need for United States investment abroad. These were too radical even to consider mentioning in the political atmosphere that prevailed when the speech was conceived and drafted. This speech vividly illustrates, by contrast, how quickly recognition of impending disaster came and how far United States foreign economic policy moved within a matter of days. The survival of nations themselves rather than the survival of liberal trading practices became the central issue. The dollar gap, reconstruction, economic integration, United States aid to help create economic conditions in which human freedom could survive—these matters suddenly pushed normal commercial policies into the background, there to remain for several years.)

The President was back in his office Friday, March 7. Before the regularly scheduled Cabinet meeting that morning he had a lengthy session with Acheson, was brought up to date on develpoments in the Greece-Turkey crisis, and read the draft message to Congress proposed by the State Department. Acheson suggested that the President go before Congress in person to deliver the message and that the idea of a radio "fireside chat" be abandoned. The President agreed. The day before, Joseph Jones had recommended this to Acheson on the grounds that the message was shaping up in a forceful way and the President's personal appearance before Congress would dramatize its importance; also, the way things were going there would not be time to prepare an effective radio speech. Acheson had readily agreed.

President Truman was unusually solemn as he opened the Cabinet meeting on the morning of March 7. He was faced, he said, with a situation more serious than had ever confronted any President. He therefore wanted to have the facts put before the Cabinet, to have a full discussion of them, and then to consider ways and means of procedure. Acheson, at the invitation of the President, then gave a full report on all that had happened in the previous two weeks with regard to Greece and Turkey, analyzed the problem posed for the United States, and pointed out its wider implications. In the ensuing discussion it became clear that all present favored the action proposed by Acheson and approved by the President, but there was considerable doubt expressed as to whether Congress could be brought to support it. Forrestal said the crisis in Greece and Turkey was just another manifestation of what had been in process of development for four years, and that if we were to have a chance of winning we would have to recognize that a fundamental struggle was going on between our kind of society and that of the Russians, and that the Russians would not respond to anything except power. He thought we would have to mobilize the talent and brains and abilities of the whole country into a single team in order to win.

Harriman and Patterson vigorously supported action. It was the consensus of the Cabinet that the President should approach Congress on immediate aid to Greece and to Turkey and that everything should be done to persuade Congress of the necessity for granting the necessary funds and authority.

At the end of the meeting the President appointed a committee headed by John Synder, and including Harriman, Patterson, Acheson, and Forrestal, to lay out a program of communication with leaders throughout the country, particularly business people, on the necessity for aid to Greece and Turkey and the larger implications of the problem. This group met the following morning in Secretary Snyder's office. At this meeting Acheson gave a preview of State Department thinking on how aid to Greece, and perhaps to other countries that might receive United States aid, should be administered. He thought it would be necessary to send an American mission that would include working parties of experts in government administration, communications, taxation, transportation, and the like, that would pitch in and do a thorough job of reconstruction. He also reported that he and Secretary Marshall agreed that there should be in Washington an office that acted as a backstop to the foreign operations and saw that all the necessary things were done at this end.

After the Cabinet meeting on March 7, the White House announced that President Truman had postponed indefinitely the Caribbean cruise for which he was to have left Washington the next day. It was also made known that congressional leaders of both parties had been invited to a conference at the White House Monday morning, March 10, in connection with the Greek crisis.

President Truman did most of the talking at that March 10 meeting, with Acheson backing him up. In addition to those present at the February 27 meeting, the congressional delegation included Senator Taft, chairman of the Republican Policy Committee; Senator Wallace H. White of Maine, Senate Majority Leader; Senator Alben Barkley of Kentucky, Senate Minority Leader; Senator Kenneth McKellar of Tennessee, ranking Democrat on the Senate Appropriations Committee; Representative Charles A. Halleck of

Indiana, House Majority Floor Leader; Representative Clarence Cannon of Missouri, ranking Democrat on the House Appropriations Committee; Representative John W. McCormack of Massachusetts, House Minority Whip; and Representative John Taber of New York, chairman of the House Appropriations Committee. There was considerable discussion and many questions were asked, but no opposition was registered. James Reston, whose close relationship with Senator Vandenberg is well known, reported (*New York Times,* March 11) that Senator Vandenberg had made it clear that he was in favor of moves to block Soviet expansion at key points, but that "he insisted that the President was obligated to explain in the most direct terms to the Congress and to the country why it was the United States was moving into these areas. The President evidently assured his visitors that he intended to lay the facts on the line." The Senator was only emphasizing again the condition he had made at the previous meeting. Reston also reported that Senator Vandenberg told the President he should instruct Secretary Marshall, then in Moscow, to explain to Stalin that the new policy of the United States was dual: (1) collaboration for peace; and (2) economic intervention in key areas to block Soviet expansion.[2]

Senator Vandenberg called a conference of Republican legislators the evening of March 10, at which he gave a talk lasting an hour on what was behind the President's forthcoming message to Congress. James Reston quoted Senator Vandenberg (*New York Times,* March 11) as saying that he hoped the President would give the Congress and the country the benefit of the "total implications" of the new policy. The Senator told the legislators that he was withholding judgment pending the President's statement, but that "this is a matter which transcends politics. There is nothing partisan about it. It is national policy at the highest degree."

Immediately after the White House meeting of March 10, both the President and Senator Vandenberg announced that the Presi-

[2] In Marshall's only talk with Stalin, on April 15, he did not put the matter as Vandenberg had proposed, but he did say that the United States was determined to assist those countries suffering from economic deterioration, which, if left unchecked, might lead to economic collapse and subsequent elimination of any chance of democratic survival.

dent would appear in person on March 12 before a joint session of the Houses of Congress to deliver a special message.

We are already acquainted with that message and with the occasion on Capitol Hill on March 12. Let us now consider the public debate the President's message set in train.

3

THE PUBLIC DEBATE

THE public discussion on United States foreign policy that followed President Truman's message to Congress was the most mature and fruitful in the history of the nation, and it continues to this day. In the intervening years the rising tide of public comprehension has supported responsible American action on the world stage that would have been unthinkable before.

The President's message posed the problem in such a way that American responsibility in the world had to be accepted or rejected. In our previous sheltered existence we had strongly disliked what we considered power politics. We now realized that positions that were being evacuated by a friendly power would not remain power vacuums but would be taken over by another power that was the avowed enemy of our way of life. There was no place to hide. The historic shield of sturdy kindred nations in Western Europe was broken.

Not only were the broad concepts of power reality debated and clarified during the Fifteen Weeks, but the mundane necessities of world housekeeping as well: political grants and loans for political purposes, military aid in peacetime for political purposes, intervention (its morality, aims, and limitations), American supervision of American aid, aid to governments of which we did not wholly approve, the calculated risk of war, the necessary choice between unpleasant alternatives. The immersion in reality was thorough, and from it the nation emerged sobered, instructed, and equipped as never before to play a responsible role in world affairs.

Practically all press, radio, and congressional observers immediately recognized President Truman's message as a landmark in American history. Commentators searched their histories for suitable comparisons and their lexicons for weighty words with which to describe the new policy. The most obvious comparison, one that was immediately and widely made, was to the Monroe Doctrine of 1823. A few typical excerpts from the press of the day demonstrate the importance that was immediately attached to the President's declaration:

> This is no issue for partisan division. This is no little problem to be dismissed with easy phrases about meddling in the affairs of Europe or pulling British chestnuts from the fire. This is a question as grave as any that has ever confronted the American people, and the answer to it may, for better or worse, decide our own ultimate destiny as a free people. (Scripps-Howard Newspapers, March 13, 1947.)

> President Truman's latest address to Congress was, beyond question, one of the most momentous ever made by an American Chief Executive. (Barnet Nover, *Washington Post,* March 13, 1947.)

> President Truman has confronted the American people with a decision which is scarcely less grave than a decision involving the declaration of war. . . . The decision that Congress, acting for the American people, must make is whether we will join issue with the already undeclared ideological war, by actively assisting those countries menaced by Russian communism, or whether we shall continue a feeble diplomacy, based on appeasement and half-hearted opposition, while the totalitarian ideology of Russia nibbles away at freedom of the peoples of the world. (*The Chronicle,* Augusta, Georgia, March 13, 1947.)

> What the President was saying was that if the American system is to survive, it must prove its value—just as the totalitarian system has been trying to prove its own value—as an article of export. . . . President Truman was asking for dollars; but he was also asking for the enthusiasm, the willingness to venture, the belief in our own values, which can prove to the shattered peoples of the world that the American system offers a working alternative to

the totalitarian order which is otherwise their only refuge. (*New York Herald Tribune,* March 13, 1947.)

The epoch of isolation and occasional intervention is ended. It is being replaced by an epoch of American responsibility. Our aim must be to establish conditions under which the United Nations and our own principles have a chance to survive. (*New York Times,* March 12, 1947.)

President Truman . . . unmistakably called for action which will launch the United States on a new and positive foreign policy of world-wide responsibility for the maintenance of peace and order. (*New York Times,* March 13, 1947.)

This is a time of decision—one of the most momentous decisions in American history. (*Christian Science Monitor,* March 13, 1947.)

President Truman's message to Congress on relief to Greece and Turkey in effect is a corollary of the Monroe Doctrine. . . . While the implications of the "Truman Doctrine" are as grave as any the people of the United States ever were called upon to face, they are no more so than those to which they were committed by the doctrine of Monroe. . . . Both the Monroe and Truman Doctrines are thoroughly and peculiarly American. The United States always has shown a keen interest in nations struggling for liberty, freedom of speech and religion, free elections and the way of life which President Truman said we must support. (William Philip Simms, *Washington Daily News,* March 14, 1947.)

President Truman's address to the joint session of the Congress, Wednesday, was historical. His speech definitely carried out the strength of this nation and the will of the citizens of the United States. The President gave proof that we have the money and the ability to help weaker nations and that we will not allow any country, even Russia, to swallow smaller and weaker countries. (*The Beacon,* Wichita, Kansas, March 13, 1947.)

Within three days it was reasonably clear that Congress and the American people would approve the course of action recommended by the President. Powerful press support rolled in from all parts of the country. Most columnists and radio commentators backed the President. On March 14 the Associated Press, the Scripps-Howard Newspapers, and many radio analysts predicted favorable action by Congress. Of the 75 congressmen who promptly commented in public on the President's request, 35 indicated support, 22 opposition, and 18 were noncommittal.

Senator Vandenberg immediately backed the President with his immense prestige. Speaking to newsmen on the afternoon of March 12, he said:

> The President's message faces facts and so must Congress. The independence of Greece and Turkey must be preserved, not only for their own sakes but also in defense of peace and security for all of us. In such a critical moment the President's hands must be upheld. Any other course would be dangerously misunderstood. But Congress must carefully determine the methods and explore the details in so momentous a departure from our previous policies.
>
> The immediate problem may be treated by itself. But it is vitally important to frankly weigh it for the future. We are at odds with communism on many fronts. We should evolve a total policy. It must clearly avoid imperialism. It must primarily consult American welfare. It must keep faith with the pledges to the Charter of the United Nations which we have all taken. . . .
>
> The plain truth is that Soviet-American relationships are at the core of this whole problem. Every effort should be made to terminate these controversies. . . .
>
> We cannot fail to back up the President at such an hour. . . . Meanwhile we must review our own foreign policy in other directions and make it consistently effective. We must proceed with calm but determined patience to deal with practical realities as they unfold. We must either take or surrender leadership.[1]

Senator Vandenberg called a meeting of the Republican Policy Conference on March 13, which was attended by all fifty-one senators, and again urged support for the President's proposed course of action.

Senator Taft did not go along with the senior Senator from Michigan. "I do not want war with Russia," Taft said to newsmen after the President's address. "Whether our intervention in Greece tends to make such a war more probable or less probable depends upon many circumstances regarding which I am not yet fully advised and, therefore, I do not care to make a decision at the present

[1] *The Private Papers of Senator Vandenberg.*

time." He indicated that he was troubled not by the economic and
financial aid, but by the aid to the Greek Army and the proposal
to send American military missions there to teach the Greeks how
to use the equipment. He thought that Truman's view accepted
"the policy of dividing the world into zones of political influence,
Communist and anti-Communist."

Senator Byrd, Democrat of Virginia, was concerned about the
expenditures involved in implementing the Truman Doctrine all over
the world, and also about the by-passing of the United Nations.
Senator Capper, Republican, of Kansas, usually opposed to the
administration's foreign policy, declared, "We have to go along with
the President. There seems to be no other alternative." On the other
hand, Senator Pepper of Florida and Senator Ellender of Louisiana,
both Democrats who usually supported the administration in foreign
affairs, promptly spoke out against the President's program on the
grounds that it was warlike and by-passed the United Nations.

It is significant that the early reactions to the Truman Doctrine
cut deeply across party lines, class and group lines, and regional
lines. Many who were known as isolationists supported it; many
recognized internationalists opposed it. There were notable defec-
tions from positions taken by nearly every established group, whether
liberal or conservative, pro-labor or pro-capital, religious or secular,
a wide variety of reasons being advanced for support or opposition.
There was little elation among supporters of the policy; in fact, to
most the prospect was grim but there seemed to be no acceptable
alternative. The opponents worked themselves up to a greater heat,
but they were mostly concerned with such matters as "by-passing
the United Nations," "aid to reactionary governments," "power
politics," and the like, and they appeared reluctant to face up to
the central issues. Among both supporters and opponents there was
some resentment at the necessity for making a decision to accept
or reject American responsibility of so sweeping a nature and a
tendency to blame the British, or the administration, or the Greeks
and Turks, or the Russians, for making a choice necessary.

In the weeks following March 12 the State Department's Office
of Public Affairs collected all available evidence of reactions to the

President's message, including nation-wide press and radio comment, opinion surveys, statements by political leaders, and views of prominent organizations and individuals. Study of this material disclosed that most public support was based on the conviction that the security and well-being of the United States required resistance to Soviet or Communist expansion and that the President's program was a necessary first step in that resistance. United in this preponderant view were Americans of diverse political persuasions who converged at a common stand from different routes: confirmed anti-Communists who had always feared communism's threat to capitalism in America; conservatives and independents who had watched with growing trepidation the rise of Soviet power; staunch liberals of the Americans for Democratic Action variety who were concerned about the safeguarding of human freedom; fervent internationalists who were convinced that peace and prosperity could be achieved in the world only through United States leadership and the full commitment of American power and resources. In view of the fears, suspicions, and sense of outrage that had been building up in the United States since V-J day against the Soviet Union, the administration recognized the danger that taking a stand against Soviet expansion might touch off a jingoistic crusade. At least partly for that reason the President's message avoided mention of the Soviet Union and pitched United States policy on a pro-freedom rather than an anti-Communist plane. There was a minimum of hysteria and jingoism in the American reaction.

Supporters of the President's policy were not all by any means confident and happy over their position. Throughout their comments ran strong notes of reluctance and misgiving. Few regarded the new policy as anything but the lesser of two evils. Most believed that the policy involved the "calculated risk" of war; some feared the projection of the United States as a direct opponent of Soviet expansion. Many contemplated with trepidation the incalculable expenditures, commitments, and risks that might be involved. Yet most affirmed their support on the grounds that failure to take action would be appeasement and isolationism, which would court even greater dangers.

Most of the outright opposition came from the extreme Left and the extreme Right of the political spectrum: from a certain school of "liberals" who had long been strongly critical of the administration's stiffening policy toward the Soviet Union, and from the "isolationists" who had been consistent opponents of all foreign-policy measures that projected the United States actively into world affairs. Thus Henry A. Wallace, Fiorello La Guardia, Senators Claude Pepper and Glen H. Taylor found themselves in the same bed with Colonel Robert McCormick, John O'Donnell, Representatives Harold Knutson and Everett M. Dirksen; and the Marshall Field papers (*PM* and the *Chicago Sun*), the *Chicago Daily News,* the *Nation,* the *New Republic,* and *Christian Century* found themselves in the same corner with the McCormick-Patterson press. The opposition of the Left emphasized that American aid to the existing Greek and Turkish governments would not promote freedom but would protect anti-democratic and reactionary regimes; and that the proposed action by-passed the United Nations and endangered its future. The opposition of the Right emphasized that the President's policy would probably, if not inevitably, lead to war; and that the American economy could not stand the strain of trying to stop communism with dollars. But both Right and Left used the full range of arguments in a bitter attack. "Power politics," "militarism," "intervention," were charged against the administration. "You can't fight communism with dollars," "the new policy means the end of 'One World,'" "the Moscow conference will be undermined," "We should not bail out the British Empire"—these were among the arguments used.

It had not been expected that Wallace and the group he represented would be very happy over a policy of firmness toward the Soviet Union, but the violence and character of his attack was not fully anticipated. Wallace and company for years had been leading exponents of using the power and public funds of the United States for aiding underprivileged groups at home and underprivileged nations abroad, they were ardent internationalists, and they were committed to the ideas and institutions of freedom. But when it came to recognizing that the Soviet Union was the enemy of freedom and to extending military aid, along with economic, to the intended victims of Soviet expansion—countries whose governments of the moment they did not like—they balked, and found all sorts of reasons for doing so. Although they approved of economic aid to Greece through the United Nations, they opposed with vehemence military aid to either Greece or Turkey even though it was clear that Greece could not recover economically, or even survive, unless the Communist military challenge to the authority of the Greek state should first be successfully met, and even though Turkey's economic health was directly dependent upon aid in resisting military and political pressures. The least that can be said was that this was partial and fuzzy thinking. In opposing the Truman Doctrine, Wallace and company in effect went back on most of their cherished beliefs, retaining in full vigor only one, and that was their blind faith that accommodation could be reached with the Soviet Union even though our side was weak and inactive. But for his failure to win renomination as Vice-President in 1944, Wallace would have been President at this critical time.

In a radio address on March 13 Wallace accused President Trument of "betraying the great tradition of America," of acting as "the best salesman communism ever had," and of plunging into a "reckless adventure" that would cause a "century of fear." He described the new policy as "utterly futile and amounting to a military lend-lease program," and said that it would require the United States to "police Russia's every border." While agreeing that economic aid to the Greek people was a necessity, he vigorously opposed a "military subsidy" to a reactionary Greek government, and considered it nonsense to assert that either the Greek or Turkish government was representative or democratic. Loans for military purposes, he said, would not stop communism, but would spread it throughout Europe and Asia. For days he led the attack against the President's proposals on the radio and in the *New Republic,* and then took off for England. There, while the Greece-Turkey aid

bill was being debated in Congress, he delivered a series of public
addresses in which he charged that his government was committed
to a "ruthless imperialism" and to war against the Soviet Union, and
advised the British to stand aloof from the United States if they
would avert war. These speeches caused great embarrassment in
England and intense indignation throughout the United States. On
the floor of the Senate, Senator Vandenberg called Wallace an
"itinerant saboteur." It was widely believed at the time that the
American reaction against Wallace's performance in Europe took
the steam out of the attack of his group at home and aided the
passage of the bill through Congress.

Two public opinion polls taken in the United States around
March 20, one by the National Opinion Research Center of the
University of Denver and one by Dr. Gallup's National Institute of
Public Opinion, disclosed a high degree of awareness of the President's proposal (about 75 per cent) and strong majority support
for economic and financial aid to Greece and Turkey. But there
was considerable reluctance to support military aid either in the
form of supplies of military advisers (one poll showed about five
to three against, and the other less than four to three against). By
about two to one those with opinions thought that sending military
supplies would make war with Russia "more likely." Nevertheless,
when asked whether we should send "military supplies" and some
"military experts" to "strengthen Turkey's defenses against Russian
pressures," 43 per cent expressed approval and 41 per cent dis-
approval. And to the question "If Communists in foreign countries
try to seize control of their governments by force, do you think it
should or should not be our general policy to help those governments put down such revolts?" 47 per cent thought it should be our
policy and 37 per cent that it should not. Nearly half of those interviewed in the Gallup poll thought that the principal reasons for the
proposed aid program was to keep communism out of Greece and
stop Russian expansion; a third conceived it as help to the needy
Greeks. And over two to one of those interviewed thought the
problem should be turned over to the United Nations, although
about half of the majority advanced reasons for not doing so.

Virtually all who for any reason opposed or who had any doubts about the President's proposals found common ground in the charge that direct and "unilateral" action by the United States would by-pass the United Nations, violate its spirit, damage its authority, and stunt its growth. This therefore became the central issue in the debate.

As we have seen, the administration did not anticipate the opposition that would arise over the by-passing issue, and had given little attention to words and procedures that might have headed off the opposition of sincere United Nations supporters. Immediately after the President spoke, however, the mistake (if it *was* a mistake, considering the problem whole) was apparent. A number of congressmen immediately commented publicly that the prestige and usefulness of the United Nations had suffered a damaging blow. Representative Thomas L. Owens, Republican of Illinois, told reporters "The United Nations died today." The Associated Press wire on March 12 carried a story from Washington that said, "President Truman all but by-passed the United Nations today in calling for quick United States action to protect independent nations from totalitarian aggression." The cry came bounding in from the most diverse quarters, from both opponents and supporters of the President's recommendations.

Senator Vandenberg immediately sensed that a mistake had been made and in his comments to reporters on the afternoon of the President's message said:

> We should proceed as far as possible within the United Nations. But that is not practical at the immediate moment because the United Nations has no relief funds; and it has not yet concluded agreements with member nations for military support. We should immediately insist in the Security Council that these latter plans be consummated. We should also seek an immediate report from the United Nations Commission investigating alleged external invasion of Greek sovereignty.

Senator Vandenberg later wrote, "The administration made a colossal blunder in ignoring the UN."

The United Nations was immediately made an issue by the

opponents of direct United States action in Greece and Turkey. It was also raised by others who did not oppose direct action. Within a week the overwhelming attachment of the Amercan public to the United Nations made itself felt in no uncertain terms, and many of the staunchest supporters of the President's policy, who were at the same time backers of the United Nations—including Walter Lippmann, Marquis Childs, Barnet Nover, and Anne O'Hare McCormick—were deploring the failure of the President to notify the United Nations and to adopt other procedures that would have brought his proposed action "within the spirit of the United Nations." Several suggested ways of remedying the "mistake."

Public discussion became intense and the issue dangerous. For perhaps the majority of the American people, the United Nations in the two years of its existence had become the halfway house on the road from isolationism to full responsibility in world affairs, and they were uncritically sold on it. At the same time, in every community there were leaders who, aware of the realities of national power and the limitations of the United Nations, nevertheless knew equally well the great potentialities of the United Nations as a peace-keeping instrument; they were saddened, even alarmed, at proposed action that, however necessary on an emergency basis, damaged the prestige of the United Nations and endangered its future development. The government contended that unless direct action was taken in Greece and Turkey the United Nations would become a shadow and war almost inevitable. The isolationists of the Right, for whom the United Nations issue was an excuse for inaction, put on a great show of anguish. The opposition of the Left, refusing to face the facts of Soviet aggressiveness and the United Nations' incapacity to deal with it, complained bitterly that the administration was destroying the chief organ through which accommodation with the Soviet Union might be reached.

Walter Lippmann was among the first supporters of direct action in Greece and Turkey to point out publicly that there was a real issue in the by-passing of the United Nations but that the damage could be repaired without impeding the President's program. In his syndicated column on March 18, Lippmann conceded the need for direct action, the inability of the United Nations to act, and even that technically we were perhaps not obliged to consult the United Nations on Greece and Turkey, as they had requested our aid. But:

> The heart of the United Nations Charter and the soul of the whole undertaking is the covenant to consult with the other members, particularly the permanent members of the Security Council, when an issue of international security and peace is raised. Undoubtedly such an issue is raised here: the President said so in his message. . . .

> It was, to put it conservatively, an oversight to have discussed our proposed action before the President announced it to the world only with the British government, and not also with the French, the Chinese, and the Russian. That, however, is water over the dam, and the mistake can be repaired. . . .

> A full explanation, and a willingness to consider objections, would meet the obligation to consult. . . . We could inform the Secretary-General of the United Nations about our proposals, and invite him to take notice of the explanations which will be offered to Congress. Mr. Austin could go before the Security Council and explain the proposals, not waiting until Mr. Gromyko attacks them. We could notify the United Nations that we shall not only explain what we intend to do and why, but also that we shall report to them at regular intervals what we have done and why. We could, moreover, invite the leading interested nations to send official observers to Greece to see for themselves what we are doing.

> The great advantage of some such action on our part is that it would at once rehabilitate the moral authority of the United Nations and would reaffirm our loyalty as a member of the organization. It would not interfere with the efficiency of our action. . . . This is the best way to answer the charge that we are doing what we have so often charged others with doing—that we are acting unilaterally and for the purpose of domination and aggrandizement. . . .

Returning to the subject three days later, Lippmann advanced another reason for clearing the proposed action with the United Nations:

> Suppose that in Greece later, or in some other wracked and hungry land, there comes into power by elections like those in Greece a government of the extreme Left, dominated by the Communists.

That could happen. It could happen elsewhere in Europe, in Asia, or even in an American republic. What happens then—if that government calls upon the Soviet Union for aid, asks it to equip and train its army, to supervise its budget, to plan and direct its economy? What under the "Truman Doctrine" do we do if the Soviet government says there is an emergency, that it has been invited to intervene, that the UN is not in position to extend the kind of help required? . . .

If we are wise, we shall seek to spread the moral risk, and not assume the whole of it as we are now doing.

In the meantime Senator Vandenberg and Acting Secretary Acheson, in consultation with the senator's colleagues on the congressional committees dealing with foreign affairs, were working out a strategy to resolve the United Nations issue. On March 20 Senator Vandenberg and Senator Connally offered as an amendment to the Greece-Turkey aid bill a lengthy preamble consisting of six "whereas" clauses (a similar amendment was introduced in the House). In these it was pointed out that Greece and Turkey had sought aid from the United States to preserve their national integrity and survival as free nations, which was important to the security of the United States and of all freedom-loving peoples; that the Security Council had recognized the seriousness of the border troubles in northern Greece and recognized that "if the present emergency is met" the United Nations might subsequently assume responsibility for that phase of the problem; that the Food and Agriculture Organization mission to Greece had recommended that Greece ask for aid from United Nations agencies and also directly from the United States and Great Britain; that the United Nations was not in position to furnish the aid so urgently required; and that inasmuch as United States aid to Greece and Turkey would contribute to the freedom and independence of all the members of the United Nations it was in conformity with the principles and purposes of the Charter.

The next step in neutralizing the United Nations issue was the summoning to Washington of Warren R. Austin, United States representative on the Security Council, and the preparation of a statement on United States aid to Greece. In this statement, which

Austin made to the Security Council on March 28, he considered the problem of Greece as a whole and analyzed its several aspects. He reported fully on Greece's appeal for aid and on policy decisions in Washington and suggested that United Nations action in Greece and United States emergency aid were complementary, directed to the same ends. He also proposed ways in which United Nations action might be speeded up, and assured the Council that the United States wanted the United Nations to equip itself as soon as possible to take over the whole job in Greece and that the United States would cooperate fully to that end.

Austin's statement went far toward reassuring those in this country and abroad who charged that the United States was by-passing the United Nations. Even greater assurance was given three days later, when Senator Vandenberg introduced another amendment to the Greece-Turkey aid bill, which, as later approved by the Senate Committee on Foreign Relations, read as follows:

> The President is directed to withdraw any and all aid authorized herein under any of the following circumstances:
>
> (1) If requested by the governments of Greece or Turkey, respectively, representing a majority of the people of either such nation;
>
> (2) If the President is officially notified by the United Nations that the Security Council finds (with respect to which finding the United States waives the exercise of the veto) or that the General Assembly finds that such action taken or assistance furnished by the United Nations makes the continuance of such assistance unnecessary or undesirable;
>
> (3) If the President finds that any purposes of the Act have been substantially accomplished by the action of other intergovernmental organizations or finds that the purposes of the Act are incapable of satisfactory accomplishment.

The amendment took most of the remaining wind out of the sails of the United Nations issue. Supporters of the President's policy who had misgivings on this score were completely reassured, some of the critics were mollified, and the sincerity of those who continued this line of attack was opened to serious question. The issue continued to be flailed, but it was practically dead.

There remains to be mentioned the grief of Andrei A. Gromyko, Soviet representative on the Security Council, over our actions. He pointed out to the Security Council on April 8 that the United States had alleged the existence of a threat to the security of Greece but had not waited to *prove* the matter to the Security Council. He thought that the United Nations Investigating Commission then in Greece should be allowed to finish its work, determine the facts, report to the Security Council, and that the Council should then decide what action, if any, it would take. The United States, in failing to await the report of the commission and in proceeding on its own, was violating its United Nations obligations. Moreover he thought that the rendering of military aid "cannot be recognized to be consistent with the purposes and principles of the United Nations," that the sending of American civil and military instructors to Greece and Turkey, even though requested by those countries, was interference in their internal affairs and a serious blow to their independence. Gromyko was firmly against foreign interference. But, considering that Greece's freedom and independence were at that moment on the point of extinction by armed Communist bands aided and supplied by the Soviet Union's Balkan satellites, his concern was something less than convincing. In fact his statement exposed Soviet strategy in bold relief and gave added reason for haste in pushing through the program.

It was fully anticipated in the State Department that one of the main arguments against the program would be that the Greek government was undemocratic, corrupt, and reactionary, and that Turkey was not a democracy and had been neutral during the war. The character of the Greek and Turkish governments ranked as an issue second only to that of the United Nations. American liberals had the most trouble with this problem: many who otherwise welcomed the Truman Doctrine balked at its specific application to Greece and Turkey.

That Greece had a restored King and that the Greek government was corrupt, reactionary, inefficient, and indulged in extremist practices was well known and incontestable; that Turkey, though making progress, had not yet achieved full democratic self-government was also patent. It was extremely easy to attack the logic of applying the Truman Doctrine to these countries. The defense of the President's proposals required far more facts and understanding, more faith, and at the same time greater realism.

As to the facts, Greece had a government as democratic *in form* as that of Great Britain, a constitutional monarchy in which the King held very little power. The then existing Parliament had been chosen a year before in elections held under the scrutiny of some fifteen hundred Allied observers and had been declared representative even though the Communist-dominated EAM had boycotted the election (if they had participated their representatives would have been in a small minority). The return of the King had been overwhelmingly ratified in a plebiscite that was also pronounced fair by foreign observers. Reactionaries were in control of the government, and in an atmosphere of fear, extremism, and impending chaos they were running things very badly; but democratic forms remained. The press was free. Political opposition, notwithstanding terrorism on both sides, was unrestricted. There was every reason to believe that with fear of guerrilla attacks on the villages and of a Communist coup in Athens removed, and reasonable economic conditions assured, the Greek people would assert themselves and create a more worthy government in new elections. The United States had to make a choice between supporting temporarily a bad democratic government and allowing an armed minority under Soviet direction to fasten a Communist dictatorship permanently upon Greece. It was not a choice between black and white, but between black and a rather dirty gray. With United States aid and pressure the gray might become a respectable white.

It was a major job of statesmanship to clarify this choice to the American people, who were not accustomed to thinking about foreign affairs in terms of a necessary choice between unattractive alternatives, both involving risk. The task was complicated by the fact that incessant Communist propaganda, echoed by fellow travelers and misinformed liberals, had been widely successful over a period of years in portraying EAM and ELAS as organizations of patriotic liberals resisting corruption, fascism, and monarchy. The unspeakable horrors perpetrated by the rebels during the civil war of 1944–45 had opened the eyes of most Greeks to the character of EAM and ELAS and had swung them far to the Right in reaction, but the opinions of a great many Americans and British had not been changed. The President's program therefore ran into considerable opposition on the American Left that was grounded in ignorance and stereotyped sentimentality.

That democracy has progressed in Turkey in the years since 1947 none will deny, but few except the best-informed experts realized then that the thoroughgoing social, economic, political, and educational reforms instituted and patiently carried out by Ataturk had already brought Turkey to the threshold of democracy. In the hotly contested elections of July 1946 an opposition party had won sixty-three seats in the Grand National Assembly. An opposition press flourished, and liberalism—as manifested in mounting political debate, education, womens' rights, free enterprise, government decentralization, and the advance of minorities—was growing. To consider Turkey in 1947 a democracy deserving of our aid required full information and a certain amount of faith.

It is not necessary to describe here, play by play, the debate on whether Greece and Turkey, as free and democratic peoples, deserved our aid under the Truman Doctrine. The issue was never resolved purely on the basis of the facts, although administration spokesmen and government information services worked hard to convey the facts. In the end realism and faith combined came to the fore: the necessity of choosing the better of two less than perfect alternatives—helping Greece and Turkey keep the doors open for democratic development, or seeing the doors permanently closed to democratic development by the force of a minority. This required the kind of faith that is a built-in feature of democratic philosophy. Considering developments in Greece and Turkey since 1947, it is plain that that faith was justified.

It is significant that American "intervention" in the affairs of foreign countries in remote continents did not become a major issue except in its United Nations context. President Truman's formal abandonment of nonintervention and neutrality as a foundation stone of American foreign policy in time of peace marked a break with American tradition dating back to the earliest years of the Republic, and will probably loom large in history. Nevertheless in 1947 the break seemed natural and inevitable. The massive intervention of the United States during two World Wars, United States membership in the United Nations, and the vivid, inescapable facts of Soviet expansion had already killed intervention as an issue in American political life. President Truman merely recognized the fact.

If the issue of intervention was a lifeless one in the United States, even more so was its gaudier twin, "imperialism." It was mostly the Communists and their fellow travelers who parroted this charge which Soviet propaganda boomed around the world. The American people not only accepted but, according to public-opinion polls, overwhelmingly approved the sending of American experts, advisers, and administrators to Greece. Members of Congress were especially impressed by this feature of the President's proposals.

Other objections, which in earlier times would have aroused intense discussion, melted rapidly under the sun of public scrutiny and hardly attained the status of issues: that the proposed policy would lead to war, that it meant the end of "One World," that it would "bail out the British Empire." It was too clear in the spring of 1947 that any other course would run a far greater risk of war, that the Soviet Union had already divided the world, and that what we had thought were British chestnuts were in fact our own.

The Senate Committee on Foreign Relations began its formal consideration of the principles involved the day after the President delivered his message. On March 13 Acheson, Patterson, and Forrestal appeared before the committee in executive session to discuss with the members the implications of the program. On the same day Senator Vandenberg invited all members of the Senate to send to him any questions they might have, and more than four hundred questions were submitted. These were consolidated into a questionnaire of a hundred and ten items and sent to the State Department. On March 28 the Department furnished a complete reply, which was immediately printed for the use of Congress. This document clarified many of the issues involved, assuaged many doubts, and contributed significantly to the support that developed in Congress.

Public hearings of the Senate Committee on Foreign Relations began on March 24 and continued through March 31, with Acheson, Patterson, Forrestal, Clayton, and Paul Porter (chief of the President's Special Economic Mission to Greece) as the principal government witnesses. Most of these, as well as Lincoln MacVeagh, Ambassador to Greece, and Edwin C. Wilson, Ambassador to Turkey, also testified in executive sessions. Public hearings of the House Committee on Foreign Affairs began on March 20 and extended through April 9, with many executive sessions interlarded, the same government witnesses appearing. The hearings were marked by an absence of partisanship and a deep sense of responsibility.

Of all the testimony before the congressional committees, that of Acheson on the first day of the Senate committee's public hearing was by far the most dramatic and the most meaningful for American policy. The hearing was held in the large caucus room on the third floor of the Senate Office Building. It was a splendid spring day and the room was overflowing with spectators and excitement. After Acheson had read his prepared statement Chairman Vandenberg courteously deferred questioning him until other members of the committee had an opportunity. Senator Connally was in fine form and obviously impatient to tear into the issues that had accumulated in the public mind. He was called on first by the chairman, and in rapid succession he put to Acheson, in the form of extended leading questions, all the major objections that had been publicly raised and gleefully joined him in knocking them down. The two of them together, the one with old-fashioned oratory and political feeling, the other with precision and a high order of logic, did an effective job. Following Senator Connally, Senator H. Alexander Smith of New Jersey and several other senators joined in the questioning. By this time it was nearly noon, and Senator Vandenberg, having noted in statements, questions, and answers a certain amount of hedging on the wider implications of the President's message, decided to wait no longer and intervened with questions of his own. He appeared determined to put a spotlight on the matter at that very session, before the noon recess, and not let anyone get the impression that the new policy was more or less confined to aid to Greece and Turkey. The significance of his intervention can be appreciated only in the light of a few statements that had been made earlier in the morning.

In his opening statement Acheson had said:

We have been asked whether this establishes a pattern for all future requests for American assistance. Any requests of foreign countries for aid will have to be considered according to the circumstances in each individual case. In another case we would have to study whether the country in question really needs assistance, whether its request is consistent with American foreign policy, whether the request for assistance is sincere, and whether assistance by the United States would be effective in meeting the problems of that country. It cannot be assumed, therefore, that this government would necessarily undertake measures in any other country identical or even closely similar to those proposed for Greece and Turkey.

Shortly thereafter Connally and Acheson had this interchange:

SENATOR CONNALLY: A good many people have propounded the inquiry, Does this mean a complete reversal of our foreign policy, and does it mean that all over the world any country that applies to us will be in such a position that we have to make them a loan or take action similar to that set forth in this bill? Is it not true that those situations will have to be deferred and met when they arise, and that each case will have to stand on its own bottom in the light of the world situation and in the light of our own situation at the time such application may be made?

SECRETARY ACHESON: That is very true, Senator Connally. That is exactly the situation.

SENATOR CONNALLY: This is not a pattern out of a tailor's shop to fit everybody in the world and every nation in the world, because the conditions in no two nations are identical. Is that not true?

SECRETARY ACHESON: Yes, sir; that is true, and whether there are requests, of course, will have to be left for the future, but whatever they are, they will have to be judged, as you say, according to the circumstances of each specific case.

Senator Smith of New Jersey was also interested in this point:

SENATOR SMITH: Mr. Secretary, we read in the papers about this being a Truman Doctrine. I gather from your excellent statement—and I want to compliment you on the statement—that the objective we are driving at here is the rehabilitation of Greece and the assistance of Turkey in her dilemma, without any necessarily wide political implications. I am troubled by the comparison of this movement of ours to the so-called Monroe Doctrine. I do not know whether you want to comment on that, or whether we have anything in our mind of that sort. Are we adopting a policy where we say the United States of America will be interested all over the world in any country that is seeking democratic freedom?

SECRETARY ACHESON: I think that what the President said was much more limited than what you now suggest to me, and very clear indeed. He proposed that we should give this aid to Greece and Turkey. He pointed out that here were two countries which had constitutional systems which were founded on democratic principles which were struggling to maintain those systems. He said it was to our interest that all peoples who had free governments and democracies, that were moving toward human freedoms, should not be coerced into giving up those institutions, and that whatever help we could extend would be in accordance with our policy. I think that is what the President said quite clearly in his message.

The definite impression was conveyed at the moment that Acheson was hedging on the global implications of the President's statement. Senator Vandenberg apparently thought so, for shortly thereafter he intervened in the discussion:

THE CHAIRMAN: Mr. Secretary, you have spoken rather generally about the fact that there may be similar demands upon us of one sort or another. You have identified one of them. May I ask you specifically what is the prospect in respect to Korea?

SECRETARY ACHESON: The prospect in respect to Korea is that there will be a requirement for expenditure of United States funds, probably over the next three years, in Korea.

Acheson explained that the Soviet government had not been willing to proceed with the unification of Korea and that this left the southern part below the thirty-eighth parallel in a very serious economic condition; it would therefore "be necessary to invest

American funds and have American funds for the purpose of getting that area for which we have responsibility going." The exact projects and the manner and extent of aid to Korea, he said, were under discussion in the State, War, and Navy Departments and a proposal would shortly be made to Congress.

THE CHAIRMAN: So we must definitely anticipate . . . a somewhat similar proposal on behalf of Korea in the near future; is that right?

SECRETARY ACHESON: Well, I do not know how similar it is, Senator. We must contemplate a proposal for American funds in Korea; yes, sir. . . .

THE CHAIRMAN: A good deal of emphasis has been put this morning upon localizing this project in Greece and Turkey so far as precedent is concerned. The President, in his message, said, and I quote:

"To insure the peaceful development of nations free from coercion, the United States has taken a leading part in establishing the United Nations. The United Nations is designed to make possible lasting freedom and independence for all its members. We shall not realize our objectives, however, unless we are willing to help free peoples to maintain their free institutions and their national integrity against aggressive movements that seek to impose upon them totalitarian regimes."

Then I underscore the following sentence:

"This is no more than a frank recognition that totalitarian regimes imposed on free peoples, by direct or indirect aggression, undermine the foundations of international peace and hence the security of the United States."

That is the end of the quotation. That would seem to suggest, Mr. Secretary, that we find it necessary to defend the United States against what might be called the chain reaction of agression wherever it occurs in the world. It would seem to raise a somewhat broader problem than this immediately localized situation.

I should like to have your comment, if you will, upon this phase of the matter. In other words, does not this statement by the President substantially broaden the concept which we are discussing this morning?

SECRETARY ACHESON: . . . what the President is talking about is an example of an attempt by direct or indirect means to take away from a free people their free institutions and substitute others. There have been various statements in the press that this was an ideological crusade. That is not what the President is talking about. He is talking about the fact that where a free people is being coerced to give up its free institutions, we are interested.

He was talking specifically about the problem in Greece and Turkey. He laid down this broad principle. He did not state, and I think no one would state, that that means that wherever this situation occurs, one must react to it in exactly the same way. The situations of different cases are utterly different, and what you could do in one case you cannot do in another case. But the principle is clear, I think. I am sure it is clear, because the President of the United States has announced it, and that for me is sufficient, that we are concerned where a people already enjoying free institutions are being coerced to give them up. Now, what can we do about it? As I pointed out a moment ago, we are already protesting against action which is being taken in Hungary which we think has this effect, but what we can do in Hungary, what we should do, the whole circumstances of that case are very different from the one we have before us. Does that at all clarify the matter?

THE CHAIRMAN: Yes. In other words, I think what you are saying is that wherever we find free peoples having difficulty in the mainte- ✓ nance of free institutions, and difficulty in defending against aggressive movements that seek to impose upon them totalitarian regimes, we do not necessarily react in the same way each time, ✳ but we propose to react.

SECRETARY ACHESON: That, I think, is correct.

There are surely few more dramatic moments than this in the evolution of an American leader or the life of the American nation. Senator Vandenberg so emphasized the words "we propose to react," and they were of such weighty import, that the effect was tremendous. At least one spectator wanted to throw his hat into the air. Senator Vandenberg's conversion from isolationism had been gradual; as he himself wrote on June 6, 1947, bipartisan foreign policy had been "quite definitely confined (1) to the evolution of the United Nations and (2) to the peace treaties in Europe." Only three weeks earlier the President and Acheson had not known how he would react to a proposal to aid Greece and Turkey. Now the senator, the most powerful Republican in Congress, was publicly approving, in fact insisting upon and himself restating, the global implications of the Truman Doctrine.

In succeeding months the word "containment" came into use to describe the administration's policy; several years later, during and after the election campaign of 1952, the policy and concept of "rollback" was advanced as an improvement. On this morning of March 24, 1947, during the hearing of the Senate Committee on Foreign Relations, the distinction between containment and rollback was clearly defined. Acheson was struck by Senator Smith's question whether the United States would be "interested" all over the world in any country "seeking" democratic freedom. This meant, in later parlance, rollback or liberation. In his reply to Senator Smith and to Senator Vandenberg, Acheson delineated the boundaries of the Truman Doctrine: it applied to countries that then had free institutions and that were being coerced into giving them up. There was to be no "ideological crusade," and by clear implication no material aid for liberation of countries already under Soviet control. And even as regards free peoples under coercion, Acheson suggested limits in the application of the Truman Doctrine: Had a request for aid been received? Was the request sincere? Did the country really need aid? Was the granting of aid consistent with American foreign policy? Would United States aid be effective in meeting the problems of that country? In other words, was it practicable to extend aid, and would that aid have a reasonable chance of accomplishing its objectives? Acheson mentioned as an example Hungary, a country surrounded by Communist-dominated states, occupied by the Red Army, and already virtually under Communist control through internal political manipulation. In this instance one could protest, and the United States was protesting, but by implication our intervention could not practicably go as far as the proposed aid to Greece and Turkey, for to attempt it would have little chance of success and would make war more than a risk—a probability. As John Foster Dulles later found out, rollback was a catchy slogan but an utterly impracticable policy. Before it was abandoned it aroused grave fears among our friends and allies abroad that the United States was going to lead the world into a new war.

In the light of events since 1947 the sharp questioning of Acheson

in the House Committee on Foreign Affairs by Representative
Walter H. Judd of Minnesota and Representative James G. Fulton
of Pennsylvania on the applicability of the Truman Doctrine to
China merits attention. Judd suggested that there was a contra-
diction in our foreign policy. "If it is a wise policy to urge, for
example, the government of China to unite with organized Communist minorities there, why," he asked, "is it a wise policy to assist
the Greek government to fight against the same sort of armed Communist minorities in Greece?" Acheson's main point in reply was
that the circumstances in Greece and in China were entirely different.
The Chinese Communists had for nearly twenty years controlled a
large contiguous geographical area with an army that had repulsed
all attempts to invade it. He described briefly the negotiations
between the Communists and the government, which General Marshall had supported, to create a unified government and army, and
admitted the negotiations had failed and fighting had broken out.
He emphasized the aid the United States had given China since
the end of the war: Lend-Lease aid of $700 million, $836 million
in surplus property, and other aid amounting to $133 million, and
he later added that we had equipped thirty-six Chinese divisions.
He suggested that this "great and vast aid" to China hardly merited
being called a "hands-off policy." The Chinese government was not
approaching collapse and facing defeat, he added, whereas in
Greece there was an imminent crisis.

Representative Judd's time had expired, but Representative Fulton, taking up the questioning, tried to get Acheson to admit that
if the Chinese government were facing defeat our policy toward
China would be different. Acheson evaded the question but insisted
there was no difference between our policy as regards Greece and
that toward China—but the circumstances were different. At the
next day's hearing Judd returned to the attack. He seemed primarily
interested in making the point that the United States had made an
enormous mistake during the war with Japan in discouraging the
Chinese government from attacking the Chinese Communists, and
since the war in encouraging an accommodation between the Chinese
government and the Communists. "As a result China is left with

internal troubles like Greece. It is difficult for me to believe that we
do not have obligations there almost as great—perhaps greater—
than those in Greece, from the point of view of the security of the
United States." Acheson seemed reluctant to discuss China policy
and several times indicated that he was not sure of the facts. He gave
no further clarification of the relation of the Truman Doctrine to
China: the circumstances were different, the United States was helping China, and there was no imminent danger of Communist victory
in China.

Only one observation is going to be made here on an issue which
even whole books and decades of perspective may not clarify con-
clusively: no geographical limitation of the Truman Doctrine was
intended, nor has it ever been made, but when the test of prac-
ticability was applied in subsequent months by Secretary of State
Marshall, Secretary of State Acheson, and the President they served,
China did not qualify for the kind of massive intervention that
would have been required to save her from Communist control.
Vast economic, military, and technical aid had already been and
was still being extended to the Chinese government. What more
would have been required? More billions? A mammoth United
States expeditionary force? And if this were done, "Would United
States aid be effective in meeting the problems of that country?"

Some years later President Eisenhower and Secretary of State
Dulles were confronted with a similar situation in Indochina. Large-
scale economic, military, and technical aid was flowing from the
United States to the French and the Vietnamese fighting the Com-
munist rebels. In the fall of 1953 and the spring of 1954 President
Eisenhower and Secretary Dulles repeatedly stated in explicit terms
that a Communist victory in Indochina, either as a result of internal
subversion or outside pressures or both, would menace the security
of the United States and the free world, and threatened United
States action that went beyond aid to the defenders—even United
States intervention to massive retaliation against unnamed countries.
But in the end they found that such action was not practicable.

If, upon the fall of China to the Chinese Reds in 1949, the administration in Washington had acted quickly, and on a large enough

scale, to strengthen the countries of Southeast Asia against subversion and aggression, and particularly to help the French destroy the Communist menace in Indochina, the situation in 1953 and 1954 might have been different. But it did not. Its aid and attention to Southeast Asia was too little and too late, and it thus became less and less practicable to save northern Indochina.

The Senate Committee on Foreign Relations unanimously approved the bill to aid Greece and Turkey and reported it to the Senate on April 3. The Senate debate opened on April 8 with an eloquent address by Senator Vandenberg and continued for two weeks. Senator Connally and other administration stalwarts swung in with strong supporting speeches. Attack came chiefly from Democratic Senators Pepper and Taylor, who held that American aid should be channeled through the United Nations, and from Republican Senators Wherry, Malone, Brooks, and others, who held that the program would lead either to war or bankruptcy. On April 22 the bill passed the Senate by a vote of 67 to 23; in addition, five senators not present or voting announced that if present they would have voted for the bill. Of those voting for the bill, 35 were Republicans and 32 Democrats; of those voting against the bill, 16 were Republicans and 7 Democrats. The bipartisan majority was the largest ever given in the Senate to any major controversial measure in the whole field of American foreign policy since the outbreak of the war in Europe.

The House Committee on Foreign Affairs favorably reported the bill to the House on April 25; only one member in a committee of 25, Representative Lawrence H. Smith of Wisconsin, signed the minority report. Debate began on May 6 and was concluded on May 8, when the House approved the bill by a vote of 287 to 107. Of those voting for the bill, 127 were Republicans and 160 Democrats; of those voting against it, 93 were Republicans, 13 were Democrats, and one was American Labor (Marcantonio of New York). The Conference Report which adjusted minor differences in the Senate and House bills passed both Houses by a voice vote on May 15. President Truman planned to sign the bill at a White House ceremony on Monday, May 19, but an illness of his mother

having called him to Kansas City, he signed the bill there in his
suite at the Muehlebach Hotel on May 22, and issued a statement
which said in part:

> The act authorizing United States aid to Greece and Turkey,
> which I have just signed, is an important step in the building of the
> peace. Its passage by overwhelming majorities in both houses of
> Congress is proof that the United States earnestly desires peace and
> is willing to make a vigorous effort to help create the conditions of
> peace.
>
> The conditions of peace include, among other things, the ability
> of nations to maintain order and independence, and to support
> themselves economically. In extending the aid requested by two
> members of the United Nations for the purpose of maintaining
> these conditions, the United States is helping to further aims and
> purposes identical with those of the United Nations. Our aid in
> this instance is evidence not only that we pledge our support to
> the United Nations but that we act to support it.

The President's declaration that one of the essential conditions of
peace was the ability of nations to support themselves economically
was not just a turn of phrase, and it extended far beyond Greece and
Turkey. It was a statement specifically intended to add to the policy
foundation of large-scale United States reconstruction aid to Europe.
Long before the congressional debates on aid to Greece and Turkey
ended, the catastrophic economic condition of Europe had moved
front center on the world stage, United States responsibilities for aiding Europe had been publicly recognized by Acheson with the approval of the President, and plans were being made in the State
Department for an early announcement that the United States would
extend aid if the Europeans would get together and draw up a common recovery program. The chapters following will describe the
steps by which the Truman Doctrine led to the Marshall Plan.

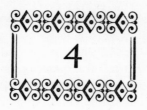

THE ACHESON INITIATIVE

EVEN as the Truman Doctrine was being drafted in the State Department, Acheson took the initiative that set three government departments to work on studies that led toward the Marshall Plan. On March 5, after his two meetings with Secretary Patterson and Secretary Forrestal, he sent them identical letters that are of central importance in the history of the Fifteen Weeks. In those letters Acheson recalled that in the course of their discussions frequent reference had been made to the fact that the Greek and Turkish problem was only a part of a much larger problem growing out of the change in Great Britain's strength and other world circumstances, and he thought it important that study be given to situations elsewhere in the world that might require similar aid. Therefore, he wrote, he had asked Assistant Secretary of State John H. Hilldring, as chairman of the State-War-Navy Coordinating Committee (SWNCC), to direct the attention of the committee to that important problem and, in consultation with the Treasury Department, to undertake a thorough study to be submitted to him or to Secretary Marshall as soon as possible.

The SWNCC on March 11 appointed a Special *Ad Hoc* Committee of three, one officer from each of the three Departments,[1] which

[1] The members were: State Department, William A. Eddy, Special Assistant to the Secretary of State for Research and Intelligence; War Department, Brigadier General George A. Lincoln; Navy Department, Rear Admiral E. T. Woolridge.

was directed to complete within three weeks a preliminary report on countries that might need emergency United States aid within the next few months, and then to refine and enlarge its studies to cover all countries that might require longer-range aid. The kinds of assistance envisaged were economic, financial, technical, and the supply of military equipment. The Committee was asked not only to determine the countries that might need aid, but in the case of each country to supply the answers to a number of questions: To what extent was the country threatened by internal or external pressures? Would it be possible, given the resources of the United States, to give assistance that would be effective? What considerations of national security and interest should govern the decision of the United States to grant or withhold assistance? What kinds of assistance would be needed? What demands would the granting of assistance make upon the resources of the United States? What arrangements should be made with foreign governments to assure the effective use of our aid in accomplishing our objectives? Was the country willing and able to help itself? What would be the consequence of failure to aid each country concerned?

The scope of the committee's terms of reference was breathtaking. Less than a month earlier it had seemed as though the foreign policy of the United States were caught in a political vise from which there was no escape, and State Department officers had gone about their daily routine with a sense of frustration and impending disaster. Now the Greece-Turkey decisions, the President's message to Congress, and the bipartisan nature of congressional and public support for the new foreign policy had broken the restraining bonds. American power was released for its world tasks, and United States foreign policy could be planned without boundary.

The Special Committee organized several groups to carry on the required studies: one on military aid, one on economic aid, one to consider what assistance might be forthcoming from international organizations, and four to study the specific situations in the countries of four broad geographical areas. To formulate the position of the State Department on the Special Committee and its various subsidiary groups, there was created a Committee on Extension of Aid to Foreign Governments (hereafter referred to as the Foreign Aid Committee), which in fact became the controlling group as regards all matters except strictly military aid. The whole effort was awkwardly organized, jurisdictions were not clear, and the machinery creaked and groaned, but the work got done expeditiously, and the product was destined to have a major impact on our foreign policy. The military aid studies made a powerful contribution—through the attitudes they engendered and the information they assembled—to the evolution of the Military Defense Assistance Program, which, inaugurated by Congress in 1949, channeled military assistance to our friends and allies abroad during the succeeding two years until it was merged with economic assistance in the Mutual Security Act of 1951. The economic, social, and political studies, done almost wholly in the State Department, became the foundation stones of the Marshall Plan.

It might be supposed that the Special Committee and the Foreign Aid Committee, considering their terms of reference and the quality and subsequent importance of their work, were heavily endowed with rank and prestige, that there was great competition for participation, and that their work was closely directed and their report eagerly awaited by the top brass of three Departments. Such was not the case in the State Department. The reasons are not entirely clear, but several may be suggested. SWNCC itself was not a policy-making organ, and even less a research mechanism; it was an interdepartmental committee that coordinated policy and action of three Departments chiefly in regard to enemy-occupied countries. Chairman Hilldring, the Assistant Secretary of State for Occupied Areas, was not widely known in the State Department; he possessed no authority over the personnel and wider operations of the Department. Acheson threw the big job of surveying the world's need for aid to SWNCC not because it was the ideal directing group, but because it was the only group that brought State, War, and Navy together below the top level, and it had an efficient secretariat. The person selected to represent the State Department on the Special Committee and to head the Foreign Aid Committee was similarly in but not of the State Department. Colonel William A.

Eddy was a newcomer from the Office of Strategic Services; pending a final decision of how much, if any, of the functions of OSS were to be transferred to the State Department, he held the title of Special Assistant to the Secretary for Research and Intelligence. He had little to do with the personnel, policy, and operations of the State Department.

These auspices automatically fixed the status of the committees as little wheels rather than big ones in the State Department, and their work as peripheral rather than central to the main stream of policy and operations. The original idea was that each of the three principal members of the Special Committee should associate with himself senior officers from his Department and that this larger central group would direct the necessary operations in each Department. But in the State Department several higher officers found themselves too busy to serve on the committee; others, after attending a meeting or two, sent subordinates. Chagrined, General George A. Lincoln, the War Department's representative and a leading power behind the whole project, suggested that the original procedural idea be abandoned as unworkable and that the three members establish several expert groups and draw into them men lower in rank, men who were interested, capable, and willing to work hard for a big idea—the men to whom the work would be turned over in any case. This was done. The Foreign Aid Committee and the subsidiaries of the Special Committee were thus composed for the most part of men of modest rank, but included some of the best-informed and hardest-working officers in the government.

These observations perhaps throw some light upon several questions: why, for example, the existence of the committees and their work never leaked to the press (leaks in the State Department, defying natural laws, usually occur near the top); and why few in the Department other than those directly engaged knew of the work or considered it important. They also suggest, at least in part, the reason why the work of the Special Committee was so little recognized in the State Department as the foundation of what became known as the Marshall Plan. Because of sheer physical limitations Acheson, having called the Special Committee into being, was not able during March and April to give it more of that personal attention which would have given its work prestige. Secretary Marshall was absent in Moscow. Clayton was ill in Arizona for several weeks preceding the President's message. Upon his return to Washington he testified on the Greece-Turkey aid bill before congressional committees, but he was mainly preoccupied with the forthcoming Geneva trade conference and the establishment of the Economic Commission for Europe. He left for Europe on April 8 and did not return until May 19. Acheson was left virtually alone at the top in the Department, during the critical period after March 12, to cope with the tidal wave of reaction to the Truman Doctrine, to direct the defense of the Greece-Turkey aid bill before congressional committees and the public, to work out a program of aid to Greece and Turkey, to backstop Secretary Marshall's negotiations in Moscow, and at the same time to direct the usual heavy stream of foreign relations.

When, upon his return to Washington from Moscow on April 28, Secretary Marshall gave top priority to the problem of Europe's need for United States aid and asked George Kennan to study the matter, Kennan found that a great deal of the spade work had already been done by the Special Committee. Moreover the experts that had been working on the foreign aid problem since March 18 were in process of refining and extending their preliminary studies for a more definitive report due for completion on July 1. There was no break in continuity as the work shifted from second to high priority.

During the spring of 1947 a number of friendly critics, aware of the implications of the Truman Doctrine, alarmed over the deterioration of economic and social conditions in Europe, and irritated by what seemed to be Washington's piecemeal approach to the problem of foreign aid, publicly took the State Department to task for not formulating a comprehensive plan. This was in fact being done by the Special Committee and its subsidiaries in the month following the President's message, and a preliminary report was completed on April 21. The economic, financial, political, and social situations in each of a dozen "critical" countries, mostly in Europe, were surveyed and estimates made of how conditions would develop within the next year. What were the status and prospects of each country's consumption and reserves of food, fuel, and raw materials? its reserves of gold and foreign exchange? its ability to supply itself from its own resources and from abroad? What political tensions prevailed, and what political and social developments could be expected, given likely economic conditions? How much United States aid could each country expect under programs already authorized?

These studies were the heart of the project, but many others were made: the United States balance of payments with the world and with each of the critical countries was projected through 1947, 1948, and 1949; and United States and United Nations commitments for loans and credits during the years ahead, in total and by countries, were figured up. In 1947 the world scarcity of food, fuel, raw materials, and transport was such that money could not necessarily buy in world markets even minimum requirements for all critical countries without a great deal of planning and control. Surveys were therefore made of how much food, fertilizer, coal, and transport and industrial machinery would be available for export from surplus-producing countries, including the United States. Estimates were made of the increase in shipping necessary to a program of foreign aid, and studies of how available shipping space might be used more effectively.

Finally, studies were made of the legislation and administrative controls that would be necessary. In view of the unlimited foreign need it was clear that if a large program of foreign aid was to be undertaken with a minimum of derangement and inflation at home, unnecessary foreign buying in the United States would have to be restricted and available supplies would have to be directed to the countries where they were most needed to support the foreign policy of the United States; this would require the retention of certain wartime controls, due to expire on June 30, over the domestic sale, transportation, and export of certain commodities.

Some of the central concepts of what later became the Marshall Plan were developed in the studies of the Economic Aid Group of

the Special Committee. Although immediate aid to critical countries was necessary, the committee recognized that the United States
could not indefinitely shore up singlehandedly the world economy or
even any substantial part of it, and that the speed and extent of
economic recovery abroad (and therefore the duration and cost of
a successful United States aid program) would depend upon the
revival of production and trade on a regional and world basis. It
therefore recommended that recovery programs in critical countries undertaken with United States aid be closely coordinated with
one another and with similar programs in other countries in that
region not receiving United States aid. As production and trade in
critical countries were integrated into healthy regional and world
trading systems, the strain concentrated upon the United States
would be relaxed. For example, Greece needed structural steel to rebuild her bridges; if she could obtain this steel from Germany or
France and pay for it with her exports she would not have to pay
dollars for it, and the cost to the United States would be correspondingly reduced. It was therefore agreed that techniques should be developed to exploit to the fullest the possibilities of mutual assistance
on a regional basis.

The committee placed special emphasis upon the revival of German production and trade in order to speed up general European
recovery, and upon the revival of production in Japan to speed up
Far Eastern recovery. Because of the great economic interdepend-
ence of all European countries, the committee emphasized that recovery should be continent-wide, including the Soviet satellites.
France needed Polish coal. Germany needed Balkan grain. It was
agreed that priority should be given to democratically oriented
countries but that trade between those countries and Soviet satellites should be encouraged and that where clear secondary advantage to Western Europe could be demonstrated and aid and
comfort to Communist-dominated countries minimized, it might
be desirable to extend financial and commodity assistance to those
countries.

In the months following Secretary Marshall's speech at Harvard
on June 5 the full energy and attention of the administration in

Washington and of every government in Europe from the Prime Minister down were mobilized and directed to studying the requirements of a common European recovery program. It is therefore hardly surprising that the work of the Special Committee was lost to sight. Nevertheless the early studies of the committee laid the foundations for the colossal structure of foreign aid that was subsequently erected and contributed directly and powerfully to the launching of the Marshall Plan.

On Monday, April 7, President Truman asked Acheson to take on a chore for him. The President had agreed many months earlier to go to Cleveland, Mississippi, on May 8 to speak at the annual meeting of the Delta Council. After the President accepted the invitation, however, a bitter intra-party fight had broken out in Mississippi over who would be appointed to succeed Senator Bilbo, who was mortally ill. President Truman decided he did not want to walk into that one and so informed his sponsors, who were disappointed but agreed to let him off the hook if he would send Acheson down to make a speech on foreign affairs. Acheson readily agreed to go.

Two days later Acheson called to his office Francis Russell and Joseph Jones, told them of the impending Delta Council engagement and of another invitation he had accepted to speak at a luncheon meeting of the state officers of the League of Women Voters in Washington on May 1, and as was his custom asked for speech suggestions. Russell and Jones, with a few hours' forewarning of the meeting with Acheson, and its nature, had had time to marshal a few thoughts. Russell was concerned about the nature of the attacks that were being made on the Greece-Turkey aid bill—that it meant by-passing the United Nations, aid to reactionary governments, steps toward war, and the like—and suggested that in one of the speeches Acheson deal directly with these issues. Jones, who for three weeks had been attending the meetings of the Foreign Aid Committee, handed Acheson the just-completed first draft of the committee's "Summary of Preliminary Conclusions" and a few of the committee's more significant working papers, and suggested that in the Delta Council speech he elaborate the economic intent of the Truman Doctrine into a comprehensive statement of our foreign reconstruction policy. The background of the suggestion, as discussed with Acheson, was as follows:

1. The studies of the Special Committee disclosed in concrete terms a portentous situation that was known only in a general way. Exports of goods and services from the United States during 1947, including projected aid to Greece and Turkey and the proposed post-UNNRA relief program, would run about $16 billion, and imports around half that. Of this huge difference between imports and exports, about $5 billion would be financed by United States loans and credits already authorized or expected to be authorized, and the remainder by foreign liquidation of reserves of gold and foreign exchange and by private remittances. Foreign ability to buy minimum needs abroad would fall off rapidly during the latter half of 1948 as a consequence of exhaustion of reserves and of United States loans and credits. The evidence overwhelmingly indicated that even the current volume and pattern of United States aid were not adequate to bring about world economic stability, support the liberal world-trading system desired by the United States, or attain the political objectives of the United States in certain critical countries. The President's Council of Economic Advisers expected a slight business recession within twelve months; if the expected export decline, due to foreign inability to pay, coincided with weakness in the domestic economy, the effect on production, prices, and employment in the United States might be most serious. Aside from the general situation, the prospects in several critical countries were immediately alarming. For example, a preliminary survey showed that France and Italy, where communism was thriving amid growing hunger, cold, and social discontent, would virtually exhaust their reserves of gold and foreign exchange before the end of the year (both countries were obliged in August and September to prohibit virtually all imports except wheat and coal). Great Britain's reserves would unavoidably sink below the panic point in 1948 without possibility of replenishment.

2. Public concern for the dark prospects for Europe, which had

started in mid-February, increased after the announcement of the Truman Doctrine as public commentators repeated in public what government officials and informed businessmen were saying in private. A month thence public alarm would probably reach proportions that would require the government to face up publicly to its responsibilities for aid.

3. It already appeared likely that the Russians would never agree, at the Conference of Foreign Ministers then meeting in Moscow, upon a settlement that would allow Germany to contribute to European recovery. The conference was highlighting not only the problem of Germany, but also the problem of European reconstruction, and Soviet expectations of profiting politically from a prostrate Europe were shown up.

4. Public interpretation of the Truman Doctrine at home and abroad was taking an undesirable tack, one that became more pronounced in succeeding weeks but which was already clearly discernible. President Truman had said quite clearly, "I believe our help [in supporting free peoples] should be primarily through economic and financial aid which is essential to economic stability and orderly political processes." Nevertheless the facts that ideological struggle had been joined by the President's message to Congress and that half the aid proposed for Greece and all that proposed for Turkey was military overshadowed in early April the economic content and intent of the Doctrine. It was not only Henry Wallace and the extremists of the Left who objected to the apparent military and ideological emphasis, but, as the spring advanced, many others who, while recognizing the necessity for military aid to Greece and Turkey, became increasingly concerned over the need of Europe for United States economic aid and considered the ideological vehicle unnecessary and dangerous and military aid irrelevant.[2]

This attitude was even more prevalent in Europe, and it was spreading. Initial reaction to the Truman Doctrine had been largely favorable and in official quarters enthusiastic. The Truman Doctrine

[2] This attitude changed radically a year later after the Communist coup in Czechoslovakia, and was altered even more after the Communists invaded South Korea in 1950, but in 1947 there were many who failed to see that the Soviet Union was aggressive and expansionist.

instantly dealt a stunning blow to communism in Western Europe and gave immediate heart and hope and resolution to those who feared or opposed it. Soviet influence ceased to expand in Western Europe from the moment the President pledged United States aid in support of free peoples. Nevertheless many in Europe had second thoughts on the Truman Doctrine that were not so favorable. What the people of Europe desperately needed was food, fuel, raw materials, and machinery with which to bring about an economic recovery that would itself check communism. Did the Truman Doctrine mean that the United States would help provide these? There was no certainty, hardly even a probability. But it was evident that the United States had picked up the ideological gage and was going to give military aid to Greece and Turkey. With the Communist issue clearly drawn for them by the United States, and without increased material strength in Europe with which to carry on the struggle for freedom, was not their condition worse than before? This was a very real question in many countries, especially in France and Italy, where middle-of-the road governments depended upon leftist and even Communist support to remain in power. The main stream of generally favorable reaction to the Truman Doctrine in Western Europe was therefore joined in early April by a substantial and swelling current of fretfulness, chiefly among liberals and Socialists, who criticized the Truman Doctrine on the grounds that it was militaristic, negatively anti-Communist and anti-Soviet, and did not meet Europe's need. This attitude was reflected back to the United States and reinforced domestic critics, who were charging that the proposed policy was warlike, would bolster reactionary governments, and was imperialistic. Congressional passage of the Greece-Turkey aid bill seemed assured by early April, but the responsibilities and promise inherent in the Truman Doctrine were becoming obscured at a time when it was clear that the Doctrine would have to be used as the basis for large-scale aid to Europe. It was important to bring public discussion back to an even keel and direct it to the next problem at hand, namely, the reconstruction of Europe.

These were the explicit considerations discussed in Acheson's speech conference on April 9. Before that day he had not seen the papers prepared by the Special Committee, but they merely served up to him in a concrete and compelling form a situation with which he was familiar. He and his staff had been greatly concerned about the bleak world outlook a year thence, with United States appropriations for foreign aid running out and with domestic controls expiring on June 30. He was aware that extreme financial and political crisis would occur in several countries long before the bottom of the barrel had been scraped unless it was well known that the United States was planning to help prevent them. After a discussion he therefore asked Jones to draft a speech laying the world economic situation and Europe's deepening crisis on the line with facts and figures, stating clearly what they meant for the United States: we would have to extend large-scale aid for reconstruction abroad, we would have to accept more imports, we would have to revive the workshops of Germany and Japan. To do this we would have to have an extension of wartime controls over the domestic sale, export, and transportation of certain commodities: Congress would have to face up to this problem. Acheson thought that a speech along these lines would in itself focus attention at home and abroad upon the economic intent of the new foreign policy announced by President Truman, and interpret the new policy in relation to the growing crisis in Europe. Jones was directed to give priority to the Delta Council speech and later to prepare some material in line with Russell's suggestion for the talk to the League of Women Voters.

This was quite an assignment, and it involved a number of subjects—for example, impact on the domestic economy, the availability of supplies, and control legislation—that were complex and hard to handle. Jones therefore raised the question whether Mr. Acheson might want to have some discussions with Dr. Edwin G. Nourse, chairman of the President's Council of Economic Advisers, Secretary Harriman, and others on his proposed speech. Acheson seemed to favor the suggestion and said he would consider it.

Things turned out differently. Three days later the Special Committee completed draft papers on some of the subjects that had needed clarification, and these were supplied to Acheson. About a week thereafter he went to discuss the matter with the President.

He told him that he wanted his authorization to put a ball in motion in the Delta Council speech. Laying the facts and figures before the President, Acheson described what he proposed to say. Working out a program of foreign aid and putting it through Congress would be a big job and require a long time, he said, but in his speech he wanted to outline publicly the dimensions of the problem and set off a public discussion that would make it necessary for the whole administration to go to work and come up with a program. He wanted it clearly understood that the administration would have to catch the ball he was going to throw out. The President agreed that the problem had to be faced and authorized Acheson to go ahead. After that, although Acheson did not rule out the possibility of high-level discussions within the government preceding his Delta Council speech, he seemed to veer away from them, and in fact the discussions never took place.

Having in mind Acheson's instructions, drawing heavily on the studies of the Special Committee, and aided by several of those who had contributed most to the economic work of the committee,[3] Jones prepared a detailed speech suggestion in outline form and on April 23 sent it to Acheson and several others in the Department for comment. On the basis of criticism and suggestions received, these notes were revised for use by Acheson in preparation for his talk at the League of Women Voters' luncheon on May 1, as he had decided that on that occasion he would give the Delta Council speech a "preliminary canter," off the record. The "canter" turned out to be a full exposition. Jones attended the luncheon, took notes on his chief's presentation, and in the succeeding days drafted the Delta Council speech. This was checked by three members of the Department staff and by John D. Clark, member of the President's Council of Economic Advisers, and taken to Acheson's office on the afternoon of May 6. Acheson departed for Cleveland, Mississippi, on May 7. The Cabinet had not seen the proposed speech at any stage, but Acheson spoke to the Delta Council with the full authority of the President.

[3] Notably Norman T. Ness, director, Office of Financial and Development Policy; H. Van B. Cleveland, Division of Investment and Economic Development; and Ben T. Moore, assistant chief, Division of Commercial Policy.

No attempt was made to build up public expectations in connection with the Delta Council speech as had been done in the case of President Truman's message to Congress. Daily news reports were taking care of that, whipping up intense interest in Europe's need for reconstruction aid. Several steps were nevertheless taken to spread the word among newsmen and columnists that the speech was officially considered an important one. Acheson had frequent informal meetings with American newsmen, but he also had lunch occasionally with three Britons—Leonard Miall of the British Broadcasting Corporation, Malcolm Muggeridge of the *Daily Express,* and Stewart McCall of the *News Chronicle*—for the purpose of explaining the background of developing United States foreign policy. As one of these occasions occurred shortly before the Mississippi speech, Acheson told his guests off the record what he was going to say and emphasized its importance as the policy of the United States. The word spread quietly among editors in Great Britain, with the result that the Delta Council speech was treated as a sensation, widely published and commented upon.

Through other channels reporters of the Associated Press, United Press, and International News Service covering the State Department, as well as a number of writers of syndicated columns, were advised of the official importance attached to the speech. They were also told that public discussion of the Truman Doctrine, in the view of the Department, had overemphasized its military aspects, whereas one of its chief meanings was that the United States was prepared to use its economic resources to help remedy the conditions of economic anarchy in which communism inevitably breeds. It was suggested that Acheson, by outlining in Mississippi a positive economic program, was going to try to bring public discussion back to the level where it belonged.

The Delta Council speech managed to make a modest appearance on page one of many of the larger daily newspapers, but most news reports were confused and distorted, with misplaced emphasis upon the reconstruction of Germany and Japan. Editorial writers, columnists, and radio analysts nevertheless saw the point, and in the succeeding three weeks, against the background of mounting news reports on the outlook in Europe, swept in with a large and swelling volume of comment and interpretation. Acheson's arithmetic suggested that Europe's need for aid was in the neighborhood of $5 billion a year for several years, and this figure promptly gained wide currency. Public discussion at home was given point and emphasis by the speech's reception in Europe, where it was published textually in many papers and its significance recognized in prominent news reportage and comment. This bounced back across the Atlantic in news stories and cables to editors. Within the State Department and other government agencies the speech acted as a powerful stimulus and instruction to staff work and discussions already in progress, and encouraged other Department spokesmen to hit the same line in prompt follow-up speeches.

The relentless, the merciless goad to decisive policy development during the month of May, as during the preceding months, was the unfolding situation in Europe, the stark facts. But the moving streams of public discussion and policy development were mingled, swelled, and given official direction by Acheson's speech in Cleveland, Mississippi, on May 8, 1947.

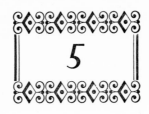

LESSONS OF MOSCOW

WHILE Dean Acheson in Washington, confronted with alarming facts and figures on Europe's condition, was reaching the conclusion that the United States would have to face up to large-scale aid for European reconstruction, Secretary Marshall in Moscow, negotiating with the Russians on the future of Germany, arrived at the same conclusion by a different route.

To the layman the Moscow Conference of the Council of Foreign Ministers, March 10–April 24, 1947, was merely another in a long and dreary round of international meetings whose proceedings were largely unintelligible and whose results were meager and usually inconclusive. There was little press build-up for the Moscow Conference, only modest interest in it, and even less expectation of important results. The fact is that it was the first and only postwar conference that deserved the title of Peace Conference, in that it was the only conference at which the victorious Allied powers tackled frontally and comprehensively the question of what kind of Germany was to be re-established in the center of Europe, what safeguards against future German aggression should be erected, what price in terms of territorial cessions, industrial controls, and reparations Germany should pay for her past crimes, and what her future relations to her neighbors to the east and west should be. These were the central problems of peacemaking. In dealing with them at Moscow the United States was obliged to decide how and

214

to what extent it would act to safeguard the freedom and promote the well-being of the continent it had helped liberate from the Nazis. Secretary Marshall and his delegation thus reached conclusions at Moscow and on the way home that made a powerful contribution to the development of United States foreign policy.

Certain principles and provisional arrangements regarding Germany had been agreed upon at Yalta and at Potsdam, but in the nearly two years since V-E Day these had been interpreted and applied in Germany by each of the four occupying powers with such cross and competitive purposes that the possibilities of agreement on a permanent settlement had receded rather than advanced. It had been agreed at Potsdam to negotiate peace treaties for Italy and the Balkan countries before attempting to settle the fate of Germany. During the course of these long, arduous, and acrimonious negotiations on secondary matters the wartime alliance had broken down, cold war between East and West had in effect been declared, and patience and willingness to make concessions had been exhausted on both sides. Therefore, it was with suspicions fully aroused and positions hardened that the Foreign Ministers of the Big Four powers —the United States, Great Britain, France, and the USSR—met in Moscow on March 10 to consider what to do about Germany and Austria. Notwithstanding the inauspicious circumstances there was a certain amount of hope that agreement might be reached. Neither the Soviet Union nor the Western nations had a preponderance of power in Central Europe. All of the Big Four had common reasons for wishing agreement. Each occupied a zone of Germany, a task unrewarding, unprofitable, and unpromising. Each wanted to prevent the rebirth of an aggressive Germany. Each realized that without an agreement that would establish in Central Europe an East-West equilibrium both the Soviet Union and the West would embark upon ceaseless and dangerous efforts to increase their strength by dominating Germany's manpower, industries, and geographic position. Each needed increased German production and each knew that a balance would have to be struck between Europe's need for a revival of German production and the danger of a strong Germany.

The agenda of the Moscow Conference included a wide range of complex and touchy problems. The American delegation went there without hope of reaching full agreement on a settlement for Central Europe, but they did expect to achieve three things: increased political and economic unity in Germany across the boundaries of the four occupation zones; agreement in principles upon a four-power treaty to keep Germany disarmed; and an Austrian treaty. They did not reach agreement on any of these things; indeed, they did not reach agreement on any item on the agenda.

No agreement was reached on political and economic unity for Germany because the Soviet Union wanted to rebuild Germany in a way that the United States, Great Britain, and France thought dangerous. At Potsdam, Stalin had agreed that peace would be best served if Germany did not have a high-powered central government and if Germany was weakened by removal of industrial plants as reparations, especially those plants that could be readily converted for war purposes. At Moscow the Russians insisted, as the price of political unity in Germany, upon a strong central government in Berlin and upon $10 billion in reparations in the form of German goods out of current German production. This supply of German goods to the Soviet Union would have required a vast strengthening rather than a weakening of the German industrial base. The Russians had found it difficult and unprofitable to remove industrial plants and establish them in the Soviet Union, had removed only half those to which they were entitled under the Potsdam agreement, and had switched to taking as reparations goods manufactured by Germans in the Soviet-occupied zone. They now wanted to turn not just the Eastern Zone but the whole of Germany into a workshop for the Soviet Union. The other three powers would have been obliged to continue indefinitely pouring hundreds of millions of dollars of goods into Western Germany to keep people alive while the Soviet Union siphoned off German production to the east. The Soviet leaders recognized the risk in restoring a strong industrial base in Germany and a strong central government (as against strong state, or Land, governments and a federal government of limited powers, proposed by the United States and Great Britain), but they were prepared to take that risk for reasons that Secretary

Marshall and John Foster Dulles pointed out in radio addresses upon their return home.

Secretary Marshall said that the United States and the United Kingdom opposed Russian plans on the grounds that a strong central government could so readily be converted to a regime similar to the Nazi and thence to the resurrection of German military power; and he referred in passing to "concealed desires" of the Russians in connection with a strong central government in Germany and to our concern over this possibility "for quite other reasons." Dulles frankly specified the concealed desires and the other reasons. He said the Russians wanted a strong central government in Berlin, located in the Soviet Zone, because they were confident they could penetrate and dominate its politics and its trade unions through local Communists and turn Germany into a workshop for the Soviet Union while avoiding the danger that German power would ever be turned against them. We, on the other hand, he said, did not want a political and economic centralization that would allow anyone who controlled Berlin automatically to control all Germany—we did not want a Germany that would be a projection into Western Europe of the totalitarian system.

The same Russian design for eventual control of Germany was revealed in connection with the United States proposal for a Four Power Pact that would guarantee for a long period—twenty-five to fifty years—the disarmament of Germany through the exercise of strict controls. This had been suggested a year earlier by Secretary Byrnes to reassure Europe that the United States would not, as after World War I, insist upon various peace-settlement terms and then withdraw from a position of responsibility for their enforcement. It meant a long-term United States commitment in Europe to insure the peace. The Soviet delegation professed to want such a treaty but loaded the treaty proposal with riders that would have committed the four powers to the kind of highly centralized and industrialized Germany that three had already rejected. The American delegation got the distinct impression that the Soviet Union did not want such a Four Power guarantee, that it did not want United States commitments in Europe and especially not in Germany, that it hoped the United States would quit Europe and go home, in which case it was confident it would be able to carry through its plan for dominating first Germany and then all Europe.

The Soviet plan for dominating Austria was blatant. The Soviet delegation insisted upon economic provisions in the treaty for Austria that would have made that country a puppet state, with a large part of its economy owned by the Soviet Union and operated free from the controls of Austrian law. The United States, the United Kingdom, and France of course refused to agree.

The first lesson of Moscow was therefore that the Russians would never agree to any settlement for Germany and Austria that would not give them an excellent chance to dominate those countries completely, from the inside.

The second lesson of Moscow was that to deal with the problem of Germany it was necessary to deal with the problem of Europe.

Given the fear and hatred unchained by the Nazi orgy in Europe, the endless horrors of war, and the suspicions that promptly divided the victorious Allies, it would have been a miracle if the problem of what to do with a defeated Germany had been approached after V-E Day with generosity and wisdom. No miracle occurred. When the Germans surrendered on May 9, 1945, not one of the Allied powers had a consistent and well-defined policy toward Germany. In each country, within each government, within each department of government, opinion on what to do about Germany was sharply divided. Revenge and determination to make Germany forever incapable of aggression, at first dominant, yielded progressively to a more moderate approach. The Potsdam agreement to administer the several occupied zones of Germany as a single economic unit pending a final settlement seemed to be a sensible and tolerant decision. The Level of Industry Agreement of March 6, 1946, recognized that Germany should retain, after reparations, sufficient resources to maintain living standards not above the European standard without external aid, but was nevertheless based upon the premise that the economic role of Germany in Europe should be greatly decreased and that there should be a redistribution of industrial power in Europe through relocation of German plants in neighboring countries. No provisional agreement for Germany would work, however, because the country was divided into four compartments, and the Russians and the French would not co-operate in carrying out the Potsdam agreement to administer Germany as a single economic unit. The result in Germany was progressive economic decay. Food and fuel rations were below the level required for life and health, other consumers' goods were practically non-existent, and inflation was mounting. Defeated, wrecked, without hope or incentive, the Germans were sinking into an apathetic, sub-human morass.

Although in their happy relaxation into normalcy Americans generally were disinterested in Germany after the war and were satisfied that the Germans had been rendered harmless and were paying for their crimes, American policy, sparked by American administrators who had a burning problem on their hands, began to recognize in 1946 that economic stagnation in Germany was inhuman and was retarding European recovery. Renewed efforts were made to get the Russians to agree to the economic unification of Germany. When these ended in failure, Secretary Byrnes, on July 11, 1946, offered to join the American Zone of Germany with any other zone, an offer accepted in principle only by the British. The British and American Zones were informally merged economically in the fall of 1946, formally on January 1, 1947, but no immediate improvement in the condition of the German people resulted. By the end of 1946 it began to be apparent that concentration upon the unattainable Potsdam goal of economic unity for Germany was blocking all other approaches to the problem.

Such was the situation in the early months of 1947 when economic recovery throughout Western Europe suddenly stalled and went into a tailspin, coinciding with the necessity for facing up to the problem of Germany at the Moscow Conference. And it was also at this time that American policy was unleashed, invigorated, and turned to positive, constructive ideas by the Truman Doctrine. In this changed climate of circumstances new ideas on Germany, or at least dormant ideas, began to grow. The focus of attention became the wider needs of Europe rather than the needs of Germany or fears concerning German revival: Germany was the economic heart of Europe; German resources and manpower were necessary to Europe; German production would have to be revived in order to serve Europe, but in such a way as to prevent German industrial power from being used as a weapon against Europe.

John Foster Dulles had been one of the first in the United States to emphasize publicly the need for a new approach to the problem of Germany. In a speech approved in advance by Senator Vandenberg and Governor Thomas E. Dewey of New York (as head of the Republican party) and delivered before the National Publishers' Association on January 17, 1947, Dulles said that the reason for economic unification of Germany was also a reason for the unification of Europe—a Europe divided into small compartments could not be healthy. All of Europe's potentialities, he continued, needed to be used, and European markets should be big enough to justify modern methods of cheap production for mass consumption. From the basin of the Rhine—the economic heart of Europe—ought to flow vitality not only for Germany but for Germany's western neighbors. This could make all Europe prosperous. The industrial potential of the Rhine basin ought therefore to be integrated into Western Europe. This could be brought about if Europe were reconstructed along federal lines, with states sharing authority over economic resources just as in the United States several states shared in the Tennessee Valley Authority. Thus could the industrial potential of Western Germany be used in the interest of the economic life of Western Europe without making the Germans the masters of Europe. The United States, Dulles concluded, should take the leadership in bringing about such a development.

Dulles was not an ordinary citizen but a Republican spokesman on foreign affairs, and his speech was widely quoted. A few weeks later Secretary Marshall invited him to accompany him to the Moscow Conference as adviser.

At Moscow, the desperate and immediate needs of Western Europe for food and fuel crowded in relentlessly upon the problem of Germany. As Secretary Marshall expressed it afterward in his radio report to the nation:

> The German negotiations involved not only the security of Europe and the world, but the prosperity of all Europe. . . . We were faced with immediate issues which vitally concerned the impoverished and suffering people of Europe who are crying for help, for coal, for food, and for most of the necessities of life, and the majority of whom are bitterly disposed toward the Germany that brought about this disastrous situation.

None of the thorny issues—reparations, plant removal, control of the Ruhr, economic unity, level of German industry, the powers of a central German government—was resolved at the conference, but the very deepening of deadlock in a setting of European desperation forced the beginning of fresh thinking. This was particularly true within the American delegation. Dulles gave quite a clear indication of this in his radio address on the conference. "We did not come home empty-handed because at Moscow we worked out policies which can be of tremendous value for the future." And as a suggestion of the general nature of those policies he said:

> As we studied the problem of Germany in its European setting, we became more and more convinced that there is no economic solution along purely national lines. Increased economic unity is absolutely essential to the well-being of Europe. . . .

There is no question that during the course of the Moscow Conference, Secretary Marshall became deeply impressed with the fact that Germany was only one facet, even though a central one, of the more complex problem of what to do to get Europe organized and functioning in such a way as to relieve the suffering of its people. His concern for this larger problem showed through in every statement made at the conference and in nearly every paragraph of the public report he made upon his return home.

The third lesson of Moscow was that the Russians were dragging their feet on a German settlement because they had acquired a vested interest in the devastating sickness of Western Europe: this was useful to them as pressure on the Western powers to force compliance with Russian terms on Germany, and in any case, if it was aggravated, it would facilitate Communist subversion and domination in France and Italy and perhaps other countries.

On April 15, 1947, nine days before the end of the conference, Secretary Marshall had a long talk with Generalissimo Stalin. He was accompanied by Ambassador Walter Bedell Smith and Charles E. ("Chip") Bohlen; Stalin by Foreign Minister Molotov and the interpreter Pavlov. The talk was frank but good-mannered. Marshall opened by stating that it was evident that the wartime sympathy of the American people for the people of the Soviet Union had cooled and proceeded to give the reasons. He mentioned a number of things, including the Soviet refusal to allow the economic unification of Germany and the Soviet position on several other issues before the conference. The conference had reached an impasse that very afternoon, Marshall continued, on the treaty for the demilitarization of Germany, and he had come to the conclusion, and would so report to the President, that the Soviet Union did not want such a treaty.

Leaving conference issues aside, Secretary Marshall observed that the United States recognized the right of any country to have the kind of political and economic system it wanted, and that one kind existed in the United States and a different kind in the Soviet Union. The United States, he volunteered, was determined to do what it could to assist those countries suffering from economic deterioration, which, if left unchecked, might lead to economic collapse and subsequent elimination of any chance of democratic survival. Our intention, he continued, was to help insofar as we could to restore the economy of such countries. We had, however, no intention of dominating or trying to dominate any country in the world. He was speaking frankly, he said, in the hope that if suspicions were cleared away it would be a good beginning toward restoring understanding between the United States and the Soviet Union.

In reply, Stalin said he did not think the situation was so tragic. He said he was more optimistic than Marshall. After all, these were only first skirmishes and brushes of reconnaissance forces on these questions. Differences had occurred before on other questions, and as a rule when people had exhausted themselves in dispute they then recognized the necessity for compromise. It was possible, thought Stalin, that the conference would achieve no great success, but no one should become desperate. Compromises were possible on all the leading questions, including demilitarization, the political structure of Germany, reparations, and economic unity. It was necessary only to have patience and not become depressed.

Incidentally, although the Truman Doctrine and United States aid to Greece and Turkey were topics of heated discussion throughout the world and of debate in the United States Congress, they were not mentioned by either Marshall or Stalin.

On the plane returning to Washington, the Secretary reviewed with the senior members of his delegation the lessons of Moscow. All agreed that the Soviet Union was stalling for time while Europe disintegrated and that the United States must initiate action to bring about European recovery. The problem was what to do and how to do it. In his radio address of April 28 Secretary Marshall mentioned Stalin's counsel of patience and added:

> But we cannot ignore the factor of time involved here. The recovery of Europe has been far slower than had been expected. Disintegrating forces are becoming evident. The patient is sinking while the doctors deliberate. So I believe that action cannot await compromise through exhaustion. New issues arise daily. Whatever action is possible to meet these pressing problems must be taken without delay.

The next day he issued a written instruction to George Kennan to consider with the Policy Planning Staff what could be done to aid European reconstruction, and to come up with ideas and suggestions. Kennan managed to have a few minutes conversation with the Secretary on his new assignment. It was so clear that the world was falling down around our ears, the Secretary said, that Congress would soon be demanding action, suggesting all kinds of bright and unworkable ideas in an effort to force the Department's hand. This would put the government on the defensive, and that was inadmissible. The Secretary said he therefore wanted to take the offensive himself. Within ten days or two weeks he wanted from Kennan a paper containing an analysis of the problem of European reconstruction and recommendations for action.

At the end of their brief talk Kennan asked the Secretary if there were any other instructions he wished to give him. The reply was: "Avoid trivia."

6

PUBLIC PRESSURES

DEMOCRATIC statesmanship, as contrasted with the mere conduct of public affairs, consists in gauging an objective situation accurately, in selecting the proper psychological moment to
expose it in public, in pointing toward solutions in policy terms
and concepts capable of evoking wide public interest and discussion, and finally in drawing from that discussion—to which the best
brains in the country have contributed—ideas as to how to carry
policy into execution and support for specific measures. Those who
criticize the government for not coming up promptly with a full-
blown plan to meet each problem simply do not know the limitations of democratic government or how government at its best
operates in a democracy. Statesmanship is a working alliance between leadership on the one hand and the bureaucracy and the
people on the other. Statesmen keep policy development moving
ahead and establish its level and direction by well-timed and well-
pitched public expositions and statements; they draw ideas and
support for its implementation from the bureaucracy and citizen
leaders. This does not of course mean that a leader may not have
or should not have specific implementing ideas of his own or that
he should not propose specific measures of his own. It means that
if he concentrates upon the unique responsibilities of his position
he stimulates the whole government and the whole people to come
forward with ideas and support, enriching and fortifying the national effort.

During the Fifteen Weeks the alliance between the nation's leaders and the people they served was in splendid working order. President Truman had laid down a broad policy. Aid to Greece and Turkey was in the congressional mill. But the problems of determining which other countries needed aid, the basis upon which aid should be extended, and especially of building up public support for such a program of aid, were colossal. At this point the partner in the alliance had gone into action. Congressmen, lesser public officials of all kinds, columnists, radio commentators, editorial writers, spokesmen for organized groups, professors, distinguished citizen leaders, ordinary citizens—had all joined in analyzing, weighing, debating, criticizing, justifying the new policy, suggesting extensions or modifications, proposing ways to carry it into effect beyond Greece and Turkey. By the middle of May the tide of public expectation was so high that it was no longer a question of whether the United States would aid Europe but when and how the initiative would be taken. There is no question whatever that Secretary Marshall's proposal at Harvard was to an important degree the consequence of public pressure built up and suggestions advanced, during the weeks following the announcement of the Truman Doctrine, in an interplay of ideas between the nation's leaders and the public. Before proceeding to consider the official evolution of the Marshall Plan, let us therefore take a look at some of the public influences that operated upon the policy-makers.

Of all the public allies of American statesmanship none compares in effectiveness with Walter Lippmann. He can be, and often is, irritating to policy-makers, and he can be, and often is, wrong, whether judged by what is practicable at the time or by later events. But on foreign policy he is more often right than wrong, and whether right or wrong he thinks ahead publicly in policy terms and concepts that are a steady challenge to official leadership. During the Fifteen Weeks he played a highly significant role in the progress of policy thinking. The day following the President's message to Congress, Lippmann expressed irritation that Secretary Marshall should be wrangling with Molotov in Moscow on secondary matters while

here in Washington the decisions [that have to be taken] call for
an estimate of how the total military and financial resources, that
can be made available, may most effectively be applied to meet
demands which arise from every quarter of the globe.

Never was it so necessary to budget our means and our commitments. Never was it so necessary to define our commitments by a
unified strategical conception as to where our available power,
prestige, money, and expertness, which are not unlimited, can be
invested with the best prospect of achieving the best that is judged
to be possible.

Also on March 13, Marquis Childs, appraising the President's
message, was concerned with the "larger picture." Western Europe
would probably need billions in aid. Childs thought we should
determine our capacity to help the world and then pro-rate the
demands that would be made upon us according to the urgency
of the needs. The *Washington Post* of March 13 looked upon aid
to Greece and Turkey as only a "starter"; the *New York Times*
made the same point. Quite generally, press and radio interpreted
the Truman Doctrine in relation to four things: the financial crisis
of Britain, with its world-wide implications; the showdown with
the Soviet Union then taking place in Moscow on the future of
Germany; the immediate distress of Europe; and the apparent desire and intention of the Soviet Union to take over the Continent.
The news magazines—*Time, Newsweek, U.S. News*—as well as
correspondents for leading newspapers, joined in building up great
expectations of United States foreign policy and acceptance of
responsibility for aiding the economic recovery of an ailing Europe.

On March 19 James Reston and Joseph Alsop foresaw vast
impending moves to carry the United States policy into effect. Lippmann on March 20 said there was no longer any doubt that the
United States would have to make a large outlay for reconstruction and peace. He proposed that we make the Soviet Union an
offer to invest a large sum as part of an over-all political settlement.
If the Soviet Union would agree to treat Europe, not just Germany,
as in economic unit, we would find it profitable to allocate a large
sum to a European economic union and make a favorable loan to
Russia in lieu of reparations. Senators Fulbright and Thomas

(Utah) and Representative Boggs (Louisiana) introduced into Congress on March 22 a resolution favoring the creation of a United States of Europe. On March 23 Herbert Hoover released a report on economic conditions in Germany and Austria, which he had surveyed at the request of President Truman, in which he concluded that

> There is only one path to recovery in Europe. That is production. The whole economy of Europe is interlinked with German economy through the exchange of raw materials and manufactured goods. The productivity of Europe cannot be restored without the restoration of Germany as a contributor to that productivity.

Hoover's report was widely quoted and commented upon; the conclusion generally drawn was that Europe's economy must be revived, with the whole of Germany included if the Russians would agree, with the Western zones included in any case.

These examples are selected from hundreds merely to suggest the scope, character, and intensity of the public discussion that followed the President's message, and to show how they conduced to further official action in implementation of a general policy.

On April 5 Lippmann produced what is surely one of the most consequential columns he has ever written, entitled "Cassandra Speaking." With exceptional gravity he told his readers that Europe was on the verge of economic collapse. None of the leading nations of Europe—Great Britain, France, Italy, and Germany—was recovering from the war or had any reasonable prospect of doing so with the means at its disposal. He suggested that he might sound sensational and exaggerated but that he was "saying only what responsible men say when they do not have to keep up appearances in public." Leaders did not dare admit the alarming condition because of the effects such admissions would have on morale. Lippmann then emphasized the desperate financial condition of Great Britain, which would probably have to withdraw shortly her occupying forces from Germany, leaving the United States isolated in Europe, face to face with the Russians, in the heart of a continent that dreaded more than anything the prospect of being used as an area of conflict between the United States and the USSR. He continued:

> The truth is that political and economic measures on a scale which no responsible statesman has yet ventured to hint at will be needed in the next year or so. To prevent the crisis which will otherwise engulf Europe and spread chaos throughout the world, *the measures will have to be very large—in Europe no less than an economic union, and over here no less than the equivalent to a revival of Lend-Lease.*[1] To deal with the crisis, if it is not prevented, the measures will have to be infinitely larger and much more dangerous.

Lippmann did not say anything that was new to many in the State Department. But he simultaneously informed the whole staff of the State Department, from the Acting Secretary on down, the entire government hierarchy, and the Congress, of his own estimate of the proportions of an adequate solution: peacetime Lend-Lease and economic union in Europe. More important, he so informed the readers of scores of newspapers throughout the country, including the nation's most influential citizens. The effects of such a statement, if it is apt, statesmanlike, well timed, and if it proceeds from one as respected as Walter Lippmann, are several: it makes top officials feel they are on the spot and challenges or encourages them to broader thinking and speedier and more effective action; it gives lesser officers arguments with which to convince their colleagues and a lever with which to prod their superiors on specific approaches; and it enlarges at once the realm of what men are inclined to regard as possible. Such were the effects of Lippmann's column of April 5. For example, when Acheson was considering what he should say to the Delta Council, that April 5 column specifically came up.

Public expectations continued to grow throughout April. *World Report* on April 15 carried a staff-written article entitled "U.S. Aid to Democracies Calls for Huge Investment Abroad— If program is carried to logical end, $21,000,000,000 would be committed in three years." *World Report* said it had reached its conclusions on

[1] Italics the author's.

the financial implications of the new United States policy "after checking with national and international experts." Though it was not clearly evident, the article was in fact a survey of foreign *needs* rather than *plans* to meet them—there were at that time no plans. *World Report* envisaged most of the aid in the form of loans and government investment, chiefly through international agencies. A few days later, on April 18, John J. McCloy, new president of the International Bank, dampened this kind of thinking by making it clear in a public address that contributions to the International Bank were merely for the purpose of providing security for private capital invested abroad: "We can't and we won't grant loans in order to accomplish political objectives. We can and we will refuse loans where the political uncertainties are so great as to make a loan economically unsound." The world had been waiting for some time for the International Bank to decide what role it would play in the snowballing financial crisis. Here it was. It put sharp limitations on the International Bank in meeting Europe's deficits, and it threw public expectation and government back with increasing force upon the idea of a large grant-in-aid program or a revival of Lend-Lease in one form or another.

Marshall and Dulles in their radio addresses of April 28 and 29 on the Moscow Conference caused a great stir by hinting that great things were in the offing. On May 1 Lippmann, taking these speeches as his point of departure, again made constructive and influential suggestions. As the Russians would not agree to a political settlement and an economic program which would allow the unification and recovery of *all* Europe, we would have to go ahead with Western Europe. Western Europe is a highly industrialized area, he said, which cannot in itself become self-supporting or solvent, but we would have to help make it so in order to induce or compel the Soviet Union to agree to a general European settlement. "For we have the resources to stimulate such a revival of Western Europe that the profit and advantage of collaborating with it will be manifest, and even compelling, in Prague, Warsaw, and Moscow."

He went on to say that this could not be done through private investment or government loans, but would have to be done by reviving in one form or another what was known in wartime as Lend-Lease. He then proceeded to suggest an essential idea of what became the Marshall Plan:

> Now as we face up to the realities of the burden, our prime consideration must necessarily be, not how to get the money back, but how to make that money promote peace and prosperity. It will not do that, I believe, if we allocate our contributions to each European government separately. That will merely put them all on the dole, whereas what is needed is a reorganization of the bankrupt economy of Europe, and then, to make the reorganization succeed, a large contribution from America of working capital.
>
> So after we have discussed the separate needs of Britain, France, Italy, and the rest, we should suggest to them that they meet together, agree on a general European program of production and exchange, of imports and exports to the outer world, and that they arrive at an estimate of the consolidated deficit for as much of Europe as can agree to a common plan. Such a consolidated deficit will be smaller than the sum of the separate national deficits. Moreover, from our point of view it would be a refreshing innovation to make our contribution not to many separate governments but to Europe—if not to all of it at first, then at least to a very large part of it. In some such way as this the contribution which we must inevitably make would serve not merely to relieve suffering but as a premium and inducement to the unification of Europe.

There are seldom any new ideas in statecraft, and Lippmann's general idea certainly was no more than fractionally original. The idea of European unity was aged, efforts to promote it legion, and European agitation in favor of it currently prodigious. Moreover there were many in the State Department, chiefly younger men of modest rank, who fervently believed that European union was the only solution to the security and prosperity of the world and persistently urged the use of American diplomacy and economic power to bring it about. Two of these,[2] young economists, members of the Department's Foreign Aid Committee, had already influenced the committee to think in terms of aid to Europe as a whole administered in such a way as to bring about economic unification, and were at that moment at work on further studies that Kennan was

[2] H. Van B. Cleveland and Ben T. Moore.

to use in carrying out the assignment given him by Secretary Marshall. But Lippmann, timing his suggestion for the psychological movement following the Moscow Conference, had a powerful impact upon policy thinking. His proposal that the European countries be asked to get together and agree upon a common recovery program and present us with a consolidated deficit was, so far as this writer can discover, original. One immediate result of his suggestion was that State Department advocates of European union began to be listened to with greater attention, and their memoranda read, by their superiors. Kennan recalls that during this period Lippmann made a very significant contribution to his thinking.

Acheson's Delta Council speech of May 8 moved both official and public discussion of foreign aid overnight to higher ground. After two months of speculating upon the intent of the Truman Doctrine, columnists, commentators, and editorial writers, who were getting low on grist, fell upon the Acheson pronouncement with avidity. And while not certain whether he was interpreting the Truman Doctrine, or extending it, or superseding it, they expressed relief and satisfaction that the administration at last appeared to be moving toward filling in the breaches in Europe's (and our own) dikes against chaos. After the Delta Council speech, the economic reconstruction of Europe was in the forefront of the thinking of all concerned with foreign affairs. The government having accepted responsibility for aiding European reconstruction, attention became centered upon how, in what spirit, for what ends it would be administered, and how much it would cost. Increasing demands were made for an over-all statement on foreign economic requirements, for a plan, accompanied by a balance-sheet.

One of the curious reactions to the Delta Council speech was that it occasioned so many invidious comparisons with the Truman Doctrine. Many commentators looked upon the Acheson pronouncement as a logical interpretation or extension or application of the Truman Doctrine; but perhaps an equal number composed of both those had supported aid to Greece and Turkey and those who had opposed it considered it a distinct "improvement." It was considered so because it "abandoned" the "emotional" rhetoric of the Truman Doctrine, descended from the "ideological" plateau where it was offering battle, omitted mention of military aid, and got down to the humanitarian and common-sense region of men's needs and the question of how much it would cost to satisfy them—for this was the only effective way to fight communism.[3] It was not surprising to the State Department, in view of the word that had been passed out and had apparently spread far and wide, that most commentators said that Acheson's speech was a conscious effort to reinterpret the Truman Doctrine in order to emphasize its economic intent and bring public discussion back from military and ideological preoccupations to the problem of economic reconstruction. But it was surprising to find that such a narrow conception of the Truman Doctrine existed even among many of its supporters, and that so many, with obvious relief, expressed dissatisfaction with it when what appeared to be a purely humanitarian and economic alternative was offered. The fact is that, had there been no Truman Doctrine, there probably would have been no Marshall Plan. As President Truman said years ago, "They are two halves of the same walnut."

While public debate churned about Acheson's foreign-aid forecast of $5 billion a year, Henry A. Wallace and Harold E. Stassen enlivened public discussion with proposals that made Acheson seem like a miser. During the middle weeks of May, Wallace went barnstorming about the country, speaking mostly at universities, violently denouncing the Truman Doctrine but urging that the United States finance a five-year-world-rehabilitation program costing $10 billion a year, at least half of which would be spent in the USSR and Eastern Europe. Stassen, speaking in Iowa on May 21,

[3] Among those taking this line were Walter Lippmann, May 10; Winston Burdette (CBS), May 9; Martin Agronsky (ABC), May 9; Raymond Swing (ABC), May 11; Joseph C. Harsch (CBS), May 11; Jennings Perry (*PM*), May 13; Thomas Stokes (*Washington News*), May 16. Among those who considered the Acheson speech an extension of the Truman Doctrine were James Reston, May 9; Marquis Childs, May 13; *New York Herald Tribune,* May 10; Elmer Davis, May 9; Stewart Alsop, May 16; Arthur Krock, May 19; *New York Times,* May 25; *Washington Post,* October 6. Dozens of leading newspapers, commentators, and magazines, commenting on Acheson's speech, launched into the grave problem of European reconstruction and United States responsibility for aid without mentioning the Truman Doctrine.

attracted national attention with a proposal that the United States adopt a "Production for Peace" program which would involve the setting aside of 10 per cent of our production each year for ten years to build world-wide peace, plenty, and freedom. Production was then running at about $210 billion a year. According to Stassen, the United States would look for returns not in money payments, but partly in raw materials and partly in guarantees of liberal trade policies, abolition of censorship, the ending of nationalization of industry, and other political and economic objectives. The United States should administer and control the program, Stassen thought. No munitions would be provided. *The program should not be directed against anyone,* but its emphasis should be positive and affirmative, its objectives the progress of all mankind and our own peace and prosperity. The *St. Paul Pioneer Press* said, "The Stassen Doctrine is the Truman Doctrine without any specific anti-Russian aims and the Wallace doctrine without appeasement." The *Des Moines Register* said the Stassen program was the only one that offered any real hope. Arthur Krock, Dorothy Thompson, Tom Stokes, and Max Lerner—just to cover the political spectrum—agreed that its general approach was sensible. The *New York Herald Tribune* commented that it was easy to tear the proposal to ribbons but it wasn't easy to outline any viable alternative. Stassen might seem visionary, it continued, but "the real visionaries . . . are those who will blindly attack him without bringing up any other answer to the desperately practical human and economic issues to which he points and of which all responsible leaders are growing more and more acutely aware."

To those interested in how foreign policy is made, it may be pointed out here that no atmosphere is more conducive to official action than that created when public figures on the Right and on the Left happen to agree, even though for different reasons, that a daring, even "visionary" course of action should be taken. The effect upon government officials is almost tangible: it raises their sights; it opens the psychological and political doors to action and invites them to pass through, bearing official proposals which, although more imaginative and effective than would otherwise have been the case, are nevertheless modest and conservative compared with those of their more daring public allies.

It was of course fortuitous that precisely at the peak of official and public concern in the United States over how to aid Europe, Winston Churchill on May 14, speaking in London's Albert Hall, made an impassioned speech in favor of a united Europe. With incomparable eloquence Churchill, then head of His Majesty's Loyal Opposition, described Europe's broken and ravished condition and marshaled facts to show that only in unity could Europe achieve security from aggression, economic well-being, and protection of a common culture. He would include in a united Europe any country whose territory lies in Europe "and which assures to its people those fundamental human rights and liberties of which our democratic civilization has been created." Pending the building up of enough popular support in Europe to bring about a federation of Europe, he made this suggestion:

> We ask, however, that in the meantime His Majesty's Government, together with other governments, should approach the various pressing continental problems from a European rather than from a restricted national angle. In the discussions on the German and Austrian peace settlements, and indeed throughout the whole diplomatic field, the ultimate ideal should be held in view. Every new arrangement that is made should be designed in such manner as to be capable of later being fitted into the pattern of a united Europe.

Churchill's speech received widespread attention in the United States, especially in the State Department, at the critical moment when minds were being made up on how to aid Europe. Entering the stream of discussion, his views colored the waters perceptibly.

Sailing along in a brisk May breeze toward an expected early announcement of a gigantic program of aid to Europe, the public allies of statesmanship in the United States ran into a squall and a few days later got temporarily stuck on a sandbar. On May 18 the *New York Times* published prominently a story from Washington to the effect that Senator Vandenberg had indicated that the passage of the $350-million post-UNRRA relief bill, which had been in the works for months, might "complete the foreign relief program in the present session." The Senator expected no new relief requests from the administration. Two days later Secretary Marshall, when asked at a press conference whether he expected that the United States would have to launch some multi-billion-dollar peacetime Lend-Lease program, replied that he did not foresee "at the present time" the need for further appropriations of the kind that had just been made (he was referring to aid to Greece and Turkey and the post-UNRRA relief measure). He added that he was not prepared to make a statement on what might happen in the future, but that the newly organized Policy Planning Staff was studying the whole situation, and he had not as yet received their report.

Something clearly had happened, and this is the story. Senator Vandenberg had been upset by Acheson's Delta Council speech, with its costly implications. And a few days after the speech he had read that Senator Alben W. Barkley, Minority Floor Leader, had told the Society for the Advancement of Science in Washington that the United States would have to provide "millions, even billions" for European reconstruction. Alarmed, Senator Vandenberg telephoned both Acheson and Marshall, and a meeting of the three took place at Blair House. The Senator was excited: Acheson had publicly said we were going to entertain enormous requests for foreign aid! And then Barkley had sounded off! What was going on? Things were getting out of hand! Was he going to be presented late in the session with a sheaf of administration requests for huge foreign-aid appropriations with the same pressure and suddenness attending the request for aid to Greece and Turkey? Secretary Marshall assured him that he had no intention of presenting any further legislative requests at that session and went on to explain why sooner or later we were going to have to undertake a very large program of foreign aid. Problems were pressing, and we had to face up to them. The whole question of foreign aid was being studied, and when presented to Congress it would be in the form of a coordinated program. As the Secretary spoke, Senator Vandenberg cooled off, and then he became interested. Concord reigned, and the parting was cordial. As usual, the Senator's initial alarm over a new idea yielded to a reasoned presentation of the facts. Within a few months he was with great eloquence and intense conviction to lead a fight in the Senate for the Marshall Plan which probably ranks as the greatest and most enduring monument of his career.

The Vandenberg and Marshall statements caused considerable momentary bewilderment, both within the government and outside. It is nevertheless notable that in spite of the sudden cutting down of early expectations there was very little public criticism of the decision. Public discussion, only slightly dampened and reduced in volume, continued as before.

One reason for this may be that after about May 20 Acheson, Kennan, and Bohlen began to talk more freely to certain reporters covering the State Department, keeping them informed on the trends of thinking in the Department and possible solutions being discussed. By that time the Policy Planning Staff, getting along with its work, had reached tentative conclusions, and the subject was discussed daily and at length at Acheson's morning staff conferences. The trend of these discussions was reported with accuracy by James Reston in the *New York Times* on May 25. Official Washington, he said, was seriously considering a different approach to the problem of European reconstruction:

> The old approach was to deal with the shattered economies of the several nations one at a time, lending now to Britain, then to France, then to Italy, etc. The new approach is based on the growing conviction that the problems of all these countries are interrelated and that Europe cannot recover by shoring up, one at at time, the various national economies.
>
> What is under urgent and thoughtful consideration is a proposal to call on the nations of Europe to suggest a more coordinated continental economy as a preliminary to the United States meeting them with a large-scale program of "continental aid."

Reston proceeded to give the arguments for a "Continental Plan." At this stage the "plan" was merely a trend of thinking that had as yet received no official sanction. Its publication, and the wide public notice it received, doubtless had some effect upon its official acceptance, for officials are frequently influenced by seeing in print, logically and concisely set forth, information and ideas of which they themselves are the source.

A "different approach" to the problem of European reconstruction was indeed shaping up. It was considered in Secretary Marshall's office on May 27 and May 28, and on May 29 the Secretary decided to make an early public statement on it. At this point, therefore, we may appropriately consider what was happening in the State Department during the month of May 1947.

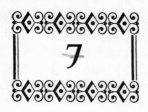

THE MARSHALL PLAN

THAT the administration would propose a program of aid to
Europe had by early May become a virtual certainty. Truman
and Acheson had agreed upon it in principle, knew its general
proportions, and had launched the idea publicly through the Delta
Council speech. Secretary Marshall had agreed with his delegation
in Moscow that some such program was necessary and upon his
return had instructed Kennan and his Policy Planning Staff to consider the problem and come up with recommendations. Vocal public
opinion in the United States was not only favorable to action but
clamorous. The tragedy of government is usually that farseeing
leaders in positions of power find themselves thwarted in their
desires and efforts to achieve new solutions by the pull of established institutions and rigid patterns of public thinking. This was
not so during the Fifteen Weeks.

The difficulty that confronted the State Department in May was
surely unique in statecraft. It was not whether the United States
should aid Europe, or even how much aid should be proposed,
but how to make the transfer of billions of dollars to countries that
had not asked for them, and would not ask for them. Normally
when foreign governments ask for aid an "action paper" comes
into being and goes through the usual channels to established
institutions, or in special cases the administration makes a specific
request of Congress. In this instance there were no "action papers,"

and there would be none. The British had the year before been granted $3.75 billion, a loan extended explicitly to end all further requests for aid. The French had just been granted loans by the World Bank and the Export-Import Bank that by normal standards were extremely large, placing further requests beyond the boundaries of dignity. The Italians had since their defeat existed on American largesse, and they needed more but were not in condition to ask for loans or to do more than make general suggestions regarding grants. The Germans, under occupation, were supported by the Allied powers with not even the possibility of asking for more than they were getting. The sums needed by most of the countries of Europe were beyond the bounds of existing institutions to contemplate. How, then, would action be initiated? And what should extraordinary United States expenditures seek to accomplish beyond filling immediate needs? These problems were almost as difficult of solution as the usually familiar hostility of Congress and the indifference of public opinion.

When Secretary Marshall on April 29 had put Kennan to work with his Policy Planning Staff and asked for recommendations within two weeks, the staff did not exist and Kennan had not yet moved over to the State Department from the War College, where he had been for nearly a year. Before leaving for Moscow, Marshall, as we know, had decided to establish such a staff and had asked Kennan to head it when his existing assignment ended in May. About the middle of April, however, the Secretary began to send back messages from Moscow to the Department making it clear he wanted the staff established without delay. Thereafter, spending a few hours each day at the Department, Kennan began to tackle such mundane matters as organization, budget, office space, and to make some approaches on staff. By the time he received his massive assignment from Marshall, Carlton Savage was working full time as executive secretary of the staff, Joseph E. Johnson had been committed to join it but had not yet done so, and that was all there was to the Policy Planning Staff, which, in fact, was not formally established until May 2. Kennan, Johnson, and Savage held their first meeting on May 5, and between this date and the production of the staff's highly consequential memorandum of May 23, the staff met only three times; a new member, Jacques Reinstein, was present at the last two meetings.

According to the State Department summary of Secretary Marshall's press conference on May 20, the Secretary, when asked whether he anticipated a multi-billion-dollar peacetime Lend-Lease program, had explained that "the Department was studying the whole situation, with all its elaborations, and that the newly organized planning committee was working on it with the help of the subsidiary agencies and the War Department so that it would have an over-all view of the situation." To say the least, this was an inflated description of what was in fact happening, and reporters not unnaturally conveyed the impression, which has since become part of the myth of the origins of the Marshall Plan, of an elaborate staff directing wide departmental and interdepartmental studies. This was not the case. In a new job with an incipient staff and a two-week deadline (he exceeded it by a week), Kennan did the only thing he could do: he confined himself to figuring out an approach to a plan for a plan, using studies of the European situation for the most part already in existence, chiefly those prepared by the Special Committee, and drawing ideas from everybody—in the State Department, elsewhere in the government, and from the public— who had any to offer. The number of people, both in and out of the government, who habitually think in concrete, practical, forward policy terms is limited. Moreover by May 1 their minds were more or less running in parallel or converging currents. Kennan set as his task to discover these currents, to check his own ideas with them, and to determine, with his staff, what seemed to be the most practicable and promising approach to the problem of European reconstruction.

The most vigorous idea currents on the subject were at that time those emanating from the economic offices of the State Department, presided over by Undersecretary Clayton. The economic staff had been built to great strength and high quality during the early favor of Cordell Hull, had been expanded during the war, and now, directed by a man regarded as the nation's foremost economic statesman, included some of the best policy and idea men in the Department. Trained as economists, they nevertheless thought in terms of security, morale, prestige, of these and all the other incentives—in addition to economic wants—that make men and governments tick. Many of them were highly articulate. Partly as a consequence of their training and partly because of the nature of the problems they were called upon to deal with, they considered barriers as the enemy of peace and prosperity—national barriers, local barriers, regional barriers, barriers to trade, to production, to the movement of persons and skills, to the convertibility of money. Many of these men had long felt that prewar national economic patterns should not be re-established on the continent of Europe, and they had been greatly preoccupied in 1946 and early 1947 in getting the United Nations Economic Commission for Europe established as an agency that would attempt to bring about a reconstruction of Europe's transport, power facilities, and production and trading patterns generally, especially for coal, steel, food, and other basic commodities, along European rather than national lines.

All this was of course a basic article of faith with Clayton, who spent most of April and May in Europe, negotiating for lower tariffs and a general pattern of liberal trading practices, attending the initial session of the Economic Commission for Europe, traveling about getting first-hand reports from leading economic and financial officials on Europe's calamitous condition, and reporting his views back to the State Department. He believed that nothing less than full economic federation of Europe and massive United States aid in its support would save the situation, and he freely said so during this period.

Partly because of the logic and persuasion of several of Clayton's younger officers, the reports of the Foreign Aid Committee during the month of April had been impregnated with the idea that aid to individual countries of Europe would be wasteful and would not necessarily bring lasting recovery unless administered so as to bring about a coordinated reconstruction program and a revival of intra-European trade. When the Moscow Conference ended in

failure and official thoughts turned to plans for the reconstruction
of Europe as a whole, three of these men [1] immediately set about
casting their ideas into the new mold. On May 9 they completed
and sent to Kennan an annotated outline of a paper on a United
States program for Europe. The study itself was not completed and
mimeographed until a few days after Secretary Marshall's speech
at Harvard, but the outline was elaborate and parts of the paper
based upon it were available during May.

These men reasoned that the primary objective of United States
policy toward Europe should be to bring about conditions in
Europe and in our relations with the USSR which would cause
Soviet leaders to decide that their interests were better served by
negotiating a political and economic settlement and collaborating
with the United States on European matters rather than continuing a policy of unilateral expansion—in other words, we should
press Soviet leaders to trade a policy of collaboration with regard
to Europe as a whole for immediate material benefits to the Soviet
Union and its satellites. A second objective should be to strengthen
Western Europe and increase its Western orientation under our
leadership so that we would be better able to resist in the event
the Soviet Union should decline to collaborate. It was uncertain
whether we could attain our primary objective, this being a matter
of Soviet choice, or whether we would have to concentrate on our
secondary objective. There were certain things that could be done
to lead simultaneously toward both without prejudicing attainment
of either. These were to bring about as quickly as possible a recovery of mass living standards in non-Communist Europe, and to
help provide the leaderless and goalless center groups in Europe,
especially in France, Italy, and Germany, which were drifting
towards extremism on the Right and on the Left, with ideological
goals and effective leadership both locally and from the United
States. What was called for, therefore, was a coordinated European
recovery program assisted and primed by the United States, a
program designed to solve immediate and pressing problems but
directed at the same time toward a strong and economically in-

[1] H. Van B. Cleveland, Ben T. Moore, Charles Kindleberger.

tegrated Europe in such a way as to fill an ideological vacuum and build mass support for center and left-of-center leadership. The initial approach should be Europe-wide in order to avoid undesirable psychological repercussions in Western Europe and to attract, if possible, the Soviet Union and the satellites. The Economic Commission for Europe was suggested as the most appropriate agency for handling such a program.

It is of course futile to attempt to trace precisely the source or destination of ideas, and it is not intended to suggest here that the ideas in this study were either wholly original or that they had a causal relationship with the proposal made by Secretary Marshall at Harvard on June 5. The least that can be said, however, is that the three men concerned articulated, added significantly to, and gathered converts for an idea pattern that developed during the month of May in the State Department—a pattern of which the writer of this book was aware at the time—and that, insofar as may be discovered, captured and reflected accurately at least part of the thinking that underlay the Marshall proposal.

There is further evidence of the pattern of Department thinking during the month of May. Secretary Marshall had some time earlier accepted, rather tentatively, an invitation to speak at the University of Wisconsin on May 24 and receive a degree, and he now wanted a speech drafted for him. Joseph Jones received the assignment. The Secretary had congratulated Acheson upon the Delta Council speech and told him that in his forthcoming address he wanted "to hit the same line." This was passed on to Jones, who, for several reasons, took the liberty of construing this meager instruction as meaning "to develop further" the Acheson line. The European situation, the climate of public and official discussion, and public expectations of leadership had all rushed ahead rapidly in the month since the Acheson speech had been planned, and especially in the four days since Acheson had spoken. Moreover they would continue to move in the next twelve days. It seemed clear that the Secretary should underwrite the aid commitment made by Acheson, but go beyond that to suggest that the aim of our policy was to help build a strong, independent, united Europe, to urge Europe to adopt that goal as its own, and to stimulate Europeans to seek our aid for its attainment.

Before Jones finished drafting the speech he was told that the Secretary had decided not to attend the University of Wisconsin commencement but that he should finish the speech and send it forward, as the Secretary would probably be making other speeches in June. On May 20 Jones sent a completed draft to Acheson with a covering memorandum, which read in part:

> In writing this draft, I have again worked closely with the economic offices and I believe this represents the line they think should be projected now. . . .
>
> Except for the first four pages which sound warnings similar to those of your speech in Mississippi, this speech is written primarily with a view to its effect abroad. The indications of suspicion and skepticism with which foreign peoples are beginning to view American aid are alarming and it would seem to be of first importance to spell out our design for reconstruction and to give a positive concept about which people of Europe especially can rally and upon which they can pin their hopes. The political and economic policy of the Department has led up to an expression of this sort, and now seems the psychological time to launch it. We have a great deal to gain by convincing the world that we have something positive and attractive to offer, and not just anti-communism.

In the draft speech itself the reasons were given why the United States would have to accept responsibility for extraordinary aid for European reconstruction. Beyond that, an effort was made in the draft to answer the question: "What is our design for reconstruction?" The most explicit answer was:

> It is one of the primary aims of the policy of the United States to promote the growth of a free, prosperous, economically integrated, and politically cooperative Europe that shall play an independent and stabilizing role in world affairs. And it is the aim of the reconstruction aid of the United States to support that policy.

Would Europe be rebuilt in its prewar economic compartments or along modern, cooperative lines, deriving strength from unity? A pitch was made to the Economic Commission for Europe to draw up plans along continental rather than national lines, pledging our aid for their realization:

> The Economic Commission for Europe can do all these things. What it actually does depends upon the initiative which the countries of Europe are willing to take and the imaginative leadership they are able to demonstrate. The United States and other non-European powers, for their part, can only promise financial and other support for cooperative European ventures and pledge their general economic and political policy in support of the growth of European unity. This we do now promise and pledge.

The chief significance of this draft speech, it must be emphasized, is that it proves that by the middle of May, even outside top-level policy discussions and apart from the work of the Policy Planning Staff, there was an idea current in the Department so strong it could be detected by a ghost. The draft speech was considered at Acheson's staff conference on May 21, following which he handed it to the Secretary, with the suggestion that the latter might want to consider making a speech along those lines on an early occasion.

By May 19 Kennan was drafting his report to the Secretary, and the subject of aid to Europe was a matter of earnest daily discussion between the Secretary and Acheson and in Acheson's top staff conferences. On that date Clayton returned to Washington from six weeks in Europe. He came back primarily to urge the President to veto a congressional bill that would have raised the tariff on wool (the President vetoed it). But what weighed most heavily on his mind was the alarming condition of Europe, and on the plane he had written a four-page memorandum on the subject. Suffering from a heavy cold, occupied in his first days back with the urgent wool matter, and then obliged to take to his bed on May 23, Clayton appears not to have circulated his memorandum outside his immediate office, or in his talks to have launched into the problem of European reconstruction, until his return to the Department on May 27. At that time he sent his memorandum to Acheson with a note saying he would like to discuss it with the Secretary. Acheson promptly sent the memorandum into the Secretary and arranged a meeting for that day. This memorandum and the conversations that ensued had a powerful impact both upon the content of Secretary Marshall's Harvard speech and probably upon his decision to make it.

In terse, economic language, Clayton wrote that we had grossly underestimated the destruction of Europe's economy by the war. We had understood the physical destruction but not the effects on production of economic dislocation, nationalization of industries, drastic land reform, broken commercial ties, and disappearance of private commercial firms through death, loss of capital, etc. The condition of Europe was steadily deteriorating. Political crisis reflected the grave economic distress. Millions in the cities were starving. The modern system of division of labor had almost broken down: French grain acreage was 20 to 25 per cent under prewar, collection of production was unsatisfactory, and grain was being fed to cattle. More consumers' goods and restored confidence in the currency were absolutely essential if the peasant was again to supply food in normal quantities to the cities.

The annual balance-of-payments deficit of the United Kingdom, France, Italy, and Germany, Clayton went on, totaled $5 billion, and this represented an absolute minimum standard of living; if it were lowered there would be revolution. England and France could hold out until the end of the year, Italy not as long as that. The principal deficit items were coal, bread grains, and shipping. Without further prompt and substantial aid from the United States, economic, social, and political disintegration would overwhelm Europe, with awful implications for the future peace and security of the world and immediate, disastrous effects upon our domestic economy. *These things must not happen,* Clayton emphasized.

How could they be avoided? Clayton thought it was not necessary to appoint a commission to study and report on our national assets and liabilities in order to determine our ability to assist Europe. The facts were well known, and our resources and productive capacity were ample. The problem was to organize our fiscal policy and our consumption so that sufficient surpluses could be made available out of our enormous production and paid for by taxation rather than by adding to the national debt. The problem could be met only if the administration should take the people into its confidence and tell them all the facts. The President and the Secretary of State should make a strong spiritual appeal to the American people to sacrifice a little to save Europe from starvation and chaos (*not* from the Russians), and at the same time preserve for themselves and their children the "glorious heritage of a free America."

Finally, Clayton was convinced that Europe would have to have from us, as a grant, $6 or $7 billion in goods for at least three years, in the form of coal, food, cotton, tobacco, shipping services, and the like. The three-year grant should be based upon a European plan which the European nations, headed by the United Kingdom, France, and Italy, should work out. Such a plan should be based on a European economic federation, for Europe could not recover from the war and again become independent if her economy continued to be divided into small, watertight compartments.

Although Clayton's memorandum was a strong one it apparently was not so compelling as the graphic oral description of Europe's breakdown which he gave Marshall and Acheson, and later other Department officers. Acheson has a vivid recollection of the intenseness and detail with which Clayton described the peasant who would not produce more than he and his family and his cattle could eat because with the money he might get from selling his surplus produce in the market he could not buy buttons or thread or cloth or farm tools; the manufacturer of buttons and thread and cloth who could not produce for want of materials and fuel and because workers, being unable to satisfy their wants with money, were refusing to work; the middleman, and everyone else for that matter, who was hoarding supplies because of mounting inflation. Not only Acheson but others in the Department testify to the vividness and impressiveness of Clayton's recitals during those days, to the sense of urgency he imparted for taking immediate action. In talking with the Secretary, he urged, as he had in his memorandum, that the Secretary and the President take the case for aid to the people and initiate a program. His was probably one of the most direct and important influences in the "triggering" of the Secretary's speech at Harvard.

It was either later the same day, May 27, or the following morning that the Secretary called a meeting in his office to consider with Kennan the Policy Planning Staff's memorandum on the problem of reconstruction in Europe. Kennan had completed it on May 23 and sent it to the Secretary with copies to Acheson, Clayton, Benjamin V. Cohen, Counselor of the Department, and Charles Bohlen, Special Assistant to the Secretary. Considering the proportions of the problem with which it dealt, the paper was a short one, running to only thirteen pages.

The Policy Planning Staff did not see Communist activities as the root of the difficulties in Western Europe, but believed that the crisis there resulted in large part from the disruptive effect of the war on the economic, political, and social structure of Europe and from a profound exhaustion of physical plant and of spiritual vigor. The situation was aggravated by the division of the continent into east and west. The Policy Planning Staff recognized that Communists were exploiting the European crisis and that further Communist successes would create a serious danger for American security, but that American aid should not be directed to combating communism as such but to the restoration of the economic health and vigor of European society. Plans designed to achieve this should be drawn up and frankly explained to the American people.

The Policy Planning Staff saw two problems in the question of American aid to Western Europe, one short-term and one long-term. The long-term problem was the restoration of economic health in Europe and the form and degree of American aid. The short-term problem was that of taking some immediate, dramatic action, chiefly psychological in impact, to create confidence that the over-all problem could be solved and that we would play our proper part in the solution. The short-term measures proposed were action to increase production of coal in the Rhine Valley and announcement of intention to grant aid to Italy.[2] On the subject

[2] As it turned out, of course, Secretary Marshall's proposal was what had the dramatic, psychological, immediate impact. Coal discussions were in fact

of the long-term plan, the Policy Planning Staff said things some of which were reproduced almost literally in the Secretary's Harvard speech:

> It is necessary to distinguish clearly between a program for the economic revitalization of Europe on the one hand, and a program of American support for such revitalization on the other. It would be neither fitting nor efficacious for this government to undertake to draw up unilaterally and to promulgate formally on its own initiative a program designed to place Western Europe on its feet economically. This is the business of the Europeans. The formal initiative must come from Europe; and Europeans must bear the basic responsibility for it. The role of this country should consist of friendly aid in the drafting of a European program and of the later support of such a program, by financial and other means, at European request.
>
> The program which this country is asked to support must be a joint one, agreed to by several European nations. While it may be linked to individual national programs, such as the Monnet plan in France, it must, for psychological and political, as well as economic, reasons, be an internationally agreed program. The request for our support must come as a joint request from a group of friendly nations, not as a series of isolated and individual appeals.
>
> This European program must envisage bringing Western Europe to a point where it will be able to maintain a tolerable standard of living on a financially self-supporting basis. It must give promise of doing the whole job. The program must contain reasonable assurance that if we support it, this will be the last such program we shall be asked to support in the foreseeable future.

The Policy Planning Staff thought that the United States should not, nevertheless, stand aside or remain aloof from the elaboration of the over-all program. The Department should undertake an independent and realistic study of the entire problem of European rehabilitation. "But we must insist, for the sake of clarity, for the sake of soundness of concept, and for the sake of the self-respect of European peoples, that the initiative be taken in Europe and that the main burden be borne by the governments of that area."

---

initiated with the British, resulting in some improvement in the coal production of the Continent, but the effect was not dramatic. The aid-to-Italy idea became swallowed up in the Marshall Plan.

It was recognized that the problem of where and in what form the initiative for the formulation of a European program should be taken was tremendously difficult and delicate. It could not be definitely predetermined by us. Presumably an effort would be made to advance the project through the Economic Commission for Europe in the form of a proposal for general European (not just Western European) cooperation. If the Russians should block action in the Economic Commission for Europe, then other countries would have to go ahead independently. But initiative should come primarily from the European nations, and the United States should not seek unduly to influence decisions.

As to procedure within the government, the Policy Planning Staff thought that the Special Committee studying policy, procedures, and costs of assistance should continue its work, but that the State Department representative should maintain close contact with the Policy Planning Staff. It also recommended that our Chiefs of Mission in a number of European countries be instructed to submit full reports on the problem of foreign aid, and that the operational sections of the Department should formulate the government's views for use in discussions with European governments and for the guidance of the American representative on the Economic Commission for Europe. Finally, it recommended that it be accepted as our general objective to undertake [3] before autumn the development of a program of European rehabilitation which would show what was expected of the United States in the way of support and submit that request for support to us by the end of the year.

At the end of the Policy Planning Staff memorandum of May 23 there was a brief separate section:

Steps should be taken to clarify what the press has unfortunately come to identify as the "Truman Doctrine," and to remove in particular two damaging impressions which are current in large sections of American public opinion. These are:

a. That the United States approach to world problems is a defensive reaction to Communist pressure and that the effort to re-

[3] The word used in the memorandum is literally "undertake," but in the context of the sentence, and of the whole paper, it was evidently intended to suggest the development of a program by Europeans.

store sound economic conditions in other countries is only the by-product of this reaction and not something we would be interested in doing if there were no Communist menace;

b. That the Truman Doctrine is a blank check to give economic and military aid to any area in the world where the Communists show signs of being successful. It must be made clear that the extension of American aid is essentially a question of political economy in the literal sense of that term and that such aid will be considered only in cases where the prospective results bear a satisfactory relationship to the expenditure of American resources and effort. It must be made clear that in the case of Greece and Turkey we are dealing with a critical area where failure to take action would have had particularly serious consequences, where a successful action would promise particularly far-reaching results, and where the overall cost was relatively small; and that in other areas we should have to apply similar criteria.

Secretary Marshall's chief officers had studied this memorandum in advance, and he opened the proceedings in his office by asking for comments. There was no significant dissent from Kennan's analysis, except that one of those present feared the Europeans might be too far gone to take any vigorous initiative, and another thought a commission of distinguished Americans should be appointed to investigate the problem, with publicity, and make a report with recommendations. Neither of these ideas attracted support. The Secretary then raised the super-questions: Is it wise to direct a proposal such as this to all Europe? What will happen if the Soviet Union should decide to come in on a cooperative recovery program?

Acheson had publicly stated in his Delta Council speech that as the world demand exceeded our ability to supply, the United States was going to have to concentrate its reconstruction assistance "in areas where it will be most effective in building world political and economic stability, in promoting human freedom and democratic institutions, in fostering liberal trading practices, and in strengthening the authority of the United Nations." Now, his opinion was that it would be a colossal error for the United States to put itself in a position where it could be blamed for the division of Europe. The psychological and political advantage of asking all

Europeans to get together would disappear if we should divide Europe by offering to help rebuild only half of it. The problem, however, was a very difficult one. If the Russians came in the whole project would probably be unworkable because the amount of money involved in restoring both Eastern and Western Europe would be so colossal it could never be got from Congress, especially in view of the strong and growing reaction against the Soviet Union. But there was a strong probability that the USSR would never come in on a basis of disclosing full information about their economic and financial condition, which was necessary if a common recovery plan were to work. It would be best to make the offer an open one and then see if and how and when the Russians would fit in. Kennan, in reply to the Secretary's questions, advised, "Play it straight." He noted that nothing had been said in his paper about who should be contributors and who recipients in a European recovery program. The Soviet Union and satellites were great producers of food and raw materials that Western Europe needed, and east-west trade was highly important. If the Russians were inclined to participate, we should confront them with the old Marxist maxim, "From each according to his ability, to each according to his need," and ask them to share fully the burdens as well as the benefits of a common recovery program. This would put the Russians in the position of making a contribution to a revival of Europe's economy or of forgoing the benefits of a program supported by the United States. Kennan was emphatic that we should not take the responsibility for defining the area that would receive American aid.

These points of view were concurred in by all the Secretary's advisers. Marshall himself did not elaborate his own views, but Acheson recalls that in subsequent conversations the Secretary was very clear and emphatic on the point that the United States could not take the responsibility for dividing Europe and that a proposal to aid European reconstruction would have to be addressed to all Europe—that he would have to take a calculated risk both as regards the Russians and Congress. The Secretary's proposal at Harvard, however, was carefully worded and guarded;

it committed us to nothing except to consider a European plan that would be worked out by Europeans and presented to us. There was not even any mention of the Economic Commission for Europe, on which the Soviet Union was represented, even though all concerned in the State Department assumed that the ECE would carry the ball. To have done so might have prejudiced European decision and action, and that was to be rigorously avoided at this juncture.

There appears to have been but little discussion at this meeting of a possible speech by the Secretary or the President in which a proposal would be made to Europe. The Secretary kept his counsel both on his own views and his plans. Kennan left the meeting with the impression that the Secretary had some scheme in mind for action on the Policy Planning Staff paper, but he rather thought the first step would be conversations through diplomatic channels with some of Europe's leaders.[4]

Late in the afternoon of May 28 Carl Hummelsine, director of the Executive Secretariat, took in to Secretary Marshall a stack of papers for signature and while there mentioned a number of lesser pending matters requiring decision. One was whether the Secretary could definitely confirm his previously tentative acceptance of Harvard's invitation to be there on June 5. The Secretary thought he would go and said he supposed he would be expected to make some remarks. Would Hummelsine see to it that something was drafted for him? Hummelsine commented that as the Secretary had no other speaking engagements coming up until the Amherst College commencement on June 16, Harvard might be a good place to make the speech on aid to Europe that had been discussed several times. Apparently as a result of this remark, Secretary Marshall asked Acheson his opinion on the idea. Acheson counseled against it, on the grounds that commencement exercises usually have poor news coverage and that the speech might fall flat. Acheson discussed the matter with his senior staff the next morning and afterward repeated to the Secretary his advice against Harvard as a springboard

---

[4] Kennan was more surprised than anyone when on June 6 he read the Secretary's Harvard speech in the newspapers. He had heard nothing further about his memorandum of May 23 and did not know that the Secretary was going to speak on the problem of aid to Europe.

for the big idea. But Marshall had been turning the matter over in his own mind, consulted others, and decided in favor of Harvard. Acheson gathered the impression that the Secretary neither wanted nor expected his proposal to receive immediate and world-wide acclaim, but that it should appear somewhat modestly and then grow in official and public thought. Secretary Marshall on May 29 sent a telegram to Harvard saying he would definitely be present on June 5, and asked Bohlen to draft a speech for him containing the proposal to Europe.

In drafting the speech, Bohlen used primarily the Kennan and Clayton memoranda. He also had the benefit of Clayton's graphic oral descriptions of Europe's situation. Whole parts of the Kennan memorandum and many of Clayton's phrases and word-pictures are clearly visible. Bohlen greatly sharpened the concept, apparent in the Kennan memorandum, and current in the Department at the time, that United States policy was directed "not against any country or doctrine, but against hunger, poverty, desperation, and chaos," and made it clear that any government that sought to perpetuate human misery and block the recovery of other countries (inferentially, by refusing to cooperate fully in a cooperative recovery program) would not receive our aid and would encounter our opposition.

Bohlen's draft speech was completed early in the week of June 2, gone over carefully by Clayton and Acheson, and taken to the Secretary. Marshall was not satisfied with the part about European initiative and rewrote it. Still not sure of it, he altered it further on the plane en route to Cambridge, Massachusetts, on June 4.

There were no conversations of any kind with representatives of other governments on the Marshall idea before the Secretary spoke at Harvard. Moreover there was no build-up, no hints to the American press that an important speech was to be delivered. Even in the Department the fact that the Secretary was going to launch the European proposal was by design and instruction kept from all but the handful who had to know. On June 4, however, Acheson invited to lunch the three British correspondents already mentioned in connection with his Delta Council speech—Miall,

Muggeridge, and McCall. Acheson disclosed that the Secretary's Harvard speech was of the greatest importance and urged the correspondents to telephone the full text of the speech to London as soon as it was released and to make arrangements with their editors in London to deliver the full text at once to Ernest Bevin, no matter where he was or what time it was. This was done. Miall went on the air to Great Britain at 3 p.m. on June 5, saying what a tremendous proposal Marshall had made, and Muggeridge and McCall telephoned the text to their editors, who rushed it to Bevin at his home.

It might be interesting to speculate on what might have happened, or not happened, had Acheson not taken these precautions. Whether true or not, the story is at least told and believed by many in the State Department that Sir John Balfour, chargé of the British Embassy, having been under persistent pressure from London to cut down the Embassy's cable expenses, decided, in the absence of the Ambassador, that this time he would save money and sent Marshall's speech to London by pouch. The next day he was deluged by excited cables from the Foreign Office: "Did Marshall really say this? Why no report?" More authentic is the story that when Bevin was finally convinced that Secretary Marshall had really said in public the words attributed to him, there was a conference of senior Foreign Office officials at which the question was debated whether Balfour should be instructed to call on Marshall and ask him if he really meant what he seemed to say. Ernest Bevin decided that one. "No," he concluded, "I don't want to ask Marshall that question. I don't want to take any chances that it wasn't meant. I want to go on the assumption that it was fully meant, and give an answer myself." So he went to work.

Thus was launched what Winston Churchill has called "the most unsordid act in history."

EPILOGUE

FOREIGN POLICY UNCHAINED

FOREIGN POLICY UNCHAINED

THE Fifteen Weeks was one of those rare times in history when shackles fall away from the mind, the spirit, and the will, allowing them to soar free and high for a while and to discover new standards of what is responsible, of what is promising, and of what is possible. It was a time when men thought not in terms of what could be done but of what should be done, when only the timid idea was banished and all others welcomed, a time of courage, of bold decision, of generous response. It was a time when American democracy worked with unexampled efficiency and inspiration to produce national agreement. It was a great time to be alive.

The *avant-scène* was as dreary and unpromising as any in our history: a little-respected Democratic President, a Republican-controlled Congress bent on political mayhem after fourteen years in the wilderness, and an apathetic and heedless public. How then could the sudden transformation of the Fifteen Weeks possibly have occurred? The convergence of historical trends was compelling, but this cannot be the whole answer, for the lost compelling moments recorded in history would add up to quite a respectable span of time. The remainder of the answer must therefore be found in the qualities displayed by the nation's leaders and in the processes that enabled statesmanship to emerge and to prevail.

There is no way of getting around the fact that it was the courage, decisiveness, clear-thinking, and informed judgment of President

Truman that opened the doors to the progress made during the Fifteen Weeks. It detracts none at all from the credit due him that he had exceptionally good advice, for his advisers were his appointees selected for qualities he admired and respected, and they operated in the climate of his administration and within the boundaries of what they thought he would support. Without considering its possible effect upon his personal popularity or re-election prospects, or whether it would mean an increase in taxes or the national debt, he made his decision on the basis of what the security of the nation seemed to require, and boldly confronted Congress and the people with their responsibilities. Moreover he knew what many men who find themselves in positions of power never learn, and that is that Americans respond more freely to big ideas than to small ones.

There is no substitute for this kind of courageous leadership. Most men are prisoners of their own limited conception of what is possible, and except in the most extraordinary circumstances most men involved in the foreign policy-making process in the government, from bottom to top, deliver their opinions and make their recommendations according to their own private estimate of what Congress and the American people will support. That estimate is usually low, somewhere near what Congress and people have demonstrably supported in the past. There is nothing reprehensible in this. It is natural, if not inevitable, that practical men in subordinate positions should act in terms of what they consider possible. Unless, therefore, the President and the Secretary of State, drawing upon a faith in the capacity of their fellow men for clear thinking and sacrifice, add the element of statemanship, unless they proclaim the policy of the United States in terms of bold, moving concepts and projects, whether or not they are fully and immediately attainable, the whole government process rocks along at a low level, policy planning is an exercise in futility, and the security and well-being of the nation may very well be jeopardized. But if with full candor and in accents of leadership they open new vistas of what is necessary and what is possible, they automatically raise the sights of the nation and release powerful ideas in the government departments, in Congress, and among the citizenry. In the ensuing public and official discussions great and practicable projects may emerge, with broad public support. This is what happened during the Fifteen Weeks.

The conservative prefers a balance-sheet approach to world affairs even in an age when his ledgers, the metal filing cases that enclose them, and the concrete and steel buildings that house them have a remarkably good prospect of being reduced to radioactive dust during his lifetime: add up the nation's revenues and armed forces in one column, and then figure out what can be done to build toward peace and security! There are legislators who profess to see the difference between national solvency and bankruptcy in the addition of several wings to the Air Force, even at a time when our margin of air-atomic superiority is disappearing. There are Cabinet officers who oppose a "Marshall Plan" for Asia at a time when that continent is in the balance between the free world and the slave, on the grounds that we are already "scraping the bottom of the financial barrel." There are writers on foreign policy who are considered sages for parading on appropriate occasions the neat homily (so obviously true!) that a nation's world commitments should not exceed its power to carry them out. During the Fifteen Weeks there were some who professed to be horrified at the President's announcement of an open-end policy of aiding free peoples. Where would it lead? There were some who urged a balance-sheet approach at a time when most of the world, hungry and desperate, seemed on the point of bargaining away freedom for food and coal. And of course the 80th Congress was busily engaged in building a smaller financial barrel so that they could publicly scrape the bottom of it. The whole nation was in a psychological barrel of its own construction.

What, indeed, are the limits of United States power? And what are the limits of United States foreign policy? Are they what we can accomplish with an existing budget, an existing level of armed force, an existing program of world economic development, an existing tax rate? Are they what we could accomplish were these increased, or decreased, by 10 per cent, or 50 per cent? Is our power what we can mobilize to fight a war once we are engaged? By what standard, and whose, can we measure our power to help build around the world in time of peace the economic, social, political, and military conditions that protect freedom and diminish the danger of war? The answer is that the limits of our foreign policy are on a distant and receding horizon; for many practical purposes they are what we think we can accomplish and what we think it is necessary to accomplish at any given time.

President Truman, Secretary Marshall, and Undersecretary Acheson rejected an approach to world problems based upon an existing financial statement and upon what the American Congress and people considered possible and necessary before the situation had been explained to them. Instead they figured out what needed to be done, explained their bold projects publicly in frank terms, and had faith that the American people would back them up. The Fifteen Weeks demonstrated the tremendous capacity of the American people to respond to courageous leadership with clear thinking, constructive ideas, and personal sacrifice. The people did not demand to know what was at the end of the road before responding, or the total cost, or the full extent of possible dangers. They wanted only to be satisfied that the direction in which their leaders pointed was good and necessary, and they pitched in with ideas, intellectual support, and with money to help get a big show on the road. This generous response, in turn, encouraged the nation's leaders to new acts of statesmanship.

Without making extravagant claims, and without forgetting that many complex factors enter into any major policy decision, it is reasonable to suggest that a number of other bold policies and actions, beyond aid to Greece and Turkey and the Marshall Plan, had their roots in the national conversion of the Fifteen Weeks: The North Atlantic Alliance and the North Atlantic Treaty Organization, the Military Defense Assistance Program, the Far Eastern programs of the Economic Cooperation Administration, the Mutual Security Program, the Point IV Program, the prompt commitment of American power against Communist aggression in Korea, the Manila Pact, the other defensive alliances that link our destiny with countries around the globe. And the process of drawing together and strengthening the free world continues, will probably continue far into the future. No doubt the greatest stimulus to our policy development since 1947 has been the Soviet-Communist challenge. But as was evident in the debates of the Fifteen Weeks and has been so often demonstrated since, the generous impulse, the humanitarian motive, the sense of responsibility for protecting freedom, the business instinct, the common-sense conclusion as to how peace and prosperity might best be secured in a world grown small and highly explosive—all these have played a powerful part, leavening, controlling, what might otherwise have been a foreign policy that sought security in a revolutionary age by purely military means.

Charles Burton Marshall [1] is of course right when he points out in his book *The Limits of Foreign Policy* that the capacity of one country, even the most powerful country on earth, to influence the policies, acts, and attitudes of another nation is limited by the obvious fact of independent sovereignty. The Fifteen Weeks suggest, however, not the limits but the infinite possibilities of influencing the policies, attitudes, and actions of other countries by statesmanship in Washington. Advancing communism was halted in Western Europe during the Fifteen Weeks by the announcement of the Truman Doctrine. Within weeks, the French and Italian governments were emboldened to drop Communist members from their Cabinets. And as a consequence of Secretary Marshall's proposal at Harvard, despair yielded to hope throughout Western Europe, sustaining free men through more than another year of extreme hardship before conditions began to improve. Greece and Turkey are today in reasonably good shape. Western Europe, free, and enjoying a remarkable degree of prosperity, is joined for defense with the United States and Canada in the North Atlantic Alliance, and NATO forces are growing in strength. As a consequence of the increased economic and social and military strength of the West, the Soviet Union of 1952 abandoned for a while its hopes and plans for an early conquest of Europe and started preaching coexistence. Considering these accomplishments, if there are limits to the capacity

[1] Formerly a member of the Policy Planning Staff of the State Department.

of our foreign policy to influence other nations, we must conclude at least that we have had room to maneuver.

Nor is it just United States money that carries such influence. Money may be, and often is, necessary to certain projects, but leadership commitment and leadership ideas are equally important. The Marshall proposal gave a powerful impetus to the movement for European unity, and that in turn stimulated projects and ideas for Atlantic unity. Within a few weeks the countries of Western Europe had formed the Committee (later the Organization) for European Economic Cooperation. The Brussels Pact of 1948, in part a product of the inspiration and hope aroused by the Truman Doctrine and the Marshall Plan, gave rise to the North Atlantic Pact and the North Atlantic Treaty Organization, and led directly to the creation of the Council of Europe. It was, in turn, in the Council of Europe that the idea of a European Defense Force was first projected; but it was a decision of the North Atlantic Council that made a European army imperative and called forth a proposal by the Prime Minister Pleven of France for a European Defense Community. This plan was strongly backed by NATO as essential to the security of the North Atlantic Community. Initiative, action, and interaction went on continuously across the Atlantic for several years.

The chief responsibilty of a world leader today is that of directing the deep restlessness of the mid-twentieth century, the seething urge for change so evident in all parts of the world, into sustained movement toward desired goals that are beyond immediate grasp but attainable with effort and sacrifice. The forward projects and commitments of a true world leader should therefore always exceed the ability at any given moment to carry them out. He must to a certain extent proceed upon faith that he can tap latent resources in the people. Most men and most nations are lonely and frustrated in this complex and dangerous world, desperately long for association with their fellow men and fellow nations in causes that hold promise for something better than that known before. If their energies are not directed by enlightened statesmanship to constructive projects, they will be exploited by demagoguery; if not used to build the conditions of freedom they will be used to forge chains and build walls. It is a dangerous thing in this age for a world leader to assume, because he sees at any given moment no major organized violence, that all is well and sit back in satisfaction, offering no new goals, no new outlets to powerful desires that surge immediately beneath the surface of apparent calm. The United States will fail to preserve peace and maintain security unless it continually enlists the active cooperation of free men, drawing upon their latent desire for sacrifice and for effort beyond the ordinary, in specific projects for building a better life for all, and shares the effort and sacrifice of the building.

It is widely recognized that American capitalism has in this century, and especially in the last twenty years, brilliantly disproved and confounded the Marxist dogma that the owner inevitably grinds down the workers, that the rich get richer and the poor poorer until the masses in revolution throw off their chains and establish a dictatorship of the proletariat. The prosperity and steady advancement of the American worker and the cooperation of American capital and labor for their mutual enrichment are facts the Communist finds difficult to explain away in selling his system to free men. It has been insufficiently realized, however, that during the Fifteen Weeks the United States challenged in the international arena the Marxist doctrine that capitalist countries, harboring within them the seeds of their own destruction and growing ever more desperate in fighting off economic, social, and political collapse, will engage in mutually destructive economic practices, will intensify their imperialistic scramble for advantages in underdeveloped regions, will war among themselves, and in the process so weaken one another that Communist dictatorship will take over. In 1947 the countries of Western Europe, impoverished and struggling for survival, were in fact strangling one another with competitive national restrictions on trade and exchange, and the world's empires could have been had by the United States for a song. The United States, declaring that freedom and democracy within democratic nations and the independence of nations from outside control depend upon the maintenance of healthy and self-supporting national economies, challenged the Marxist creed by advancing the proposal that nations work together in unity, using their economic and financial resources in concert for a common economic recovery that would safeguard their common democracy, independence, and free institutions; and by pledging the great economic, financial, administrative, and technical resources of the world's leading capitalist democracy to assistance in the common effort. Inspired self-help, mutual aid, and United States aid! It is understandable why the Communists turned the fury of their invective on the Truman Doctrine and Marshall Plan. These refuted the very heart of the Communist creed, and visions of early triumph vanished. The new policy is, however, infinitely more than a policy of containment of Soviet-Communist expansion. It is a constructive policy of building throughout the free world the conditions not only of peace but of a good life.

Only a beginning, of course, has been made. Brilliant early successes have been achieved. But we have yet to build in Western Europe and in the Atlantic Community more than a partial foundation for that organic unity of our economies, political systems, and armies which is necessary if we are to resist the persistent and prolonged efforts that will be made to divide, weaken, and destroy us. And although in Asia and other underdeveloped regions we have made a start with economic-development programs, technical assistance, and military aid, we have traveled only a few steps down a long, long road.

The responsibility that rests upon the United States to lead, inspire, and aid free men and free nations to draw ever closer together, and together to build ever stronger the conditions of freedom, is heavier than any that has ever rested upon any nation. It is also the greatest challenge and opportunity ever offered to any nation to save its own life and its own soul.

APPENDIX

INDEX

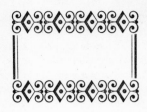

PRESIDENT HARRY S. TRUMAN'S ADDRESS BEFORE A JOINT SESSION OF CONGRESS, MARCH 12, 1947

Mr. President, Mr. Speaker, Members of the Congress
  of the United States:

The gravity of the situation which confronts the world today necessitates my appearance before a joint session of the Congress.

The foreign policy and the national security of this country are involved.

One aspect of the present situation, which I wish to present to you at this time for your consideration and decision, concerns Greece and Turkey.

The United States has received from the Greek Government an urgent appeal for financial and economic assistance. Preliminary reports from the American Economic Mission now in Greece and reports from the American Abassador in Greece corroborate the statement of the Greek Government that assistance is imperative if Greece is to survive as a free nation.

I do not believe that the American people and the Congress wish to turn a deaf ear to the appeal of the Greek Government.

Greece is not a rich country. Lack of sufficient natural resources has always forced the Greek people to work hard to make both ends meet. Since 1940, this industrious and peace loving country has suffered invasion, four years of cruel enemy occupation, and bitter internal strife.

When forces of liberation entered Greece they found that the retreating Germans had destroyed virtually all the railways, roads, port facilities, communications, and merchant marine. More than a thousand villages had been burned. Eighty-five per cent of the children were tubercular. Livestock, poultry, and draft animals had almost disappeared. Inflation had wiped out practically all savings.

As a result of these tragic conditions, a militant minority, exploiting

269

human want and misery, was able to create political chaos which, until now, has made economic recovery impossible.

Greece is today without funds to finance the importation of those goods which are essential to bare subsistence. Under these circumstances the people of Greece cannot make progress in solving their problems of reconstruction. Greece is in desperate need of financial and economic assistance to enable it to resume purchases of food, clothing, fuel and seeds. These are indispensable for the subsistence of its people and are obtainable only from abroad. Greece must have help to import the goods necessary to restore internal order and security so essential for economic and political recovery.

The Greek Government has also asked for the assistance of experienced American administrators, economists and technicians to insure that the financial and other aid given to Greece shall be used effectively in creating a stable and self-sustaining economy and in improving its public administration.

The very existence of the Greek state is today threatened by the terrorist activities of several thousand armed men, led by Communists, who defy the government's authority at a number of points, particularly along the northern boundaries. A Commission appointed by the United Nations security Council is at present investigating disturbed conditions in northern Greece and alleged border violations along the frontier between Greece on the one hand and Albania, Bulgaria, and Yugoslavia on the other.

Meanwhile, the Greek Government is unable to cope with the situation. The Greek army is small and poorly equipped. It needs supplies and equipment if it is to restore the authority of the government throughout Greek territory.

Greece must have assistance if it is to become a self-supporting and self-respecting democracy.

The United States must supply that assistance. We have already extended to Greece certain types of relief and economic aid but these are inadequate.

There is no other country to which democratic Greece can turn.

No other nation is willing and able to provide the necessary support for a democratic Greek government.

The British Government, which has been helping Greece, can give no further financial or economic aid after March 31. Great Britain finds itself under the necessity of reducing or liquidating its commitments in several parts of the world, including Greece.

We have considered how the United Nations might assist in this crisis. But the situation is an urgent one requiring immediate action, and the United Nations and its related organizations are not in a position to extend help of the kind that is required.

It is important to note that the Greek Government has asked for our aid in utilizing effectively the financial and other assistance we may give to Greece, and in improving its public administration. It is of the utmost importance that we supervise the use of any funds made available to Greece; in such a manner that each dollar spent will count toward making Greece self-supporting, and will help to build an economy in which a healthy democracy can flourish.

No government is perfect. One of the chief virtues of a democracy, however, is that its defects are always visible and under democratic processes can be pointed out and corrected. The government of Greece is not perfect. Nevertheless it represents eighty-five per cent of the members of the Greek Parliament who were chosen in an election last year. Foreign observers, including 692 Americans, considered this election to be a fair expression of the views of the Greek people.

The Greek Government has been operating in an atmosphere of chaos and extremism. It has made mistakes. The extension of aid by this country does not mean that the United States condones everything that the Greek Government has done or will do. We have condemned in the past, and we condemn now, extremist measures of the right or the left. We have in the past advised tolerance, and we advise tolerance now.

Greece's neighbor, Turkey, also deserves our attention.

The future of Turkey as an independent and economically sound state is clearly no less important to the freedom-loving peoples of the world than the future of Greece. The circumstances in which Turkey finds itself today are considerably different from those of Greece. Turkey has been spared the disasters that have beset Greece. And during the war, the United States and Great Britain furnished Turkey with material aid.

Nevertheless, Turkey now needs our support.

Since the war Turkey has sought financial assistance from Great Britain and the United States for the purpose of effecting that modernization necessary for the maintenance of its national integrity.

That integrity is essential to the preservation of order in the Middle East.

The British Government has informed us that, owing to its own difficulties, it can no longer extend financial or economic aid to Turkey.

As in the case of Greece, if Turkey is to have the assistance it needs, the United States must supply it. We are the only country able to provide that help.

I am fully aware of the broad implications involved if the United

States extends assistance to Greece and Turkey, and I shall discuss these implications with you at this time.

One of the primary objectives of the foreign policy of the United States is the creation of conditions in which we and other nations will be able to work out a way of life free from coercion. This was a fundamental issue in the war with Germany and Japan. Our victory was won over countries which sought to impose their will, and their way of life, upon other nations.

To ensure the peaceful development of nations, free from coercion, the United States has taken a leading part in establishing the United Nations. The United Nations is designed to make possible lasting freedom and independence for all its members. We shall not realize our objectives, however, unless we are willing to help free peoples to maintain their free institutions and their national integrity against aggressive movements that seek to impose upon them totalitarian regimes. This is no more than a frank recognition that totalitarian regimes imposed on free peoples, by direct or indirect aggression, undermine the foundations of international peace and hence the security of the United States.

The peoples of a number of countries of the world have recently had totalitarian regimes forced upon them against their will. The Government of the United States has made frequent protests against coercion and intimidation, in violation of the Yalta agreement, in Poland, Rumania, and Bulgaria. I must also state that in a number of other countries there have been similar developments.

At the present moment in world history nearly every nation must choose between alternative ways of life. The choice is too often not a free one.

One way of life is based upon the will of the majority, and is distinguished by free institutions, representative government, free elections, guarantees of individual liberty, freedom of speech and religion, and freedom from political oppression.

The second way of life is based upon the will of a minority forcibly imposed upon the majority. It relies upon terror and oppression, a controlled press and radio; fixed elections, and the suppression of personal freedoms.

I believe that it must be the policy of the United States to support free peoples who are resisting attempted subjugation by armed minorities or by outside pressures.

I believe that we must assist free peoples to work out their own destinies in their own way.

I believe that our help should be primarily through economic and financial aid which is essential to economic stability and orderly political processes.

The world is not static, and the *status quo* is not sacred. But we cannot allow changes in the *status quo* in violation of the Charter of the United Nations by such methods as coercion, or by such subterfuges as political infiltration. In helping free and independent nations to maintain their freedom, the United States will be giving effect to the principles of the Charter of the United Nations.

It is necessary only to glance at a map to realize that the survival and integrity of the Greek nation are of grave importance in a much wider situation. If Greece should fall under the control of an armed minority, the effect upon its neighbor, Turkey, would be immediate and serious. Confusion and disorder might well spread throughout the entire Middle East.

Moreover, the disappearance of Greece as an independent state would have a profound effect upon those countries in Europe whose peoples are struggling against great difficulties to maintain their freedoms and their independence while they repair the damages of war.

It would be an unspeakable tragedy if these countries, which have struggled so long against overwhelming odds, should lose that victory for which they sacrificed so much. Collapse of free institutions and loss of independence would be disastrous not only for them but for the world. Discouragement and possibly failure would quickly be the lot of neighboring peoples striving to maintain their freedom and independence.

Should we fail to aid Greece and Turkey in this fateful hour, the effect will be far reaching to the West as well as to the East.

We must take immediate and resolute action.

I therefore ask the Congress to provide authority for assistance to Greece and Turkey in the amount of $400,000,000 for the period ending June 30, 1948. In requesting these funds, I have taken into consideration the maximum amount of relief assistance which would be furnished to Greece out of the $350,000,000 which I recently requested that the Congress authorize for the prevention of starvation and suffering in countries devastated by the war.

In addition to funds, I ask the Congress to authorize the detail of American civilian and military personnel to Greece and Turkey, at the request of those countries, to assist in the tasks of reconstruction, and for the purpose of supervising the use of such financial and material assistance as may be furnished. I recommend that authority also be provided for the instruction and training of selected Greek and Turkish personnel.

Finally, I ask that the Congress provide authority which will permit the speediest and most effective use, in terms of needed commodities, supplies, and equipment, of such funds as may be authorized.

If further funds, or further authority, should be needed for purposes indicated in this message, I shall not hesitate to bring the situation before the Congress. On this subject the Executive and Legislative branches of the Government must work together.

This is a serious course upon which we embark.

I would not recommend it except that the alternative is much more serious.

The United States contributed $341,000,000,000 toward winning World War II. This is an investment in world freedom and world peace.

The assistance that I am recommending for Greece and Turkey amounts to little more than 1 tenth of 1 per cent of this investment. It is only common sense that we should safeguard this investment and make sure that it was not in vain.

The seeds of totalitarian regimes are nurtured by misery and want. They spread and grow in the evil soil of poverty and strife. They reach their full growth when the hope of a people for a better life has died.

We must keep that hope alive.

The free peoples of the world look to us for support in maintaining their freedoms.

If we falter in our leadership, we may endanger the peace of the world —and we shall surely endanger the welfare of our own nation.

Great responsibilities have been placed upon us by the swift movement of events.

I am confident that the Congress will face these responsibilities squarely.

UNDERSECRETARY OF STATE DEAN G. ACHESON'S ADDRESS BEFORE THE DELTA COUNCIL, CLEVELAND, MISSISSIPPI, MAY 8, 1947

You who live and work in this rich agricultural region, whose daily lives are concerned with the growth and marketing of cotton and corn and other agricultural products, must derive a certain satisfaction from the fact that the greatest affairs of state never get very far from the soil.

When Secretary of State Marshall returned from the recent meeting of the Council of Foreign Ministers in Moscow he did not talk to us about ideologies or armies. He talked about food and fuel and their relation to industrial production, and the relation of industrial production to the organization of Europe, and the relation of the organization of Europe to the peace of the world.

The devastation of war has brought us back to elementals, to the point where we see clearly how short is the distance from food and fuel either to peace or to anarchy.

Here are some of the basic facts of life with which we are primarily concerned today in the conduct of foreign relations:

The first is that most of the countries of Europe and Asia are today in a state of physical destruction or economic dislocation, or both. Planned, scientific destruction of the enemy's resources carried out by both sides during the war has left factories destroyed, fields impoverished and without fertilizer or machinery to get them back in shape, transportation systems wrecked, populations scattered and on the borderline of starvation, and long-established business and trading connections disrupted.

Another grim fact of international life is that two of the greatest workshops of Europe and Asia—Germany and Japan—upon whose production Europe and Asia were to an important degree dependent before the war, have hardly been able even to begin the process of reconstruction because of the lack of a peace settlement. As we have seen, recent efforts at Moscow to make progress towards a settlement for Germany and Austria have ended with little accomplishment. Meanwhile, political instability in some degree retards revival in nearly every country of Europe and Asia.

A third factor is that unforseen disasters—what the lawyers call "acts of God"—have occurred to the crops of Europe. For two successive years unusually severe droughts have cut down food production. And during the past winter storms and floods and excessive cold unprecedented in recent years have swept northern Europe and England with enormous damage to agricultural and fuel production. These disasters have slowed down the already slow pace of reconstruction, have impeded recovery of exports, and have obliged many countries to draw down irreplaceable reserves of gold and foreign exchange, which had been earmarked for the importation of reconstruction materials, for the purchase of food and fuel for subsistence.

The accumulation of these grim developments has produced a disparity between production in the United States and production in the rest of the world that is staggering in its proportions. The United States has been spared physical destruction during the war. Moreover, we have been favored with unusually bountiful agricultural crops in recent years. Production in this country is today running at the annual rate of 210 billion dollars.

Responding to this highly abnormal relationship between production in the United States and production in the rest of the world, the United States Government has already authorized and is carrying out an extensive program of relief and reconstruction. We have contributed nearly 3 billion dollars to foreign relief. We have taken the lead in the organization of the International Bank for Reconstruction and Development and the International Monetary Fund, and have subscribed to these two institutions to the extent of almost 6 billion dollars. We have increased the capacity of the Export-Import Bank to make loans abroad by almost 3 billion dollars. We have made a direct loan of $3\frac{3}{4}$ billion dollars to Great Britain. We are proposing this year to contribute a half billion dollars for relief and reconstruction in the Philippines, and a billion dollars to relief in occupied areas. The President's recommendations for aid to Greece and Turkey to the extent of 400 million dollars and for post-UNRRA relief to the extent of 350 million dollars are still under consideration by Congress. And there are a few other smaller items.

These measures of relief and reconstruction have been only in part suggested by humanitarianism. Your Congress has authorized and your Government is carrying out a policy of relief and reconstruction today chiefly as a matter of national self-interest. For it is generally agreed that until the various countries of the world get on their feet and become self-supporting there can be no political or economic stability in the world and no lasting peace or prosperity for any of us. Without outside aid, the process of recovery in many countries would take so long as to give rise to hopelessness and despair. In these conditions freedom and democracy and the independence of nations could not long survive, for hopeless and hungry people often resort to desperate measures. The war will not be over until the people of the world can again feed and clothe themselves and face the future with some degree of confidence.

The contribution of the United States towards world livelihood and reconstruction is best measured today not in terms of money but in terms of the commodities which we ship abroad. It is commodities—food, clothing, coal, steel, machinery—that the world needs, and it is commodities that we must concentrate our attention upon.

Our exports of goods and services to the rest of the world during the current year, 1947, are estimated to total 16 billion dollars, an all-time peace-time high. Before the war our exports of goods and services fluctuated around 4 billion dollars annually.

It is difficult to imagine 16 billion dollars' worth of commodities. This represents one month's work for each man and woman in the United States, one month's output from every farm, factory, and mine.

Let me give you another indication of the extent of our exports. The volume of commodities now moving out of east coast and Gulf ports of the United States is twice as great as the peak volume which moved out of those ports during the war when we were transporting and supplying not only our own huge armies abroad but a tremendous volume of lend-lease supplies.

Our exports this year are perhaps the maximum, in quantity, that is likely to be exported abroad in the next few years. At the same time these exports are probably the minimum that we should make available to the world.

It is extremely difficult under present circumstances to increase the volume of our exports further. For in this country, too, there is a great demand for commodities, and foreign customers must compete with American customers. The character and composition of our exports will probably change, with lesser quantities of food, fuel, and raw materials being exported and increased amounts of steel, machinery, and other manufactured products going abroad. But the total volume of exports is not likely to increase substantially until the world gets soundly on its feet and a genuine world prosperity may carry a healthy multilateral trade to higher levels.

In return for the commodities and services which we expect to furnish the world this year, we estimate that we will receive commodities and services from abroad to the value of about 8 billion dollars. This is just about half as much as we are exporting. This volume of imports is equal to about two weeks' work of all the factories, farms, mines, and laborers of the United States, and consists largely of things which are not produced in this country in sufficient quantity. We wish that the imports were larger, but the war-devastated world is just not able to supply more.

The difference between the value of the goods and services which foreign countries must buy from the United States this year and the value of the goods and services they are able to supply to us this year will therefore amount to the huge sum of about 8 billion dollars.

How are foreigners going to get the U.S. dollars necessary to cover this huge difference? And how are they going to get the U.S. dollars to cover a likely difference of nearly the same amount next year? These are some of the most important questions in international relations today.

Of this year's difference between imports and exports, more than 5 billion dollars is being financed by loans and grants-in-aid from the

United States Government, through such instruments as direct relief, the Export-Import Bank, the International Bank, the International Fund, and the loan to Great Britain. Funds for this purpose have already been authorized by Congress. The remainder of this year's deficit will be covered by private investments, remittances of American citizens abroad, and by drawing down the extremely limited foreign reserves of gold and foreign exchange.

But what of next year, and the year after that? Continued political instability and "acts of God" are retarding recovery to a greater degree than had been anticipated. The extreme need of foreign countries for American products is likely, therefore, to continue undiminished in 1948, while the capacity of foreign countries to pay in commodities will probably be only slightly increased. Under existing authorizations, considerable sums will be available to offset next year's deficit. But these funds will taper off rapidly during the latter part of 1948. The need, however, will decline very little if at all.

This is not a bright picture. But we must face up to the facts on the rate of world recovery. It has been widely overlooked that after the first World War it was only in 1925 that the world arrived at the 1914 level of economic activity. And World War II was many times more destructive than World War I. In the late war nations planned on a vast scale and executed with new and tremendously improved weapons the destruction of the enemy's economic resources, with enormous success. Recovery will therefore be correspondingly slow.

One more thing to be considered is that as great as is our supply of commodities and services to the world during the current year, it is still far short of what the people of the world need if they are to eat enough to maintain their physical strength and at the same time carry on essential measures of reconstruction and become self-supporting. This will be true until the other workshops and granaries of the world are back in full production.

What do these facts of international life mean for the United States and for United States foreign policy?

They mean first that we in the United States must take as large a volume of imports as possible from abroad in order that the financial gap between what the world needs and what it can pay for can be narrowed. There is no charity involved in this. It is simply common sense and good business. We are today obliged from considerations of self-interest and humanitarianism to finance a huge deficit in the world's budget. The only sound way to end this deficit financing is by accepting increased quantities of goods from abroad. There can never be any stability or security in the world for any of us until foreign countries are able to pay in commodities and services for what they need to import and to finance their equipment needs from more normal sources of investment.

Today in Geneva our negotiators are meeting with representatives of 17 other countries in an effort to negotiate a mutual reduction in trade barriers and an agreement upon fair rules to govern international trade. This is one of the ways in which we are attempting to face up to the realities of international life. The Geneva conference must succeed. The International Trade Organization must be established.

The Geneva conference must succeed not only because of the emergency supply and financial situation that exists today, but also because our position as the world's greatest producer and creditor nation demands that for a long period to come we accept an ever larger volume of imports. When the process of reconversion at home is completed, we are going to find ourselves far more dependent upon exports than before the war to maintain levels of business activity to which our economy has become accustomed.

The facts of international life also mean that the United States is going to have to undertake further emergency financing of foreign purchases if foreign countries are to continue to buy in 1948 and 1949 the commodities which they need to sustain life and at the same time rebuild their economies. Requests for further United States aid may reach us through the International Bank, or through the Export-Import Bank, or they may be of a type which existing national and international institutions are not equipped to handle and therefore may be made directly through diplomatic channels. But we know now that further financing, beyond existing authorizations, is going to be needed. No other country is able to bridge the gap in commodities or dollars.

This leads directly to a third imperative for our foreign policy. Since world demand exceeds our ability to supply, we are going to have to concentrate our emergency assistance in areas where it will be most effective in building world political and economic stability, in promoting human freedom and democratic institutions, in fostering liberal trading policies, and in strengthening the authority of the United Nations.

This is merely common sense and sound practice. It is in keeping with the policy announced by President Truman in his special message to Congress on March 12 on aid to Greece and Turkey. Free peoples who are seeking to preserve their independence and democratic institutions and human freedoms against totalitarian pressures, either internal or external, will receive top priority for American reconstruction aid. This is no more than frank recognition, as President Truman said, "that totalitarian regimes imposed on free peoples, by direct or indirect aggression, undermine the foundations of international peace and hence the security of the United States."

The fourth thing we must do in the present situation is to push ahead with the reconstruction of those two great workshops of Europe and Asia—Germany and Japan—upon which the ultimate recovery of the two continents so largely depends. This is what Secretary Marshall meant when he reported to the nation on April 28 that action on behalf of European recovery cannot await "compromise through exhaustion," and that we must take whatever action is possible immediately, even without full Four Power agreement, to effect a larger measure of European, including German, recovery. European recovery cannot be complete until the various parts of Europe's economy are working together in a harmonious whole. And the achievement of a coordinated European economy remains a fundamental objective of our foreign policy.

Finally, in order to carry out an economical and effective policy of relief and reconstruction along the foregoing lines, your Government is going to need the extension by Congress of certain executive powers over the domestic sale, transportation, and exportation of a limited list of commodities. Such controls have been in effect during the war and are still in effect under the President's war powers, but are due to expire June 30th of this year. It is vitally important that these controls be renewed. It is commodities that are needed in critical areas abroad, not just money. It is wheat and coal and steel that are urgently required to stave off economic collapse, not just dollar credits.

Your Government must therefore be able to insure equitable distribution of supplies as between the domestic economy and the export demand. This requires the extension of allocation powers with respect to a limited list of commodities certified by the Secretary of State and the Secretary of Commerce as critical to the foreign economic policy of the United States. Powers to assign priorities directly to producing firms will be necessary for a still more restricted list of items. At the same time, a continuation of export controls is required in order to direct exports where we want them to go and to cut down unnecessary and undesirable foreign buying in the domestic market.

Power to assign priorities on transportation is also needed. This power is needed in order to insure the efficient use of transportation facilities, particularly freight cars. Without such authority it will be difficult to move bulky export commodities such as coal and grain in the required quantities.

Finally, certain legislation which would enable the Maritime Commission to insure maximum availability and efficient use of shipping is required in order to insure the success of our export programs with respect to bulky items such as coal and grain.

Legislative proposals of this nature have been presented to Congress, or will be presented in the near future. It is of the greatest importance to the foreign economic policy of this country, and thus to the security and well-being of the nation, that these powers be granted.

There is a story going the rounds about a man who, after listening to an extended lecture on the grave financial and economic difficulties of northern Europe and Great Britain, remarked, "And, just think, all the trouble was caused by a blizzard."

I think we will all agree that something more than a blizzard has caused Europe's current difficulties. But last winter's blizzard did show up the extremely narrow margins of human and national subsistence which prevail in the world today, margins so narrow that a blizzard can threaten populations with starvation and nations with bankruptcy and loss of independence.

Not only do human beings and nations exist in narrow economic margins, but also human dignity, human freedom, and democratic institutions.

It is one of the principal aims of our foreign policy today to use our economic and financial resources to widen these margins. It is necessary if we are to preserve our own freedoms and our own democratic institutions. It is necessary for our national security. And it is our duty and our privilege as human beings.

SECRETARY OF STATE GEORGE C. MARSHALL'S ADDRESS AT THE COMMENCEMENT EXERCISES OF HARVARD UNIVERSITY, CAMBRIDGE, MASSACHUSETTS, JUNE 5, 1947

I need not tell you gentlemen that the world situation is very serious. That must be apparent to all intelligent people. I think one difficulty is that the problem is one of such enormous complexity that the very mass of facts presented to the public by press and radio make it exceedingly difficult for the man in the street to reach a clear appraisement of the situation. Furthermore, the people of this country are distant from the troubled areas of the earth and it is hard for them to comprehend the plight and consequent reactions of the long-suffering peoples, and the effect of those reactions on their governments in connection with our efforts to promote peace in the world.

In considering the requirements for the rehabilitation of Europe, the physical loss of life, the visible destruction of cities, factories, mines, and railroads was correctly estimated, but it has become obvious during recent months that this visible destruction was probably less serious than the dislocation of the entire fabric of European economy. For the past 10 years conditions have been highly abnormal. The feverish preparation for war and the more feverish maintenance of the war effort engulfed all aspects of national economies. Machinery has fallen into disrepair or is entirely obsolete. Under the arbitrary and destructive Nazi rule, virtually every possible enterprise was geared into the German war machine. Long-standing commercial ties, private institutions, banks, insurance companies, and shipping companies disappeared, through loss of capital, absorption through nationalization, or by simple destruction. In many countries, confidence in the local currency has been severely shaken. The breakdown of the business structure of Europe during the war was complete. Recovery has been seriously retarded by the fact that two years after the close of hostilities a peace settlement with Germany and Austria has not been agreed upon. But even given a more prompt solution of these difficult problems, the rehabilitation of the economic structure of Europe quite evidently will require a much longer time and greater effort than had been foreseen.

There is a phase of this matter which is both interesting and serious. The farmer has always produced the foodstuffs to exchange with the city dweller for the other necessities of life. This division of labor is the basis of modern civilization. At the present time it is threatened with breakdown. The town and city industries are not producing adequate goods to exchange with the food-producing farmer. Raw materials and fuel are in short supply. Machinery is lacking or worn out. The farmer or the peasant cannot find the goods for sale which he desires to purchase. So the sale of his farm produce for money which he cannot use seems to him an unprofitable transaction. He, therefore, has withdrawn many fields from crop cultivation and is using them for grazing. He feeds more grain to stock and finds for himself and his family an ample supply of food, however short he may be on clothing and the other ordinary gadgets of civilization. Meanwhile people in the cities are short of food and fuel. So the governments are forced to use their foreign money and credits to procure these necessities abroad. This process exhausts funds which are urgently needed for reconstruction. Thus a very serious situation is rapidly developing which bodes no good for the world. The modern system of the division of labor upon which the exchange of products is based is in danger of breaking down.

The truth of the matter is that Europe's requirements for the next three or four years of foreign food and other essential products—principally from America—are so much greater than her present ability to pay that she must have substantial additional help or face economic, social, and political deterioration of a very grave character.

The remedy lies in breaking the vicious circle and restoring the confidence of the European people in the economic future of their own countries and of Europe as a whole. The manufacturer and the farmer throughout wide areas must be able and willing to exchange their product for currencies the continuing value of which is not open to question.

Aside from the demoralizing effect on the world at large and the possibilities of disturbances arising as a result of the desperation of the people concerned, the consequences to the economy of the United States should be apparent to all. It is logical that the United States should do whatever it is able to do to assist in the return of normal economic health in the world, without which there can be no political stability and no assured peace. Our policy is directed not against any country or doctrine but against hunger, poverty, desperation, and chaos. Its purpose should be the revival of a working economy in the world so as to permit the emergence of political and social conditions in which free institutions can exist. Such assistance, I am convinced, must not be on a piecemeal basis as various crises develop. Any assistance that this Government may render in the future should provide a cure rather than a mere palliative. Any government that is willing to assist in the task of recovery will find full cooperation, I am sure, on the part of the United States Government. Any government which maneuvers to block the recovery of other countries cannot expect help from us. Furthermore, governments, political parties, or groups which seek to perpetuate human misery in order to profit therefrom politically or otherwise will encounter the opposition of the United States.

It is already evident that, before the United States Government can proceed much further in its efforts to alleviate the situation and help start the European world on its way to recovery, there must be some agreement among the countries of Europe as to the requirements of the situation and the part those countries themselves will take in order to give proper effect to whatever action might be undertaken by this Government. It would be neither fitting nor efficacious for this Government to undertake to draw up unilaterally a program designed to place Europe on its feet economically. This is the business of the Europeans. The initiative, I think, must come from Europe. The role of this country should consist of friendly aid in the drafting of a European program and of later support of such a program so far as it may be practical for us to do so. The program should be a joint one, agreed to by a number, if not all, European nations.

An essential part of any successful action on the part of the United States is an understanding on the part of the people of America of the character of the problem and the remedies to be applied. Political passion and prejudice should have no part. With foresight, and a willingness on the part of our people to face up to the vast responsibility which history has clearly placed upon our country, the difficulties I have outlined can and will be overcome.

EXCERPTS FROM PRESIDENT HARRY S. TRUMAN'S ADDRESS AT A JEFFERSON DAY DINNER IN WASHINGTON, D.C., APRIL 5, 1947

Out of the silence of oppressed peoples, out of the despair of those who have lost freedom, there comes to us an expression of longing. Repeated again and again, in many tongues, from many directions, it is the plea of men, women, and children for the freedom that Thomas Jefferson proclaimed as an inalienable right.

When we hear the cry for freedom arising from shores beyond our own, we can take heart from the words of Thomas Jefferson. In his letter to President Monroe, urging the adoption of what we now know as the Monroe Doctrine, he wrote:

Nor is the occasion to be slighted which this proposition offers of declaring our protest against the atrocious violations of the rights of nations by the interference of any one in the internal affairs of another.

We, like Jefferson, have witnessed atrocious violations of the rights of nations.

We, too, have regarded them as occasions not to be slighted.

We, too, have declared our protest.

We must make that protest effective by aiding those peoples whose freedoms are endangered by foreign pressures.

We must take a positive stand. It is no longer enough merely to say "we don't want war." We must act in time—ahead of time—to stamp out the smoldering beginnings of any conflict that may threaten to spread over the world.

We know how the fire starts. We have seen it before—aggression by the strong against the weak, openly by the use of armed force and secretly by infiltration. We know how the fire spreads. And we know how it ends.

Let us not underestimate the task before us. The burden of our responsibility today is greater, even considering the size and resources of our expanded nation, than it was in the time of Jefferson and Monroe. For the peril to man's freedom that existed then exists now on a much smaller earth—an earth whose broad oceans have shrunk and whose natural protections have been taken away by new weapons of destruction.

EXCERPTS FROM UNDERSECRETARY OF STATE DEAN G. ACHESON'S ADDRESS AT THE COMMENCEMENT EXERCISES OF WESLEYAN UNIVERSITY, MIDDLETOWN, CONNECTICUT, JUNE 15, 1947

We . . . can, and should, help within the limits of our capacity those who wish to help themselves. It was such an action that President Truman proposed to Congress on March 12 in connection with Greece and Turkey and to which the Congress so overwhelmingly responded. This was not a novel proposal or an invitation to a crusade. It was typically and traditionally American.

This country has always responded to people struggling to attain or maintain their freedom. We have done so because it is important to us that they shall succeed. Sometimes we can do much, sometimes little, but the response is always there. It was there in the case of Hungary and Poland and Italy. It was there throughout the nineteenth century in the struggle of the Latin American states to obtain and keep their freedom from the encroachments of European powers. It underlay our efforts for decades to help China in her struggle against foreign subjugation.

So President Truman was acting and the Congress was acting in the truest and soundest American tradition. The case was an extreme one because Greece was near the abyss. But the principle was as old as our country. It is a sensible and hard-headed principle that where our help can be effective to enable people who are sincerely striving to remain free and solve their own problems, that help will be given.

We should, and I hope will, continue to act in this way—not waiting for extreme crises to develop, not attempting to carry all the burdens of the world or to solve all its problems, but responding in a thoroughly realistic way to the proposals of those who are exhausting every possibility of their own efforts and powers of cooperation with others to maintain places where free men may remain free.

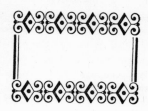

INDEX

Obscurity of Total Detail

For
State U.S. Publications